EXPERIENCING

PRAYER

Rev. Tom Sampson
Regards and Peace

The author's share of proceeds from the sale
of this book shall be assigned to the
Chicago Theological Seminary, for use in
its work with the homeless.

EXPERIENCING
PRAYER

TWENTY DIFFERENT STUDIES TOWARD
AN UNDERSTANDING OF PRAYER.
FOR INDIVIDUAL REFLECTION OR
GROUP DISCUSSION.

REVEREND TOM SAMPSON

James C. Winston
Publishing Company, Inc.

TO SOW THE FALLOW SOIL

Trade Division of Winston-Derek Publishers Group, Inc.

First printing

PUBLISHED BY JAMES C. WINSTON PUBLISHING COMPANY, INC.
Nashville, Tennessee 37205

Library of Congress Catalog Card No: 93-61290
ISBN: 1-55523-659-6

Printed in the United States of America

To my wife, Jo.
Her constant support and
incisive evaluation of the text
have made this book possible.

CONTENTS

RESOURCES AND FOOTNOTES
Appreciation.
Inventory of prayers.
Authorities quoted, with page reference.
Recommended books.
Footnotes.

PREFACE

And so I say to you, ask, and you will receive; seek and you will find; knock, and the door will be opened. For everyone who asks receives, the one who seeks finds, and to the one who knocks, the door will be opened (Luke 11:9–10).

Scripture and the promises of our Lord, such as the quotation above, make some tantalizing assurances. Every one who asks will receive, and the door to the future will be opened for all those who knock. Little wonder that many people, failing to find their asking or knocking answered, become frustrated with religion. Among such persons is my friend Elizabeth.

Elizabeth's dilemma:

Elizabeth is a faithful and devout home-maker and community worker. She has an active faith, and seeks to practice the religious life. Recently, however, she wrote to me about her frustrations. I share part of her letter because I feel she expresses the quandary many of us have about our faith and our understanding of prayer.

> The Bible asks why we ask for things, solutions, etc., (when God knows what we want and need),

then tells us to ask whatever we want in the name of Jesus and we shall have it. I'm paraphrasing poorly, but it has seemed contradictory and sometimes frustrates me.

Haven't I the right to ask that someone be relieved of pain? God knows that pain exists. Is it His will that suffering should continue? It seems a reasonable prayer, yet we know that pain is here to stay. Nevertheless, I go on praying. . . .

Oh well, for those of us who rely on prayer, it is our strength and comfort.

I find Elizabeth's last sentences significant. She is frustrated with unanswered prayer, as many of us are at times, but she says, "Nevertheless, I go on praying," and even adds, "Oh well, for those of us who rely on prayer, it is our strength and comfort." Elizabeth wants to believe in prayer yet she finds it difficult. She seems to be saying there is a God who answers prayer but she is not sure how to pray. She prays in spite of herself.

Elizabeth's dilemma is often our dilemma.

Certainly Elizabeth is not alone in her questions about faith and prayer. Although many theologians have called prayer the very center of religion, it remains for many of us, as for Elizabeth, difficult to understand. It is my hope that these pages will be of value to all the Elizabeths (and Harrys) who are searching to experience the promises of faith and prayer.

How to use this book.

This book is divided into twenty chapters.

The topic of each chapter is sufficient unto itself.

Each chapter can be a resource for study about prayer.

Each chapter deals with a main aspect of everyday living; such as, Forgiveness, Suffering, Healing, Temptation, as well as Confession, Salvation, and Social Change.

Every chapter has the same form:

A scriptural quotation about the topic.

A brief commentary on the text.

A one or two page essay on the special prayer subject.

Several testimonies of prayer-related experiences.

A final page of questions for discussion, plus a selected famous prayer.

This book purposefully presents different understandings of prayer.

Prayer is a widely practiced spiritual discipline. As such, it defies the complete understanding of any of us. Therefore, I purposefully offer varied understandings of prayer in hopes that the reader will be challenged to come to his or her own personal convictions about prayer, as he or she is led by the Will of God.

The different insights about prayer are documented by quotations from some of the best known theologians and authorities on prayer, such as:

John Baillie, Jacques Ellul, Dietrich Bonhoeffer, Carlo Carretto, P. T. Forsyth, Emily Herman, Georgia Harkness, Soren Kierkegaard, Perry LeFevre, Kenneth Leech, Reinhold Niebuhr, Henri Nouwen, Thomas Merton, Walter Rauschenbusch, and Evelyn Underhill; as well as others.

More than sixty men and women co-authors tell of their personal experiences with prayer.

Some persons report that they have been healed physically and emotionally. Many testify how prayer has saved them from sin. A few explain that prayer has filled their lives with peace and joy in the face of hardship and danger. Others tell what it means to be prayed for during their time of adversity. There are those who share their prayers of confession as well as their prayers of thanksgiving.

INTRODUCTION

What is Prayer?

> *So Samuel went and lay down in his place. The Lord came and stood there, and called, "Samuel, Samuel," as before. Samuel answered, "Speak; thy servant hears thee." The Lord said, "Soon I shall do something in Israel which will ring in the ears of all who hear it,"* (I Samuel 3:9–11).

Samuel's experience is symbolic of prayer. God speaks to Samuel, Samuel talks back to God. They interact with each other. God and a person communicate. Their conversation is an excellent introduction to the process of prayer.

Prayer is Divine-human contact. Prayer is both talking and listening. Prayer is a dialogue. Prayer is telling God what is on our hearts and minds: "O that I might have my request, and that God would grant what I hope for," (Job 6:8). And prayer is listening for God's response. A Psalmist cries out, "I called to the Lord in my distress and he answered me," (Psalm 120:1). The God, man-woman relationship.

Definitions of prayer:

1. "Prayer is the spiritual longing of a finite being to return to its origin," (Paul Tillich, Professor of Theology).

2. Prayer is, "Discovering our creative depths in the center of the self and finally in God," (Teilhard de Chardin, theologian and scientist).

3. "Prayer is the raising of the heart and mind to God, whether done mentally, individually, collectively, privately, or in public," (Roman Catholic catechism).

4. "Praying means breaking through the veil of existence and allowing yourself to be led by the vision which has become real to you, whatever we call that vision: 'the Unseen Reality'; 'the total Other'; 'the Numen'; 'the Spirit'; or 'the Father,' " (Henri J. M. Nouwen, Roman Catholic priest).

Prayer is relationship with God.

Prayer is the experience of contact with the ultimate Power. Prayer is our response to the initiative of God. Prayer is countered by the response of God. Prayer is a way for God to contact us and for us to contact God. Prayer is an effort by finite persons to connect with the Source of all things by the aid of the Holy Spirit. Prayer is the desire to become one with God. Prayer assumes, through faith, that there is the ultimate Power which can be called upon for help, direction, support, meaning, justice and peace. Prayer is the process by which we become partners with our Creator. Prayer is the two-way street with God by which we express petition, intercession, confession, forgiveness, thanksgiving, and adoration.

Prayer is not talking to God so much as listening to God.

It seems natural to talk. Most of us are quite good at it. In fact, the urge to tell others about ourselves or about the things we know dominates most of our relationships. So when it comes to prayer, we are very likely to conclude that prayer means more talking, that is, telling God what is on our mind or heart. As a matter of fact, we shouldn't waste our time. God knows us better than we know ourselves. We don't have to tell God anything. Instead, because of our limited human knowledge and narrow view of what life is all about, we need to listen to what God has to say to us. Such listening is prayer. Perhaps a better way of saying what we mean is expressed by Soren Kierkegaard, the Danish theologian:

> The "immediate" person thinks and imagines that when he prays, the important thing, the thing he must concentrate upon, is that God *should hear* what He is praying for. And yet in the true, eternal sense it is just the reverse: the true relation in prayer is not when God hears what is prayed for, but when the person praying continues to pray until he is *the one who hears,* who hears what God wills. The "immediate" person uses many words and, therefore, makes demands in his prayer, the true man of prayer, only *attends.*[1]

CONCERNING THE THEOLOGY OF PRAYER.

> *I will be with you and I will protect you wherever you go . . . for I will not leave you until I have done all that I have promised.*

xix

Jacob woke from his sleep and said, "Truly the Lord is in this place and I did not know it," (Genesis 28:15–16).

The text above introduces us to one of the great religious experiences of Jacob's life, when he came into direct contact with God, and did so quite unexpectedly. Indeed, Jacob's experience is often our experience. God comes when God wills. God seeks us when God wishes to do so. Our response to the initiative of God is prayer.

Prayer rests on many foundations:
   1. Prayer is founded upon belief in God as being above and independent of, yet at the same time within our world.
   2. Prayer is based on the belief in the personal nature of God.
   3. Prayer reflects the power of the Holy Spirit, which can comfort, direct, support, and save us.
   4. Prayer is based on the conviction that human beings can have communication with God.

Toward an understanding of prayer.
   We need to establish in the very beginning what we mean by prayer. A helpful introduction to the understanding of prayer is offered by Dr. Perry Le Fevre, theologian, and professor with the Chicago Theological Seminary:

> The theology of prayer is not an esoteric or peripheral matter for the religious life of the individual or the community, for prayer is the fundamental religious act. Living religion presupposes a responsiveness in the reality which transcends the human. only worthy of commitment—the other responds.

However this other is conceived it is the awareness of this responsiveness which is at the heart of faith and of living religion and which makes it possible to understand what Luther meant when he said that "faith is prayer and nothing but prayer."[2]

God acts through us.

Whenever we pray, it is God who has inspired us to pray. Contact between humans and God originates with God. It is God through the Holy Spirit that gives our prayers their values and meanings. Prayer is the process which discloses the purposes of God. When we pray, we open our selves to the influence of God, says the authoritative writer on spiritual matters who always signed himself "P. T. Forsyth."

> There is no such engine for the growth and com-
> mand of the moral soul, single or social, as prayer. . . .
> It plants us at the very centre of our own personali-
> ty, which gives the soul the true perspective of
> itself; it sets us also at the very centre of the world
> in God, which gives us the true hierarchy of things.
> Nothing, therefore develops such "inwardness" and
> yet such self knowledge and self control. . . .
> Nothing puts us in living contact with God but
> prayer, however facile our mere religion may be.
> And therefore nothing does so much for our origin-
> ality, so much to make us our own true selves, to
> stir up all that it is in us to be, and hallow all we
> are . . . It opens a fountain perpetual and luminous
> at the centre of our personality, where we are sus-
> tained because we are created anew.[3]

Peter Forsythe wrote *The Soul of Prayer* in 1916. It has been a classic on prayer ever since.

> When Daniel learned that this decree had been
> issued, he went into his house. He had had windows
> made in his roof-chamber looking toward Jerusalem;
> and there he knelt down three times a day and offered
> prayers and praises to God (Daniel 6:10).

The prophet Daniel was noted for his loyalty to the law, as well as his heroism and devotion. He was also a man of humility and spiritual vision. It is good to know these things about him, but an even more revealing insight into his character is witnessing him at prayer. Daniel combined prayer with praise. He prayed for courage to meet his persecutors and he praised God because of his belief and faith. It would be helpful to know what was Daniel's source of faith. He could have based his faith (and prayer) on a number of sources, even as we experience the basis for our own faith today.

The traditional sources for belief in prayer.
Traditionally, the belief in prayer has been grounded on several different authorities:

the authority of *Scripture*,
the teaching of *Jesus Christ*,
what the *Church* says,
the wisdom based on *reason*,
the personal *testimonies of faith*.

The choice of resources today.

Scripture is always an authority for prayer. The teachings of Jesus are also primary for our learning about prayer. Nor can we ignore the counsels of the theologians of the Church. And reason, for many, has a role.

I must say, however, that the emphasis of this book is on personal testimonies of prayer. Not that I have rejected the other sources for spiritual understanding. Not at all. In fact, these pages offer many quotations from the Bible and many insights about prayer from theologians. But my main emphasis is on contemporary personal experiences of prayer. How prayer gives life meaning today; how it helps people live more courageously in our time; how it encourages justice, resists despair, and confronts evil.

I seek to respond to the many individuals, in and out of the Church, who say, "I've heard the authorities but I need to experience God in my own life," or "I think the Bible stories are too much a part of history. I want to feel the Spirit now." This book addresses these attitudes. All of the testimonies herein reveal an awareness of the presence of God today, and the reality of prayer now; of which the following account from a parishioner is an example:

> I have felt strangely moved by a presence I do not understand yet acknowledge because of its influence upon me. I have felt convicted. I have received peace. I have been healed. I have been forgiven. These experiences have been pervasive, memorable, and influential upon my whole life. I feel that no human could know me so well as to speak to my secret conditions. I conclude that I have been known by some outside Power. So I find my faith and my prayers relate to some extent to

the Bible and the Word, but more deeply to the living experience of the Presence of God.

Back to the basics.

This book does not ignore the revelation of the Word in Scripture, the authority of the Church, or the teachings of Jesus about prayer. As a matter of fact, I want to make scripture and theology more meaningful by presenting a plethora of actual prayers of today with the conviction that prayer reflects and illuminates both scripture and theology. For example, consider the statement of the Psalmist: "I faint with longing for the courts of the Lord's Temple. My whole being cries out to the living God," (Psalm 84:2). Notice how the testimony of a modern individual of faith reflects some of the feelings of that Psalm.

> I pray because I cry. I have cried continuously ever since my first cry out of the womb. I am not sure what I cry for, but I know life is not complete and I cry to find that which will fulfill me. Perhaps I cry for recognition or for acceptance or for love. In some periods, a little of these things will temporarily satisfy me but only for a short time. Then my cry breaks out again. I know I am not whole enough. There is always something more for which I yearn. I cry for a response from that which created me, my Creator. My restlessness is only assuaged when I throw myself upon the mercy of God in prayer.

In conclusion.

Let me emphasize also that this a resource book. It offers insights into many areas of the prayer experience. Not every part will be of equal value to every reader. Take what you need and leave the rest. Let me add that I do not provide answers about prayer so much as I try to encourage the reader, by prayer examples, to explore his or her own life of prayer. In that respect, this volume is not so much a book *about* prayer as *of* prayer.

Part One:
THINGS YOU SHOULD KNOW ABOUT PRAYING

SOME PLAIN DIRECTIONS FOR ALL PRAYERS

Our praying is really our response to God.

> *They shall not toil in vain or raise children for misfortune. For they are the offspring of the blessed of the Lord and their issue after them; before they call me, I will answer, and while they are still speaking, I will listen. As a mother comforts her son, so will I myself comfort you, and you shall find comfort in Jerusalem* (Isaiah 65:23–24, 66:13).

The Old Testament prophet Isaiah expresses a fundamental Christian belief: God anticipates our every need. In scripture terms, the belief is stated as, "Before they call to me, I will answer and while they are still speaking, I will listen," as above. Hence, prayer is really responding to the initiative of God. Our search for God is simply our surrender to God's concern for us.

This understanding of prayer is traditional in the Christian concept of prayer. The famous French spiritual leader of the Twelfth Century, Bernard of Clairvaux, also expresses this insight.

Do you awake; well, God, too, is awake.
If you rise in the night-time,
If you anticipate to your utmost
your earliest awakening,
You will find God awakening you.
You will never anticipate your own awakeness.
In such a relationship you will be rash if you
    attribute any priority, and prominent share to
    yourself;
For God loves, both more than you love,
and before you love at all.[1]

Because so many relationships in life depend upon our initiative, many of us are likely to feel that things will not get done unless we do them. We probably feel that the act of praying is up to us. But such is not the case. Our praying starts with God.

Although at first glance it may seem unacceptable, the theological insight about prayer is that God starts the prayer process. We do not begin prayer, any more than we begin the love between ourselves and our parents. My mother and father learned about love before I was born. I did not know what love was until they first loved me. They began the significant relationship of bonding and loving. So it is with God. God loves us before we know what the word love means. God is the Great Initiator. God is our first Lover.

Examples of the initiative of the Spirit of God are everywhere. The composer explains, "It was not I who created the masterpiece. It was a force within me which formed the music in my soul. I merely put it on paper." In like spirit, the former Secretary of the United Nations, Dag Hammerskjold, wrote in his Markings:

You take the pen, and the lines dance.
You take the flute, and the notes shimmer.

2

You take the brush, and the colors sing.
So all things have meaning and beauty,
in that space beyond Time where you are.
How, then, can I hold back anything from you?[2]

This same insight about the initiative of God and the Spirit in prayer is observed by the Quaker writer and spiritual leader Thomas Kelly, in his classic and often quoted *Testament of Devotion*,

> We may suppose these depths of prayer are our achievement, the precipitate of our own habits at the surface level settled into subconscious regions. But this humanistic account misses the autonomy of the life of prayer. It misses the fact that this inner level has a life of its own, invigorated not by us but by a divine Source. There come times when prayer pours forth in volumes and originality such as we cannot create. . . . Our prayers are mingled with a vaster Word, a Word that at one time was made flesh. We pray, and yet it is not we who pray, but a Greater who prays in us. . . . All we can say is, Prayer is taking place, we are joyfully prayed through, by a Seeking Life that flows through us into the world.[3]

So finding God is really letting God find us.

Though we rebel and think we are independent, the fact remains that we are caught in God's design, and fashioned by it more than we realize. While we consume our lives with petty human plans, God the Creator is always at work, lovingly and sacrificially shaping the world as God wills the world to be. Blaise

Pascal, religious philosopher and author of *Pensees* (which suggests that in order to find the meaning of life, we can look to Jesus Christ), is reported to have said, "I would not have sought Thee, if Thou had not called me."

As a present day example of how we are moved by the influence of God, a pastor in Illinois tells of his awareness of the Inner Voice.

> As a youngster following my confirmation service, which I took seriously, I heard an "inner voice" compelling me to make the pastoral ministry my vocation. This insistent "voice" pushed me to tell my parents and my pastor of my intention. Needless to say, they were not impressed, to my surprise. I must admit I didn't see myself as a model of Christian virtue, particularly the meek and mild part. I prided myself on being the toughest kid in my part of Chicago. So I guess I shouldn't have been surprised at the dubious attitude of most of my family and friends. Frankly, I did not see how God could use a kid like me either. But I had no doubt about the voice or its meaning. The only thing I could figure out was that somehow my experience with city gangs could be useful.

God waits for us to share in the work of continuing Creation.

God is waiting for us because we have been created as God's instruments to share in furthering God's plan and purpose as revealed to us through the prophets and apostles. We are not indispensable. If we reject or fail in our responsibility in answering God's call, God will find other ways to guarantee the fulfillment of God's Will.

4

We cannot ask to be excused from being co-creators. We have the model for creation before us, in that we have been created in God's image as revealed to us. We have the imprint of the urge to create within us. It cries for expression amid our loins and our souls. As Saint Augustine is often quoted as saying, "My soul is restless until it finds rest in Thee."

Choose your own place, time, and habits.

"When you pray, go into a room by yourself, shut the door, and pray to your Father who is there in the secret place; and your Father who sees what is secret will reward you," (Matthew 6:6).

Jesus was a pray-er. Very early in the morning he got up and went out to a lonely spot and remained there in prayer (Mark 1: 35). Before Jesus chose his disciples he spent time in prayer. "During this time he went out one day into the hills to pray, and spent the night in prayer to God. When day broke he called his disciples to him and from them he chose. . . ." (Luke 6:12). After the feeding of the five thousand followers, he sought renewal of his soul. "After taking leave of them, he went up the hillside to pray," (Mark 6:46).

It helps to have a regular place to pray.

If we choose a particular place and reserve it for prayer, we may find that whenever we return there, prayer will seem more natural and may come easier. For example, William Law, a disciplined religious guide of the Eighteenth Century, tells in his book *A Serious Call to a Devout Life,* about the importance of choosing one place and using it specially for prayer.

> If you were to use yourself, as far as you can, to pray always in one place, if you were to reserve that place for devotion and not allow yourself to do

anything common in it . . . or if any particular part of a room was thus used, this kind of consecration of it as a place holy unto God, would have an effect upon your mind and dispose you to such tempers, as would very much assist your devotion.[4]

Special places to pray come in various sizes and colors.

My friend, John, lost his father when he was in college. The separation had been hard on him because they had a very close relationship. But John found a way to deal with his loneliness and emptiness. Whenever he faced a difficult matter, he would wonder what his father might advise. So he would leave his friends and retreat to a particular campus bench. The same one he and his father had often used to discuss life together. "I would tell my Dad about my problem and then I would listen for his answer," John told me. "I found it so helpful to be in his presence in that way. His continuing companionship in spirit, but so real, helped me through some hard decisions."

Our invisible "place."

When I talk about *place*, I mean more than just a physical location. Instead, I am also suggesting a place in the mind or soul to which we can retreat in spirit. Ignatius Loyola called this a "composition of place" in his *Spiritual Exercises*. Such a "place" in the heart is where we can retreat for inner quietness and meditation. Such an invisible place can be held in our soul even when we are surrounded by interruptions. In fact, Thomas Kelly, an American Quaker whose life was filled with spiritual counseling, tells how he understands the invisible place.

Walk on the streets. Chat with your friends. But every moment, behind the scenes, be in prayer,

6

offering yourself in complete obedience. I find this internal continuous prayer-life absolutely essential. It can be carried on day or night, in the thick of business, in home or school.[5]

Journeying to a scripture "place."

Many people find that putting one's self back into a biblical incident is a helpful way of finding a prayer-place. For example, imagine for the moment that you are among those who are present when Jesus heals the man at the pool (John. 5:2–9). As you come upon the scene, talk to some of the bystanders. Notice how Jesus interacts with the crowd. What is it like for you to be in His presence? Then He turns and faces you, as if inviting you to speak. What do you say? He asks you, "Tell me about yourself." What do you tell him? Look around, what are the other bystanders doing? How do you feel about being there? Stay with the adventure for some time while absorbing the mood and ambience of the occasion. Then say goodbye and come back from your imaginary visit.

Now, take a personal inventory of your experience. What was it like? What did you learn about yourself? Such guided "trips" can be quite revealing. They enable us to recognize our priorities, some of our hidden parts of mind and spirit, as well as some of our desires and reservations.

The importance of your own prayer time.

Jesus *"spoke to them in a parable to show that they should keep on praying and never lose heart,"* (Luke 18:1).

Jesus must have had some individual way of praying. Perhaps it developed since his childhood and became more disciplined as he faced increasing pressure from his opponents. His example suggests that we need to look at our praying more seriously, as we face our own unpredictable times. For help in this growth, we can turn again to "P. T. Forsyth."

7

Go into your chamber, shut the door, and cultivate the habit of praying audibly. Write prayers and burn them. Formulate your soul. Pay no attention to literary form, only to spiritual reality. . . . To formulate your soul is one valuable means to escape formalizing it. This is the best, the wholesome, kind of self examination. Speaking with God discovers us safely with ourselves. . . . Face your special weaknesses and sin before God. Force yourself to say to God exactly where you are wrong. When anything goes wrong, do not ask to have it set right without asking in prayers what it was in you that made it go wrong. It is sometimes fruitless to ask for a general grace to help specific flaws, sins, trials, and griefs. Let prayers be concrete, actual, a direct product of life's real experiences. Pray as your actual self, not some fancied saint. Let it be closely relevant to your real situation.[6]

The depth of prayer may not depend upon the time spent in praying.

For most of us, our time for prayer is often relatively short. In reality, prayer doesn't take any time at all. It doesn't take any more time than it takes me to tell my wife that I love her. Prayer, like love, is an attitude, a state of mind. When I think of love or prayer, the thought is instantaneous, whether it be "I love you," or "God be with me." The feeling of love and the awareness of God come so quickly, time is of no consequence. A friend in Illinois describes his kind of instant prayers:

Many of my prayers are silent "quickies." They are like "shooting one up there." I'll be in the middle of a project and a thought will cross my mind—

something in need of some prayer time. So I'll shoot up a quickie prayer to God, then return my attention to my project. Many of my quickie or "flash" prayers throughout the day become subjects of my more earnest and concentrated prayers later, when time can be set aside for well-focused and uninterrupted prayers melded with deep meditation (listening to what God has to say to me).

On the other hand, if it meets our needs, we should regulate our time in prayer.

There are occasions when we need to take time to pray. Sometimes we want to be more deliberate about it. For example, Dietrich Bonhoeffer, the noted German pastor who was a leader of the Church protest movement against the war-lord Hitler, reported that he gave an hour a day to prayer and meditation.

He divided his hour into three periods: one-third for meditation on a chosen text, one-third for prayer based on scripture, and the last third on prayers of intercession for special persons or events. "Intercession means no more than bringing our brother into the presence of God," he says.

Obviously such a prayer program takes time.

Prayer is an investment which pays double-digit dividends.

When we consider how little time prayer really needs, it is surprising that prayer is not more popular; especially when we observe how much it often accomplishes. For the small investment in prayer, lives have been moved from despair to hope, from ruin to a second chance, and from death to life. Experienced pray-ers report that a moment in prayer can bring inner peace to a time of stress, counteract a sinful impulse, heal a broken heart, or bring about miracles which we cannot really explain.

9

The excellent returns for an investment in prayer were publicized by Jeremy Taylor, a Seventeenth Century cleric of vast learning, in his book of spiritual advice *Rule and Exercises of Holy Living*.

> If we consider how much of our lives is taken up with the needs of nature, how many years are wholly spent before we come to any use of reason . . . how imperfect our discourse is made by our evil education, how many parts of our wisest and best years are spent in business and unnecessary vanities . . . that little portion of hours that is left for the practice of piety and walking with God, is so short and trifling, that were not the goodness of God infinitely great, it might seem unreasonable of us to expect from Him eternal joys.[7]

The importance of your own prayer habits.

"*Samuel continued in the service of the Lord, a mere boy with a linen ephod fastened round him. Every year his mother made him a little cloak and took it to him when she went up with her husband to offer the annual sacrifice,*" (I Samuel 2:18, 19).

Young Samuel is a good example of the proverb, "Start a boy on the right road, and even in old age he will not leave it," (Pr. 22:6). Every year, as he grew taller and stronger, Samuel's mother, Hannah, made him a new jacket, symbolic of the fact that as he matured in wisdom and faith she also encouraged his religious habits. So it is not surprising that he grew up to hold deep convictions of faith. In fact, he became a judge in Israel, an inspired prophet, and influenced the course of his country's history. *Early prayer can lead to later results.*

An experienced pastor tells how his upbringing stood by him throughout his life.

I was a lucky fourth sibling in a loving, congenial family in a church-centered farm community in Iowa. I was what I have sometimes referred to as "prayer conditioned." Like Horace Bushnell who grew up "never having known himself to be other than Christian," I grew up in an environment of home and church nurtured in prayer. Prayer was a daily practice, free-form mostly, very genuine, even if at times wordy and repetitive. It came naturally and was never left only for the preacher to lead. It guided daily life, and it was good. Now, after a lifetime of experiences in my pastoral vocation, I still hark back to the voice of my immigrant Swedish father at the breakfast table on the farm, reciting his everyday litany at "family devotions." It is a benediction! He didn't know how lasting an impact he had on this son of his. He didn't know it was setting the spirit of prayer for me forever.

How many of us make the effort to be models of faithfulness for those younger people who may be evaluating us as patterns for their own religious development? How many of us practice good habits of prayer in the creation of meaningful character, either ours or in others? Not idle questions in this era of family separations. Do we know where our children are?

An example of the spiritual power of well established habits of prayer.
Le Chambon is a small town in Southern France which played an extraordinary role in protecting Jews who were able to escape from Germany during the Nazi era of persecutions. When historians asked how a whole village hid thousands of Jewish children and adults in the face of constant threat of discovery and death, it was learned that the residents had developed their courageous

resistance through their own experience as persecuted Huguenots years and years before. Their courage, as well as their cunning for saving lives, was based on their long established habits of faith.

If we do not practice to deepen our spiritual life, costly habits can invade our lives.

Anyone who has tried to cure himself or herself of an established bad habit knows the difficulty of the undertaking. Many are the failed resolutions, only to promise oneself that the next time it will be different. Alas, so often "the next time" is not different. We repeat the same old habit. The pattern we have slipped into seems to fulfill something inside of us, even though we may not like it. Nor do people of faith have it much easier. Years ago, Thomas a Kempis, one of the world's best known "religious," who is known for his prayer classic *Imitation of Christ*, observed that "if one ingrained habit a year could be changed, it would be an accomplishment!"

A personal example:

I became convinced of the importance of good prayer habits in an unusual way. To describe my experience takes a little background explanation. Clergy are not exempt from the same temptations which many parishioners face. Laziness, lust for sex or power, fear of failure, individual conceit, evasion of the call of the gospel, desire for personal popularity—all these are known among clergy of every kind. Nor have I been an exception. Many a week through a number of years in my life I found myself grappling with temptation. I won some battles but I lost a lot, too. Whichever was the case, I was always conscious of the fact that all too soon Sunday would roll around again. Then I knew I would have to stand alone in my pulpit before my congregation, face to face before many friends and strangers who expected the most of me as their pastor. And I knew, too, that as we shared the church sanctuary together, God would also be present. Each Sunday forced upon me a subtle judgement I could not evade. How could I deal with the Word of the Lord for others and hide my own iniquity and weaknesses. In fact, the spiritual pain proved to be so great at times that I resolved in any way I could, to avoid such a confrontation with my Lord. That is when I developed a regular prayer life which eliminated, at least to some extent, the temptations which afflicted my life.

Prayer is an attitude.

> *Give yourselves wholly to prayer and entreaty; pray on every occasion in the power of the Spirit. To this end keep watch and persevere, always interceding for all God's people; and pray for me, that I may be granted the right words when I open my mouth, and may boldly . . . make known his purpose, for which I am an ambassador in chains* (Ephesians, 6:18–20).

When Paul was writing to the Ephesians, he used the military term "keep watch" to emphasize how constantly vigilant in prayer believers should be. Prayer is not just a one time event; it is a life habit. It is important to be alert to the use of prayer at all times. If we say a person lives a life of prayer, we are not saying he or she prays on many occasions, rather we are referring to his or her basic attitude toward God. A "life of prayer" is not necessarily a life filled with individual prayers; it is a life pervaded by the attitude of prayer. The experienced writer on spirituality Peter Forsyth, explains:

The note of prayer becomes the habit of the heart, the tone and tension of its new nature; in such a way that when we are released from the grasp of our occupations, the soul rebounds to its true bent, quest, and even pressure upon God. It is the soul's habitual appetite and habitual food. . . . Prayer is not identical with the occasional act of praying. Like the act of faith, it is a whole life thought of as action.[8]

Prayers from the heart reveal the deep faith of our souls.

A widow recently wrote to me, telling of the terminal illness of her husband. "Near the end of his long travail," she wrote, "his suffering became mine too. I had reached the point in my prayers when all I could say was, 'God help me through another day and night.' Through those months, I could only repeat again and again, 'God help me.' " Then she added, "I don't know, but I do know (and knew then) that God did and does help me all the time."

Another friend told me about her soul-wrenching divorce and the years of turmoil and trouble which they brought to her and her children. She said, "After years of praying to end the relationship, I could only pray, 'If it be thy will, let this cup pass from me.' I was exhausting my own strength and found the prayer helped me to go on."

For these pray-ers, the courage and spiritual strength of prayer were the rewards of years of faith-filled living.

A former pastor, and now a hospital chaplain, reports:

But, for me, my prayers, and my reaching up to the power that sustains me is something I have shared in for so long, that I can scarcely remember when it wasn't a part of my conscious relationship with

14

God. I really have to say that at some point in my early years, I decided that my conversations with God did not depend upon formal "verbal address," but rather on conscious awareness, that without the Creators' sustained help, I would not be able to accomplish God's will for my life.

Prayer is more than short official formalities.

Prayer is not so much a short appeal to God at a dinner or civic event in order to get the event started, as prayer is a sustained relationship.

Prayer is communicating with God as love is communicating with a loved one. We would no more think of stating our love for our spouse only on occasional brief greetings. Instead, our love is an attitude which permeates all of our relationship. So it is with prayer. Prayer is not only an occasional reaching-out to God; it is a continual love for God. Of course, there are special times when prayer can be a short event, but, more significantly, it is a long-term, ground-swell expression of faith and belief.

Of all the chaplains of the United States Senate since 1949, few will be so long remembered as Rev. Peter Marshall. Part of his influence was due to the fact that he would not let the members of the Senate assume that the traditional Prayer of Invocation ended with the Amen.

> Eternal Father of our souls, grant to the members and officers of this body a sacred moment of quiet as they take up their duties of the day. . . . Let them not think that when this prayer is said, that their dependence upon Thee is over, and forget Thy counsels for the rest of the day.[9]

Prayer is both a state of mind as well as involvement in life.

Theologian Perry LeFevre puts the matter succinctly when he writes, in *Radical Prayer:*

> Prayer in Christ or in the Spirit is both attitude and action grounded in trust in what is in fact ultimately trustworthy, the reality which transforms human existence toward the good. It's aim is to make God's intention our own. Prayer exists wherever this is the guiding aim.
>
> In this sense an attitude of prayer can characterize every aspect of our lives. We can pray without ceasing. Our basic attitude or orientation can be one of openness to God's transformation. Any act has the possibility of being guided by this intention for every act has some bearing on the becoming of the self and communities.[10]

Prayer can be a strong foundation of faith which enables us to negotiate our daily challenges, as this writer reveals.

> When I think about prayer, I consider two facts of my life—deficits and gifts. My deficits seem so great that at times I'm not sure I should write about prayer at all. Currently I work a full time job and hold responsibilities with three other organizations. A husband and three teenage sons share my life. This does not lead to a contemplative lifestyle, and I have become adept at excusing myself from private devotions. Yet, it seems that God has heard the longings of my heart, even when words seemed inadequate or nonexistent. God has given gifts;

two birth-children and an adopted son, a chance to return to graduate school and opportunities to accept callings in pastoral ministry and social work. I did not earn these gifts by right living or right praying. But I would most like to talk about the times when God has answered, even when I could hardly find the words; of times that blend grief and anger into an agony with a quality all its own, times of such pain that my words were too terrible to repeat in a book about prayer, times of terror for a child's life, times of anger at unjust systems, times of rage at my own religious denomination, times of grief at my own failures. Then it seems that God has read the yearnings of my heart. And grace has come. God has responded, not because I prayed rightly but because God kept listening and loving. What I do wish to affirm is that God hears prayer even when we hardly pray; and God answers prayer in ways we neither deserve nor expect.

This account is a reflection of so many of our own lives. We too have deficits, such as daily vexations, family crises, and disappointments. We too have gifts, such as children, the chance for education, and the opportunity to work. But how many of us stop to acknowledge the presence of God by saying, "I did not earn these gifts by right living or right praying."

But such concerns only reveal part of this writer's faith journey. She also includes her dark experiences of grief, anger, terror, rage, and agony.

17

Prayer is a partnership with God.

Some biblical references pertain to God as Creator and to us as partners with God. Responsibility for sharing with God in being architects of the future is a traditional part of Christian history and theology. Moses saw himself as an agent of God when, in God's name, he contended with the oppressive Pharaoh of Egypt to let Moses' people go (Ex. 7:16). Deborah, the activist judge, rallied Israel to throw off the oppressors in her time (Ju. 4:4–23). Esther, a young Jewish woman, saved her people from cruel persecution (Es. 4:13–16). The prophet Amos interpreted his assignment from God to be a crusader for the rights of the poor (Am. 5:21–23). Jesus of Nazareth said the purpose of his life was, as a representative of God, "to proclaim the year of the Lord," (Lu. 4:18).

Different understandings of God may affect how we will be partners.

If we understand God to be Father (or Mother), the implication is that union with God is union with a guardian, or a king. Under this definition, prayer becomes a relationship in which we are subordinates, as a child.

On the other hand, if we understand God as Creator, we discover a whole new concept of prayer. A creator is one who brings into being, who originates, and who is still creating. If then we are as parents creators of life and as citizens fashioners of a better world, prayer becomes not the role of a child to an authoritative parent, but rather a participant in the God-process of renewing and remolding.

Using this definition of prayer, the pray-er becomes a partner with God. The thought of prayer as a child dependent upon a loving father or mother is greatly enhanced. Prayer now becomes the act of sharing with God in the very active process of helping to make all things new.

18

Our responsibility as partners with God.

When we understand ourselves to be partners with God, then we see our life in a new light. We are expected to work with God to help accomplish God's will. Not only are we called to improve our individual lifestyles and save ourselves from greed, selfishness and prejudice, by renewing a right spirit within us, but we are urged to reconstruct our world more in keeping with the purpose of God. For example, faith in God and belief in Jesus Christ calls us to work for racial equality, for the rights of women, for better care of the environment, for recognition of the needs of the homeless, and for the opportunity to work for all God's people. Such a sense of responsibility is emphasized by biblical scholar, Walter Brueggeman, when he says, "What God does first and best and most is to trust his people with their moment in history. He trusts them to do what must be done for the sake of his whole community."

We have every reason to co-create a new world with God.

If we are creations of God, if we are related to God in that we have been created by God, if we are children of God, if we are created in God's image, if we are heirs of God, if we are a chosen people, then in recognition of our particular position we have a responsibility to live up to our inheritance. No one can fully claim to be exempt from taking some part in the re-creation of our society. In fact, one who speaks with much enthusiasm about this accountability is the Roman Catholic theologian, Matthew Fox, when he writes in *Original Blessing*.

> We are God's images, and God trusts us with that divine power of imagination. We have been entrusted by God with our capacity to imagine and to birth. If we are truly "God's work of art," as Paul says we are . . . then surely we have no excuse for

19

not trusting the creative powers within us. Imperfection is no excuse; failure is no excuse; sin is no excuse; suffering is no excuse. Who, after all, has the right to be excused or to excuse him- or herself from the divine plan of the universe.[11]

Pray as the Spirit moves you.

> *Two men went up to the temple to pray, one a Pharisee and the other a tax gatherer. The Pharisee stood up and prayed thus: "I thank thee, O God, that I am not like the rest of the men, greedy, dishonest, adulterous; or for that matter, like this tax gatherer. I fast twice a week; I pay tithes on all I get." But the other kept his distance and would not even raise his eyes to heaven, but beat upon his breast, saying, "O God, have mercy on me, sinner that I am." It was this man, I tell you, and not the other, who went home acquitted of his sins (Luke 18:10–14).*

Jesus' parable and impromptu prayer.

This parable says a lot about how we pray. The Pharisee observed the rules of religion: praying, fasting, and tithing. He was intent upon fulfilling the law. Thus the Pharisee was "dressed in his own spiritual self-esteem." He saw no need to grow in the Spirit. He insulated himself from any new understanding of who he was.

On the other hand, the tax-gatherer prayed directly from the heart. In his extremity he did not refer to Hebrew liturgy. Perhaps he did not know enough of it. By contrast, with humility the tax-collector was open to new awareness. He felt a need to know more about life and God. Therefore, it is not surprising that Jesus said,

"It was this man, I tell you, and not the other, who went home acquitted of his sins."

The use of impromptu or spontaneous prayers

There is no special way to pray. Even the disciples, after several years of direct companionship with Jesus, asked him to teach them how to pray (Lu. 11:1). Although he suggested the Lord's prayer, Jesus prayed extemporaneously throughout his ministry. In so doing, he taught that prayer is a matter of spirit rather than form, that it is concerned with purpose instead of method, and that prayer is not dependent upon design but upon desire. Indeed, there is no one right way to pray, just as there is no one correct way to love. Like loving, different people express their praying differently, with honesty and sincerity as basic ingredients.

An example of an individual's personal prayer.

An excellent illustration of a non-liturgical prayer is that of Abbe Michel Quoist, who served as pastor of a busy city parish in Le Havre, France. Abbe Quoist has written prayers which reflect the personal extemporaneous spirit. In his book, *Prayers,* is this prayer called "The Telephone."

> I have just hung up; why did he telephone?
> I don't know . . . Oh! I get it . . .
> I talked a lot and listened very little
> Forgive me, Lord: it was a monologue and not a
>   dialogue.
> I explained my idea and did not get his;
> Since I didn't listen, I learned nothing,
> Since I didn't listen, I didn't help,
> Since I didn't listen, I didn't commune.

21

Forgive me Lord, for we were never connected, and
now we are cut off.[12]

Short spontaneous prayers from the heart can carry God's concern.
A former Navy man told me that it was his opinion that
prayer is not a product of design so much as it is an outpouring of
motive, not "pretty words, so much as interior hope." As he spoke
of his experience during wartime, he revealed that prayer was
always on his heart, if not on his lips.

> I was in service in WW II. My very best friend was
> my own pastor's son. He was home going to college
> with the goal of becoming a Dr. My nightly prayer
> was for him to be successful in that goal. And then
> I would close with, "If possible, let me return home
> safely."
> I was aboard the aircraft carrier *Intrepid*, known
> as the floating coffin of the Navy. There was not
> for me the foxhole mentality. That simple prayer
> for my friend was adequate for me. Both parts were
> accomplished.

Prayers do not have to be long to be effective. Just one sentence of prayer by the tax-gatherer earned him God's mercy. "O
God, have mercy upon me, sinner that I am," (Lu. 18:13). A
prayer of only a few words brought Paradise to the thief on the
cross. "Jesus, remember me when you come to your throne," (Lu.
23:42). The very short prayer of the dying martyr, Stephen: "Lord,
do not hold this sin against them," (Ac. 7:60) so moved callous
Saul that he accepted Christ. All of which reminds us that the
efficacy of praying is not in the length but in the depth of faith.

Examples of short prayers which are in popular usage.
"Lord make me according to thy heart," (Brother Lawrence[13]).

> God be in my head and in my understanding.
> God be in my eyes and in my looking.
> God be in my mouth and in my speaking.
> God be in my heart and in my thinking.
> God be at my end and at my departing.
> (Sarum Primer Prayer[14]).

Of course, many "extemporaneous" pulpit-prayers have been well planned before hand. A former church executive, now living in Connecticut, writes,

> I have a habit of working over my "pulpit prayers" for hours in advance, writing them out and rewriting them. This got me into trouble in my early parish. I had one member who all but quit the church over the minister's "canned prayers." "That ain't prayin'," he said. "Prayin's when you wrestle with the Spirit, right there and then, not reading something from a piece of paper." I stood my ground. "I'll try to improve my reading, John," I said (and did). "But remember that I've wrestled with the Spirit for hours in advance of Sunday. Remember I've been scouting out God's territory, then reporting to you on what I found. I've tried to distill it all in words I hope will be vivid and incisive enough to evoke your own better prayers. I can— and do from time to time— 'wrestle here and now' with the Spirit from the pulpit, but I usually come

away feeling bad that I've rambled and haven't been at my best by expressing it on the spur of the moment."

The pastor who gave this account has had much experience. He knows how important it is for a person to be known where the Christian community gathers. When our name is heard, when our needs receive attention, then we feel we are somebody. When we are known in the gates, as the psalmist expressed it, then we know we can belong. Such public sharing of prayer in corporate worship breathes Spirit into the community. When a person leaves church with the awareness of "I was heard, I was accepted, I was listened to," that person knows that his or her participation in the worship event was spiritually rewarding.

The role of prayer in the pastor's life and the life of the church.
Praying is certainly among the most important aspects of Ministry. Congregations often grow or decline in relation to the way the Spirit is revealed in the pulpit. In fact, because that is the case, it encourages faithful parishioners to sometimes ask penetrating questions.

How does the Spirit pray through the pastor? Is the praying (and preaching) the result of reading books, or does it come from experience of being the suffering servant? From which aspect of the faith do the sermons and prayers most often originate—from logic and reason or faith and inspiration? Does the pastor allow himself or herself to be vulnerable to the Spirit? Is he or she secure in the Faith? Was the clergyperson "there when they crucified my Lord?" Can the pastor share his or her own spiritual pilgrimage? Does he or she reveal the presence of Jesus Christ, the Holy Spirit, and God?"

Be guided by prayers prepared by others.

> *Lord, thou hast examined me and known me. Thou knowest all, whether I sit down or rise up. Thou hast discerned my thoughts from afar . . . For there is not a word on my tongue, but thou, O Lord knowest them all. . . . Where can I escape from thy spirit . . . If I climb up to heaven thou art there . . . If I say, "Surely darkness will steal over me . . ." darkness is no darkness for thee. . . . Watch lest I follow any path that grieves thee; guide me in the everlasting ways (Psalm. 139:1–7, 11, 24).*

This 139th psalm is one of the greatest of all psalms. Some call it the "crown of the Psalter." Others say it is "the Old Testament's highest conception of the relationship of God to the individual." The psalmist's main theme is that we are cared for by God, hence it is a prayer of faith. It is an appreciation that God is aware of every aspect of our lives. To pray this prayer is to lift our understanding of God to its supreme level.

None of us could write such a grand concept of God. The prayer is one of the many psalms which can be used in place of our own prayers when we meet a dry prayer time.

The importance of the prestructured prayers.

Printed prayers, or official prayers, can be most helpful in our prayer life in several ways.

1) When we have lost the enthusiasm for our own prayers, they can act as pump-primers.

2) There are times when persons of faith must write for those of us whose faith is in question. We need the fresh insights of others' prayers to cleanse and renew our own spirits.

3) When we make up our own prayers, we may unconsciously overlook hidden aspects of our lives about which we really should be praying. Using the prayers of others, can lead us into areas of our own lives we need to confront but may try to avoid.

Howard Thurman, the thoughtful spiritual leader and author of *Meditations of the Heart*, reminds us, "A man may share in his prayer his concern for peace in the world and yet, in his own little world, be unwilling to change his private attitude of antagonism or prejudice toward his fellows."[15]

When there is nothing left in life but prayer in any form.

One of the nation's worst airplane disasters took place at O'Hare field on a clear May day several years ago. Two hundred and seventy-three persons perished in sight of friends and relatives who had gathered to see them take off. My friend was chaplain at O'Hare at the time.

He told me that, besides concerned officials of all kinds, the local clergy from different churches immediately arrived. They were assigned to counseling with the distraught friends, supporting them by prayer, helping in contacting relatives, and making necessary family arrangements. Their main purpose was to console.

"There are times and places in life," he said, "when there is absolutely nothing left except you and your faith. Prayer alone is the expression of who and what you are. It is the essence, the response of the soul to the Creator. Standing in the midst of chaos and tragedy, nothing existed except prayer. The young folks—those who had faced little if any tests of life—needed the most help. Older folks I found more accepting of fate. Many knew God was there with them in all times and conditions.

"Supporting those who actually worked in the burned-out wreckage was also critical. The firefighters, police, security, medical teams, and airport personnel, sometimes cried as they con-

26

fronted body parts amidst charred death and destruction. They often thanked me, as I moved among them with short prayers or scripture. I found the Serenity Prayer helpful. I prayed over many unidentifiable bodies, commending them unto the care and love of God. The Lord's Prayer at times was the only word heard among the workers in the carnage. Nothing else made sense at a time like that!"

I asked my friend about praying for those who were lost. "All of us are in the hands of God," he said. "We pass through stages of life, of which death is just one stage. What more can we do than pray that the care and love of God go with us? A number of times, amid the tears and anguish of relatives and rescuers, I prayed the words of the hymn, 'O God, our help in ages past, Our hope in times to come. Our shelter from the stormy blast, And our eternal home.' "

Prayer has more than an on-the-scene value. For those who survive, it is necessary to keep open their relationship to the future; that is, to mourn with the support of prayer today but also to help establish a spiritual foundation for the needs of tomorrow. Prayer helps bridge the gap. If the memories of past sufferings have been surrounded with the care and love of God, a base has been created to move meaningfully into the later adjustments of living.

Discussion questions about "Plain Directions."

1) All of us experience ideas and feelings which come to us as if from out of nowhere. Some people say this is evidence of the creative activity of the Holy Spirit and of God. What is your opinion?

2) Some people pray in quick, spontaneous bursts of inspiration. Is that how you pray or is your prayer life more controlled? Please share the ways you find prayer most helpful, rewarding, and meaningful.

3) The Quaker spiritual leader, Thomas Kelly, suggests that he does, and that we can, pray for a person even while we are with a friend in conversation. Do you ever talk about everyday matters and at the same time hold the acquaintance in your inner prayers?

4) As you look at your life through prayer, do you feel your way of life is really Christian?

5) Many persons have found particular devotional books to be to their liking, in contrast to others. Please share the titles and authors of spiritually oriented books which have been most helpful to you.

6) Please share an experience in your life which led you to believe that God has taken, or is taking, a direct personal interest in you.

A prayer example of partnership with God, by Nikos Kazantzakis.

> My prayer is not the whimpering of a beggar nor a confession of love. Nor is it the trivial reckoning of a small tradesman; give me and I shall give you.
>
> My prayer is the report of a soldier to his general. This is what I did today, this is how I fought to save the entire battle in my sector, these are the obstacles I found, this is how I plan to fight tomorrow.
>
> My God and I are horsemen galloping in the burning sun or drizzling rain. Pale, starving, but unsubdued we ride and converse.
>
> "Leader," I cry. He turns his face toward me, and I shudder to confront his anguish. Our love for each other is rough and ready, we sit at the same table, we drink the same wine in this low tavern of life.[16]

The Lord's Prayer
is the Model For All Our Prayers

Once in a certain place, Jesus was at prayer. When he ceased, one of his disciples said, "Lord, teach us to pray, as John taught his disciples." He answered, "When you pray say . . ." (Luke 11:1, 2).

A few background facts about the Prayer.

The greatest prayer in all Christendom. A model that was suggested by Jesus Christ for the prayer development of his disciples. A prayer which is to teach what prayers should include.

The prayer is found in both Matthew (ch. 6:9–13), and Luke (ch. 11:2–5). The two forms probably come to us from different regions of Palestine, and certainly from different biographers of Jesus.

In Matthew, The Lord's Prayer is part of the Sermon on the Mount. It is included in Christ's remarks about how not to pray (as the hypocrites do, in public and for show), but rather to pray in secret.

In Luke, the prayer is offered in answer to the disciples request to be taught how to pray. This version of the prayer is probably the oldest. It is also the shortest. Luke is concerned with setting the spirit and attitude for prayer.

The Lord's Prayer is composed of seven petitions. After an introduction, the first three emphasize the Glory of God. The position of the first three implies that our human personal needs are to be subordinated to the Will of God. The remaining four petitions express human needs. Altogether, the seven parts suggest the seven most important concerns for which men and women ought to pray.

Some explanations of each phrase or sentence of the prayer.

Our father: We affirm our conviction that God is, that God hears, that God cares for us. We are persons of every background: labor, business, or politics who acknowledge our united praise for God. Whereas the Old Testament saw God as Creator and Judge, we pray to God as Father to emphasize the family intimacy with which we revere God. Our praying with others establishes a community of faith which is bound together by reliance upon God.

THE GLORY OF GOD:

who art in heaven (found only in Matthew): We recognize that God is out of our human reach, beyond our understanding, mysterious "ground of our being." Yet in faith we understand God to be approachable. We find inspiration in the majesty of our God. How majestic is thy name in all the earth.

hallowed be thy name: We pledge our respect and reverence of the greatness of God. We commit ourselves, along with others, to the acknowledgement that there is none other than God.

Thy Kingdom come: We proclaim that it is God's Kingdom which will prevail, not ours. We declare that the reign of God has already begun. God's Kingdom is coming. We know it will supplant the corrupt kingdoms of this world. We pray to take part in its establishment. We take sides with God and join with God in bringing in the Kingdom. We believe that the arrival of the kingdom is independent of us.

Thy will be done on earth as it is in heaven (omitted in Luke's version): (The Jews believed that God ruled the heavens, thus it is natural to pray that God will someday rule the earth. The perfection of heaven will someday be on earth.) We state our belief that the coming of the Kingdom will be the fulfillment of God's will. We shout our anticipation, for we know the will of God is unfolding. We show our utter confidence in the eventual rule of God on earth. We surrender our will that God's will be done. We pray that what has been done in heaven will be done on earth.

PRAYING FOR OUR HUMAN PERSONAL NEEDS:

Give us this day our daily bread: We confess our need for daily sustenance, necessary to maintain physical life, as well as nourishment to maintain spiritual life. We request the plain necessities of living. We only have the right to ask God for our daily needs. We use our because we recognize that we are not alone, instead we are part of the human family, every other person needing nourishment even as we do. We use the words give us, not as a demand, but to acknowledge that we are dependent upon God.

Forgive us our debts (sins, trespasses): We ask to be released from our evasions, our hypocrisies, our prejudices and our deceits. We are saying that our sin corrupts others and their sin enmeshes us, so we pray together for forgiveness. We are addressing our prayer to God for we believe that it is God who can most fully forgive us. We cannot earn our own forgiveness, else we would do

31

good works, so we pray for our unmerited forgiveness according to the Will of God.

as we forgive our debtors: We recognize that we will not be forgiven until we forgive others. We see the failures in the lives of others and realize that we see them for they are our own. In another sense, we are saying that we cannot expect God's forgiveness if we are unwilling to forgive ourselves. We pray in the present tense, not to forgive and be forgiven tomorrow or someday, but today. Even as we ask for forgiveness, our faith tells us that we are already forgiven.

and lead us not into temptation: (*temptation* can mean "trial" or "testing," rather than evil enticement):
1) Grant that we fail not in the time of testing.
2) We admit to God that we are tempted and turn to God for help. We pray for the strength to meet our temptations.
3) We remind ourselves that the greatest temptation is to separate ourselves from God, to forget God, to take God for granted and to reject God. We pray that we will not fail the greatest test of all; that is, to commend our spirits unto God.

but deliver us from evil (or from the Evil One): We admit evil is an influence in life, a force to be reckoned with. We ask deliverance from the dark forces of injustice, unrighteousness, selfishness, strife, adultery and idolatry; which seek to overcome us. We pray to be kept from the worst evil, that of being alienated from God. We use the word us, not just "for me and my son John," because all of us in our community need to be delivered from the evils that plague us as a society. We use the word evil because we know that God will know what the evil is for each one of us.

THE DOXOLOGY:

For thine is the power and the glory, forever and ever: This is not included by Luke. Possibly it is a later addition, or this may have been in the original prayer but omitted in subsequent translations. It was usual in Judaism to conclude prayers with a "doxology," that is, "lines giving and uttering praise." The early Christians often followed this custom. The doxology is a statement of confidence in the present and ultimate reality of the Kingdom of God, a reiteration of the assurance, which all the followers of Christ have, that God's will and power are supreme!

Amen: Very often an abused word to which we pay too little attention, such as, "Now's the time to move on to something else." But really a closing act of reaffirmation of what has been prayed. For some worshippers, the "Amen" is a deliberate, quiet recommitment to the messages of the prayer. For others, it can be a shout of approval, a joyous testimony for the Word as expressed in the prayer; a declaration of enthusiastic support.

The Lord's Prayer is a good teaching model for prayer.

If we did not have the Lord's Prayer for a model, our prayers would probably reflect our human self-interest. Instead of allowing us to center on self, the Lord's Prayer gives us helpful guidelines for our relationship with God. In fact, the theologian Karl Barth points out

> It was not by chance that Jesus gave us a formulary in the Lord's Prayer. . . . God teaches us how we are to pray, for we have so many things to ask. And we think that what we desire is so important. We cannot pray by ourselves. He, therefore, starts us with all our needs and problems on a certain path by which we can bring everything to him.

33

This discipline is necessary. If it is absent we must
not be surprised that we cry out in a void. . . . Let
us be content with possessing this formula of the
Lord's Prayer.[1]

Why it is important to learn to pray.

The difficulty that we face when we consider prayer is that we
overlook where we come from. Most of us are immersed in a society which is frenetic, stressful, hyperactive, restless, noisy, animat-
ed, and constantly on the go. Then someone suggests prayer,
which brings to mind such images as silence, aloneness, quietness,
leisure, and reflection.

Because of this contrast in experience, there are those who say
that prayer must be a learned experience, that we have to learn
how to pray. Among those of such a conviction is the German
theologian Dietrich Bonhoeffer. Of his advice that prayer has to
be a learned process, Perry LeFevre writes:

He makes it clear that Christians must learn to
pray. We must not assume that the heart can pray
by itself, that the wishes, hopes, sighs, laments,
rejoicing are Christian prayer. Prayer does not
mean just pouring one's heart out. We must learn
to pray, we must turn to him who taught us to pray
by using "not the false and confused speech of our
hearts," but the "clear and pure speech which God
has given us in Jesus Christ." And this speech of
God is the speech that meets us in the Scriptures.

If the disciples, who spent the greater part of three years with
Jesus, had to ask, "Lord teach us to pray" (Lu. 11:2), it is not
unreasonable to assume that we, in the midst of all of our distractions, also need to learn to pray.

An example of how the discipline of prayer can be invaluable support even through years of crisis.

The Lords Prayer teaches us a fundamental lesson about life. Prayer is the resource for victorious living, as the prayer-life of this family reveals.

> My father suffered a stroke and was moved to rehabilitation. While there, he developed a blood clot which caused his leg to discolor. My mother visited him regularly and pointed this out to the nurses. After several of these conversations, my mother noticed that my father's leg had turned black. The doctor was immediately called and sent my father to the hospital. He had gangrene which was poisoning his body. We were so sure that he was dying that we called the minister to plan the funeral. I can remember vividly the pain I felt at the impending loss of my father. It hurt physically. I kept resorting to prayer for comfort and strength to overcome my fear of loss and to be able to rejoice in my father's life. From prayer, I felt a physical sense of burden lifted and knew that Jesus was sharing my burden and that I could indeed be there for my mother and brother—I had Jesus with me. The doctors placed a tourniquet on my father's leg, the infection was shut off, but his leg was sacrificed. He had that leg and later his other leg amputated and lived in a nursing home for another seven years. Those were hard years as we watched him disintegrate before our very eyes. But we had faith, and our burdens of care were eased. We learned to love in a different way, too.

Prayer enables us to see beyond years of tragedy. The writer reports, "Those were hard years . . . but we had faith and our burdens of care were eased." Prayer brings peace when there is no peace. She also says, "We learned to love in a different way." Prayer brings new insights to situations which we may not have understood before but later see in a more hopeful and rewarding way. Indeed, this whole testimony reflects an occasion which is remembered, not with bitterness at its length or suffering, but with thanksgivings and peace of mind. Prayer saw the family through.

Why many persons only pray In Jesus' Name.

And Peter said (to the crippled beggar): "I have no silver or gold; but what I have I give you: in the name of Jesus Christ of Nazareth, walk," (Acts 3:5–7).

Once when they were on their way to the place of prayer. (Paul was being harassed by a slave girl.) She did this day after day . . . until Paul said, "I command you, in the name of Jesus Christ to come out of her," (Acts 16:16–18).

Why should prayers be in the name of Jesus Christ?

There are a number of good reasons for praying only In Jesus Name:

1) When we say we should pray in the name of Jesus, we mean in His spirit, with His attitude, or emulating His dedication.

2) Many persons feel we should pray only in Jesus name because it is in Christ that salvation is found.

3) When we pray In His name we identify with our Lord and we associate that about which we pray with Him. For example, it is hard to pray selfishly and then add "In Jesus Name."

4) When we combine Jesus with our prayers, we are suggesting that what we pray about should be subordinated to Him. To pray

for anything less would be depreciating His spirit and our prayer as well.

5) Attaching *In His Name* to our praying may help keep our concerns in sync with the spirit of Christ, and may redirect our prayers toward nobler visions than we might choose ourselves.

6) From a biblical viewpoint, another reason for praying only In Jesus' Name is found in the Gospel of John. "If you ask anything in my name I will do it," (John 14:13). "I chose you. I appointed you to go on and bear fruit, that shall last; so that the Father may give you all that you ask in my name," (John 16:16).

In summary, Dietrich Bonhoeffer felt very strongly that every prayer should be offered "In Jesus' Name." He claimed this gave authority to prayer. He said it would call into being the supernaturalness of the powers of Christ. In like manner, the Danish theologian, Soren Kierkegaard, observed:

> To pray in the name of Jesus is to pray in such a way that it is in conformity with the will of Jesus. I cannot pray in the name of Jesus to have my own will, The name of Jesus is not a signature of no importance, but the decisive factor . . . it means to pray in such a manner that I dare name Jesus in it . . . he steps forward for us, steps into the place of the person praying.[3]

But how about those who lived before Jesus of Nazareth?

To conclude that only the prayers which are offered in the name of Christ reach God would seem to eliminate all those who believe in God without being aware of, or believing in, Jesus as Christ. For example, were the prayers of Abraham, Isaac, Rebekah and Ruth, as well as others of the Old Testament, really of no account and perhaps ineffectual? Were their prayers not heard by God because they did not pray *In Jesus' Name?*

Praying "The Jesus Prayer."

A special prayer which seeks to develop the relationship between the pray-er and God is The Jesus Prayer. "Jesus Christ, Son of God, Saviour, have mercy upon me."[4] This particular prayer has been in use for more than fifteen hundred years. It is usually prayed when repeated over and over in rhythm with breathing. It is based on oneness with God (the objective of all prayers) and on growth, from love of self to union with God, through Jesus Christ.

An excellent example of the use of The Jesus Prayer is found in the book *The Way of a Pilgrim*, which was written in about 1880. Almost nothing is known of the author except that he lost his wife by death after a very few years of marriage and then vowed to live a life of simplicity and complete devotion to God. He planned to depend only upon a faith-relationship with people for his spiritual and physical support. The book is an account of his travels through Russia as he records all kinds of experiences, people and circumstances, most of them testing his faith. He writes that he never found life a loss because his prayer held him in the support of God. His opening sentence in his journal suggests the spirit of his travels:

> By the grace of God, I am a Christian man, by my actions a great sinner, and by calling a homeless wanderer of the humblest birth who roams from place to place. My worldly possessions are a knapsack with some dried bread in it on my back, and in my breast pocket a Bible. And that is all.[5]

Discussion questions about "The Lord's Prayer."

1) Some words in the Lord's Prayer are translated differently. For example, sometimes we say, "Forgive us our debts." At other

times, we may use the word "sin" or the word "trespasses." Do you have a preference? Why?

2) Thomas Merton believes that every person is really seeking God. He says, "There is a natural desire for heaven, for the fruition of God in us." How do you respond to this statement?

3) A foreign couple who have just moved into your neighborhood observe you going to, and coming from, church. One day they ask you what faith and prayer mean to you. What would you tell them?

4) All of us have different ways of praying. Please describe the form and type of prayer which is most comfortable for you.

5) If you pray for "our daily bread," what are you doing so that others may have their daily bread, too?

6) The Lord's Prayer uses the phrase, "Lead us not into temptation." It is a difficult reference for many people. Does God lead us in such a direction? Does God really tempt us? If so why? Is God testing our depth of faith? How have you come to terms, if you have, with the phrase?

7) We don't use the words "Kingdom" and "heaven" often. Please define what these references mean to you.

8) Is there a particular passage of the Bible which has greatly influenced your life? If so, please share why it means and why.

9) Sexist language, such as "Our Father," proves questionable for some people. Does the Lord's Prayer point to God as male? How do you feel about the male references?

"The Jesus Psalter," Anonymous, (Circa 1200–1500[?]).

> Jesus, grant me the grace to fix my mind on Thee, especially in time of prayer, when I directly converse with Thee. Stop the motions of my wandering head, and the desires of my unstable heart, and

my many vain imaginings. O beloved of my soul, take up all my thoughts here, that mine eyes, abstaining from all vain and hurtful sights, may become worthy to behold Thee face to face in Thy glory for ever. Amen.[6]

Understanding Different Aspects of Prayer

Our temperament may affect our type of prayer.

> *Then he made the disciples embark and go on ahead to the other side, while he sent the people away; after doing that he went up the hillside to pray alone* (Matthew 14:22–23).

Of course, we do not know how, or in what way, Jesus prayed when he retreated so often. Perhaps he prayed in various ways, either to reflect how he felt or to fit the situation he faced. Today, when we practice prayer, we are discovering that our temperament, as much as the occasion, often dictates how we pray. In fact, the way we pray may depend upon our type of personality.

The relation of prayer to temperament.

For many years there has been a growing interest in the differences of personality types. Important insights were gained through the publication of the Myers-Briggs Type Indicator in 1962, and more recently there has been concern about the connection between our personality type and our spirituality. Chester P. Michael, a spiritual life authority, and Marie C. Norrisey, a parish worker, editor and author, have written *Prayer and Temperament*, in which they claim that our personality definitely influences the way we pray.

> All indicators point to a close relationship between our innate temperament and the type of prayer best suited to our needs. Introverts will prefer a form of prayer different from Extraverts. Intuitives approach God from a point of view different from Sensers. Feelers pray in a different way than Thinkers. Judging persons want structure in their prayer life, while Perceiving persons want flexibility.[1]

Our temperament traits can be related to our method of praying.

Each of us understands the world from our individual background and temperament. And what holds true with our viewpoint of the world, appears true of our interest in prayer. We pray according to our personalities and temperaments. Some of us are very methodical, always wanting things neat and in order. Hence we are likely to pray in an orderly fashion. Others may not mind clutter, being more willing to spend time on ideas or creative arts, so their prayer life may be more spontaneous, original, and less organized. Still others may be action-minded and want their prayers to accomplish definite objectives. And there are those who use their prayer time for meditation and reflection. They may pray in the spirit of contemplation.

Different types, or ways of praying, in keeping with our personality.

Michael and Norrisey list four different types of prayer and show how each satisfies different temperament types.

1) Augustinian prayer might be generally described as taking words and events from the Bible and putting them into our life today. What do they mean to us for our time? This type of prayer understands scripture as God's Word to us.

2) Franciscan spirituality is concerned, like Saint Francis, with the beauty, wonder, and love in the present world. It responds to nature and to all created things with a spontaneous free spirit. It is interested in helping people appreciate spirituality. Such prayers will lift up special concerns for the poor and a plain lifestyle.

3) Thomistic spirituality is more disciplined and more concerned with what the mind tells us. It reflects a scholarly approach. Such prayers may evidence a more intellectual interpretation. They may emphasize rationality. Prayer here is an "orderly progression of thought from cause to effect."

4) Ignatian spirituality, like the "Spiritual Exercises" of Ignatius Loyola, is organized and disciplined, severe and determined in its adherence to planned spiritual development. It encourages pray-ers to introduce themselves into past Biblical events and to relive what it must have meant to be present when those things were taking place.

These different viewpoints of prayer are not exclusive and the lines cannot be rigidly drawn between them; nevertheless, describing their differences may help to explain why some kinds of prayers turn us off while others attract us.

The Benedictine method of praying.

Researchers Michael and Norrisey say that a prayer which is basic to all the varieties above is the Benedictine method of prayer.

> This ancient type of prayer has probably been used
> by Christians more often than any other method of

prayer. This is understandable since it employs all four psychological functions and therefore is an ideal form of prayer for all the different types and temperaments of personality.[2]

The Benedictine form of praying can be characterized by four prayer states:

The first state suggests that you read for devotional nourishment. When you come to a word, phrase, or event which jumps out at you, stop and take note of what it says to you.

Then proceed to the second state. Give your mind and soul over to meditation and reflection. Repeat the word, phrase, or event over and over and wait for God's message. Don't hurry. Be receptive.

After you feel you have exhausted your thoughtfulness, move to the mental or verbal prayer-response. Now is the time for personal dedication and commitment to follow what has been revealed to you.

If you are prepared for it, a fourth aspect can be added. Here, some pray-ers experience a subtle mysterious union with spiritual forces.

Summary

We should not minimize these insights about prayer styles, but it may be fair to assume that God hears the intent of our prayers more than their form. Varieties may certainly clarify our expressions of faith, but the final emphasis should be to pray our feelings with little worry about their form. "Give yourselves wholly to prayer and entreaty, pray on every occasion in the power of the Spirit," (Eph. 6:8).

The value of a prayer group.

"For where two or three have met together in my name, I am there among them," (Matthew 18:20).

What a prayer group is.

A prayer group is a small, intimate gathering, united in a common commitment which, through regular group discipline, seeks spiritual power and direction. It is often composed of six or eight persons, even up to twelve; (though when one formed around Jesus, eleven would have been a better number). The participants meet regularly to share each other's spiritual journey and often to work for some common cause. Such gatherings are called "fellowship groups," or "prayer cells," or "faith-growth" meetings. They may be referred to as "sharing groups," or "spiritual encounter sessions," or they may be referred to as faith-groups, spiritual-life groups, and confrontational groups.

The purpose of prayer groups.

Prayer groups may be formed for any number of reasons. A group of individuals may want to study the Bible and, in pursuing that goal, find themselves sharing each other's lives with such rewards that they continue in that direction. Some groups are formed for fellowship and stay for the spiritual experience. Others may be organized to meet some community or personal emergency. Some groups arise out of need for more personalized prayer. Others come into being because of the need for support and sharing during times of serious sickness or death.

Prayer groups can be the heart of the Church.

Although prayer groups are sometimes close to the heart of a church body, they are often misunderstood and overlooked. Because they are small and not given much publicity, they can be tragically missed by those who only see the church as a community institution, a social and cultural center, and just a place for public worship on Sunday morning.

John and Mary Doe were church members. They attended often and took part in the affairs of the parish. They were well liked and could be depended upon when help was needed. They supported the church because they found the members friendly.

Although the Does were part of the church, their real interests were elsewhere. John plotted and planned to be president of his company, Jane frequented the nearby city stores to make their home prestigious; both cultivated the right people in town. Then John received a business promotion, and he and Mary left town quite hastily and without many farewells. In fact, many church members never had a chance to say goodbye.

Far from being a good example of church loyalty, this story is really a tragedy. A tragedy because the Does were willing to be part of the organization but not a part of the experience! They used the church socially but never really felt its spiritual meaning. They attended the church but never gave themselves to the faith. They satisfied their outer natures but failed to cultivate their inner spirits!

Perhaps the Does heard about the prayer groups in their church. If so, the suspicion is that they did not dare to join. The spiritual intimacy, and self-revealing sharing, and commitment to a common cause would have been too risky. They might have had to reveal their real selves. Unfortunately they only saw the public, worshiping congregation. They never experienced the healing part of the church within the church.

Prayer groups serve a different purpose than the programmed church service.

Out of necessity in many instances, the regular church service is programmed worship. Open to the public and available to unnumbered attendees, the customary Order of Service offers a dependable routine which visitors and strangers may follow. Because it is a public experience of worship, intimate details of spiritual life, although raised up in prayer, certainly cannot be addressed as much as may be necessary. For these reasons, the church service serves the believer differently than the prayer-group experience.

Prayer groups are likely to be the heartbeat of a church. Meeting in smaller numbers and often for a longer time, they can reach more intimately into the lives of individual believers. Those who share their prayers together also share their innermost lives with one another. Such sharing leads to concern for each other which is deeper than most social relationships. Trust is developed at such a level that old unwanted personal lifestyles are often changed. New ways of living the spiritual life of faith and action are discovered.

Prayer groups develop such awareness of the role of God in re-creating the world that they often become energetic engines for social change. They can be powerful, deeply committed agents for renewing the spirituality of the local church.

A look inside of a prayer group.

A layperson tells how a spiritual life support group deals with threatening personal and social problems, and how the members are sustained by their community of faith.

> We are eleven confessing, troubled souls of ages
> from thirty to sixty and variously challenged by ills
> in our society, the world and our individual lives.
> We do not dwell in the dark; we continue to seek
> enlightenment. Hope, not despair, drives us. We
> are continually present for each other, and,

47

through sharing, gain strength, find direction, give and receive comfort.

We gather for three or four hours about twenty times a year. Early each year we retreat for an entire day. We never separate without prayer, for others as well as for ourselves. We may not always be in agreement, but we are always aware of the joy—spiritual joy some say—our sharing produces within us. Apparently when we are alone we do not always feel this joy, though just thinking about the group can often resurrect it. Most of us still have some difficulty with open prayer, and we continually struggle to articulate our understandings of spirituality. So be it.

As we hear and see God in each other's words and actions, we find it easier to see and hear our Creator's call on our lives. What needs to be done for others as well as ourselves? How do we cooperate with our Creator? Spirituality, to us, is living all days in God's grace with power to praise, love and act.

Perhaps "acting" is the common necessity in our lives to produce joy over and over. Each of us seems driven to take action outside the group; to give, to share, to comfort, to heal. Our individual pains seem to determine the direction in which we find our joy.

What is going on in this faith-oriented support group?

1) They are not always in accord with each other but they keep at it and find their common search for self, and faith calls them to be accountable to each other.

2) Their sharing produces understanding and acceptances of differences.

3) By being open to one another, they discover God in each other.

4) Developing trust enables them to find their own spiritual depths.

5) Their personal growth in the Spirit moves and even drives them to help others in very specific ways.

6) Even when separated, the spirit of the group continues to give them spiritual and emotional support.

The spirit of a Prayer Group.

A superintendent of a state conference describes his experience with a prayer group.

> My greatest experience with prayer was when I organized three prayer/support groups in a former parish. I joined one of the groups and we met every Thursday night from 9:30 P.M. to 11:00 P.M. There were eight people in our group, men and women, and intergenerational. The primary purpose was to share our lives with each other and to engage in intentional, intercessory prayer.
>
> Each session we went around and shared our joys and sorrows, our struggles and our accomplishments. We also indicated areas of intercessory prayer for our lives, for our families, friends, and concerns for "far neighbors" throughout the world. The frankness and openness of the sharing was profoundly transforming! We agreed to be in intercessory prayer each day at 11:00 A.M. for each member of the group and for their shared concerns. No one

49

in the group was to acknowledge their intercessory prayers for those for whom they were praying. All I can say is that miraculous events took place: healing, restoration of broken relationships, new insights given or received, a sense of community and caring!

Out of this group came the development of the Caring Fellowship Visitation Program. Eventually twenty-five persons were trained through monthly sharing sessions. These people worked with me to call on the sick and shut-ins, new member prospects, inactive members and the general membership. When I left the church after twelve years of ministry, the congregation was truly a "family."

Prayer groups, faith groups, or support meetings are very important ways of discovering our own spiritual foundations. No church should ever be without one or even several.

It is significant that this writer, who may have had considerable religious knowledge because of his leadership in the church, claims his greatest experience with prayer was when he was part of a prayer group. It affirms what many spiritually-oriented authorities say; the discovery of the spiritual life and insights of prayer are rarely, if ever, made alone.

That such is the case is evidenced by his comment that, after the members of the group has shared deep feelings with each other, they found that "the sharing was deeply transforming." Indeed, this is the key to such groups. We discover ourselves through what others and what prayer reveals to us. Only as we share do we receive. In opening up to others our own fears and doubts, and our concerns about faith and God, do we find the gifts others have, and God has, for our own spiritual development.

The value of corporate worship.

"Then he began to teach them and said, 'Does not scripture say, "My house shall be called a house of prayer?" But you have made it a robber's cave,' " (Mark 11:17, 18).

Jesus is quoting Isaiah here (ch. 56:7). He is emphasizing the traditional role of the Church and prayer. Unfortunately, as he suggests, people often try to make church something else. Spiritual matters and prayer should be among the main concerns of every gathering of believers.

Spirituality and prayer among the early Christians.

Certainly concern for others, expressed in the lifestyle of prayer, was a characteristic of the early faith communities. Paul talks about church members being bound together as the Body of Christ, each one being dependent upon the other (Col. 3:13). In his Letter to the Thessalonians, he uses the family oriented phrase, "Brothers, pray for us," (I Th. 5:25). All in all, church members are called to be caring, forgiving, helping, serving, accepting and loving.

The Church is a community of the spirit.

An insightful authority concerning public worship and the Christian Church is Dietrich Bonhoeffer, whose understanding of the Church is explained by Professor LeFevre.

> Christian community is a community of the spirit,
> transcending and including unlikeness, the weak
> and the strong, those who will go on living with us
> through sin and need. Christian community is not
> based on some wishful idea of religious fellowship . . .
> reached through spending a few days together.

51

Christian community is grounded in faith, faith in what Christ has done and made possible. What Christ has made possible is just this kind of spiritual community which can continue in spite of difference, in spite of sin, in spite of triviality and weakness. Because Christian community has this character, Bonhoeffer holds that "the most direct way to others is always through prayer to Christ" and that "love of others is wholly dependent upon the truth in Christ."[3]

Bonhoeffer thus attacks one of the most common errors we make about the Church. It is not a social community of people who just like to be together. Nor is it an organization which individuals join for rewards such as influence over others, power, or community prestige. Instead, it is a faith community in which people care for each other, pray for each other, sacrifice for each other, and give themselves in faithfulness to each other; not only because it seems right but because faith demands it—even when such action may be seen as unreasonable. In addition to his comments above, Bonhoeffer goes on to say, "If you are a member of the church, your prayer is necessary for all its members . . . the blood of the church is the prayer of intercession one for another."

The role of the Church.

The church is a place to give and receive care and support, as well as prayers; a fact which was impressed upon me by this note I received from a former parishioner who wrote following the loss of her husband.

I miss John very much. I could never get him to go to church with me as you know. He spent so much time at the tavern. I have found so much help from my church friends. They have done so much for me. I must tell you, not one of John's drinking pals at the saloon, whom he called his best friends, came to the funeral. And not one of them have contacted me since John went.

An account of why another person looks to the example of the Church.

How often we see the fallacies and inconsistencies of the Church. We forget that what the Church stands for gives courage and meaning to so many who struggle with despair and doubt. A friend, who came to church whenever his travels allowed, which was not often, told me,

> You asked why I come to church. I'll tell you. As you know, I sell steel for a living. I don't know how much you know about selling but sometimes, though not always, it's a pretty rough game: cut-throat competition, under-table deals, broken promises, cheating on accounts, shady billings, and the like. Frankly, I come to church, when I can, to remind myself what the world under God is supposed to be like. I need my faith renewed.

The importance of corporate worship to individual faith.

An example of the significance of sharing with others in the gathered community of believers—the Church—comes from a former executive of a large metropolitan association of churches. He writes,

> My prayer-life was given birth by my membership in the Household of Faith, the Church. Why pray? When to pray? How to pray? All have been formed

for me by my life in Christian communities from my birth. In times of separation from a praying community, I live a prayer-less life. I then live life as though it is totally my own doing.

How significant his last sentence is. Without the presence of the Church, he finds himself at loose ends. Without the caring community of faithful believers, he finds life relatively empty. Without the contact with others through prayer, he lives solely for himself. Without the model of the faith, which the Church preaches and commits herself to, he finds himself dependent upon his own individual values.

The benefits of prayer and the spiritual life depend upon cultivation.
God provides the Spirit to inspire our lives but it is up to us to cultivate it. Like anything else, faith and prayers do not mature unless we exercise and practice them. A student of Matthew Fox gives a clear picture of cultivation or lack thereof.

When I have been attentive to the creative gifts within me, I have been free to pray and grow as a human being. When I have cooperated in the denial of these gifts, or when I have chosen to set them aside, I have withered. My love of life has suffered. I have stopped praying. I have become small and cynical or I have driven myself to the point of exhaustion and burnout. I have become a compulsive worker trying to make up in my work what I have denied in my most creative self.[4]

The role of public prayers in the community of faith, i.e. the Church.

54

Some churches, but not all by any means, set aside a definite time during public worship for the sharing of prayers by members of the congregation. One of my correspondents for this book reported,

> In the course of corporate worship when our congregation chooses to pray, we usually identify persons and/or causes which are of import to those of us present. For the duration in which the individual or cause is named, she/he is held in the spiritual focus of the whole praying community. We ask the blessing of God on the person or concern named. I am reluctant, sometimes unable, to define to God what the blessing should be. But because of fifteen years or more of experience in this style of praying, I believe such prayers are deeply felt by those involved and bring support, forgiveness and comfort in times of crises. The corporate prayers of our congregation are consistently the remembered part of our worship. Both persons who have contributed to the praying and those who have received God's promises are willing at subsequent prayers to be named or to name someone. In this way, it is apparent the whole service is vitalized by the presence of the Spirit.

Our participation in a Retreat moves us forward.

> *Cornelius said, "Four days ago, just about this time, I was in the house here saying the afternoon prayers, when suddenly a man in shining robes stood before me. He said, 'Cornelius, your prayer has been heard*

and your acts of charity remembered before God,' "
(Acts 10:30, 31).

This story of Cornelius reflects the experience of those who set aside time to retreat from the world in order to reflect and pray. New and shining resources often appear. Withdrawing from the pressures of everyday life allows new perspectives on ourselves and our society to develop. Hours of silence bring new vigor and new enthusiasm so that we return to the world with better awareness and deeper purpose.

Definition of a retreat.

There is a profound difference between a religious retreat and a business conference. A conference is people centered; a retreat is God centered. The schedule of a conference features discussion, while the program of a retreat includes individual reflection. At a conference one talks to others; at a retreat one listens to his or her inner-self. A conference is the epitome of busyness; a retreat allows time for simplicity and solitariness. The purpose of conference is to share information and express an opinion. The purpose of a retreat is to listen and to reflect.

We attend a conference to study, to solve a problem, to express an opinion, to promote a program, and to learn about some new concern. During the conference there is much talking, discussing, arguing. The characteristics of a retreat, on the other hand, are quite different. A retreat may feature silence, meditation, free time for individual apartness, devotional reading, personal journal writing, sometimes fasting, and always prayer.

What happens on a retreat? A retreat is . . .

. . . an opportunity to set aside our concerns about getting and spending. It is a chance to nourish our inner person.

. . . the time to lay aside argument or reason and enjoy unhurried reading, thinking, meditating, and prayer.

. . . a chance to be quiet in mind and body; to allow the healings of silence to restore our soul.

. . . a time for confronting ourselves, accepting ourselves, and rededicating ourselves to ideals we may have overlooking in the pressures of every day.

. . . an occasion to ask the questions: Who am I? What is the purpose of my life? How am I doing? What is my relationship to God?

. . . an opportunity to restore the balance between body and soul.

. . . a time to commune with God, as we understand God.

A new retreatant describes his experience.

"Bring your Bible," they said. I said, "No way." Not away for a whole weekend with guys I didn't know. But a longtime friend pushed. I went.

We drove to the lakeside cabin after work Friday, chose our beds, dumped our stuff, and were off to supper. Plenty of good food. No Bible yet. Except for my friend, the others were all strangers. Spent the evening getting to know each other. Everyone was friendlier than I expected. Pop, wine and crackers ended with the Bible and prayers. I found it interesting.

Saturday morning was different. A guest leader spoke. No, he just shared. What did our faith mean to us? Some introduction to Bible stories which could apply to our own lives. We shared more experiences. Some guys really have problems. I didn't think men could be so open. I didn't talk much.

During lunch, lots of laughter, jokes, kiddings. Spent the afternoon walking the beach with two of the guys. More talk, I told them how hard it was for me and my family when I was laid off. It felt good to talk about it.

Saturday evening. More sharing. What was life all about? Where did God and religion fit in? More serious now. Personal experiences, individual problems, life histories. At the end, one guy read a spiritual meditation, prayer. We were all pretty close. I felt I was among friends who cared for each other and for me, too.

Late breakfast on Sunday followed by a short religious service. A talk about sharing and trusting in God by the leader. Free time to pack up our stuff and load the cars. Lunch, then many heartfelt good byes: "It's been a great retreat"; "John, I hope things work out for you"; "Bill, prayers for your job." Firm hand shakes all 'round. A hug or two.

I really hated to see the retreat bust up. I found some new friends. I understand my self more. I think about God more. As a matter of fact, I might go again.

The value of a Spiritual Director.

"Adapt yourselves no longer to the pattern of this present world, but let your minds be remade and your whole nature thus trans-formed. Then you will be able to discern the will of God, and to know what is good, acceptable and perfect," (Romans 12:2).

Soren Kierkegaard, the significant Danish theologian, tells a memorable story which emphasizes the importance of having an experienced director for prayer-development, rather than trying to do everything ourselves. I paraphrase his parable.

> Once upon a time there was an exceedingly rich coachman who had a hobby of show horses. After watching, from his porch, how his master-trainer disciplined the horses of his stable, he decided to train some himself. So he went abroad and purchased several outstanding animals.
>
> Just as soon as he brought them to his farm, he began to exercise them according to his own ideas. Though he did so every day, it soon became apparent that the creatures were not responding well. They seemed dull in spirit and lethargic in pace. After some weeks, in despair the owner turned over his new acquisitions to the master of his stables.
>
> "I can't do anything with these horses," he complained. "Take them yourself and see what you can do."
>
> So the master-trainer undertook a professional exercise program. And with what a difference! Within a comparatively short time, the animals seemed eager and were as fit as when they were first bought.

Kierkegaard draws the lesson that it is wiser to have a spiritual counselor who can understand what we may need, instead of trying to learn about spiritual growth ourselves. Indeed, what such a counselor can do, is defined by Thomas Merton, the well known Roman Catholic priest and Spiritual Director.

Spiritual direction is not merely the cumulative effect of encouragements and admonitions which we all need. It is not mere ethical, social or psychological guidance. It is spiritual.

It is important for us to understand what this word "spiritual" means here. There is a temptation to think that spiritual direction is the guidance of one's spiritual activities, considered as a small part or department of one's life. You go to a spiritual director to have him take care of your spirit the way you go to a dentist to have him take care of your teeth. This is completely false!

The spiritual director is concerned with the whole person, for the spiritual life is not just the life of the mind, or of the affections, or of the "summit of the soul," it is the life of the whole person.[5]

There are professional and semi-professional Spiritual Directors.

Though the term Spiritual Director is often identified with a clergyperson, many others fill the role with greater or less spirit and insight, such as the religiously oriented psychotherapist, the hospital chaplain, or the pastoral marriage counselor. Again, Thomas Merton helps interpret the role.

The director is one who knows and sympathizes, who makes allowances, who understands circumstances, who is not in a hurry, who is patiently and humbly waiting for indications of God's action in the soul. He is concerned not just with this or that urgent problem, this or that sin, but with the whole life of the soul. He is not interested merely in our actions. He is much more interested in the basic

60

attitudes of our soul, of our inmost aspirations, our way of meeting difficulties, our mode of responding to good and evil. In a word, the director is interested in our very self, in all its uniqueness, its pitiable misery and its breathtaking greatness.[6]

The value of a Prayer Friend.

There are significant requirements of a prayer friend. He or she should be a person who has the talent to listen; a person who has been on his or her own journey; someone who is not easily shocked, and who knows when to encourage and when to counsel. A prayer friend is one who will lead a compassionate, disciplined prayer life even though separated; who will share in his or her spiritual discoveries; who will be willing to deal with personal weaknesses and fears; who will share in journal writing; who will give support during the darknesses of prayer; as well as share in the creative silences of spiritual renewal.

Examples of prayer friends.

Several excellent examples of prayer friends appear in the Bible. For example, David and Jonathan in the Old Testament (I Sam. 18:1–5); as well as Paul and Barnabas in the New (Acts 13:1–4).

In that unsurpassed religious epic, *Pilgrim's Progress,* by John Bunyan, Christian has a prayer friend in Hopeful. They support each other in all kinds of trials. When they almost drown in the river just before reaching the small wicket gate, it is Hopeful who keeps Christian's head above water and his spirits high, as he calls out, "Be of good cheer, brother, I feel the bottom and it is good."

Finding a prayer-friend.

Friends are not hard to find but a prayer friend is another story. Not everyone is willing to be as open as being a prayer friend implies. Nor is it easy to establish a sense of trust deep enough with another person so that prayers of the most probing nature can be shared, the most excruciating fears be surfaced, or the past possible erosion of character rehearsed. But if such a sharing relationship with a prayer friend can be established, its dividends are significant.

Our progress in prayer may result in a real inner battle.

> *Jacob was left alone, and a man wrestled with him . . . the man . . . struck him . . . The man said, "Let me go. . . ." but Jacob replied, "I will not let you go unless you bless me." He said to Jacob, "What is your name?" The man said, "Your name shall no longer be Jacob, but Israel, because you strove with God and with men and prevailed," (Genesis 32: 24–29).*

When Jacob found himself alone, he had time to think about his past life. Memories of some shady deals came to plague him, such as the time he defrauded his brother Esau out of his birthright. He was also conscious of his alienation from God. What followed was an all night struggle with himself and God. It was a battle involving Jacob's total commitment. It was a violent and exhausting combat which demanded all of his strength as he cried, with recurring insistence, "I will not let you go." He kept demanding that the one with whom he wrestled reveal himself. As the French religious philosopher, Jacques Ellul, affirms,

Israel, God's combatant, or he who wrestled with God, such is the name which everyone who prays should bear, for prayer is striving with God. Prayer cannot be a listing of benefactions which we expect from an obvious and all-powerful intervention. It must be a demand with respect to the hidden God to reveal himself, to declare himself and enter into our situation.[7]

Prayer may involve serious combat with ourselves and with God.

Our growth in prayer is sometimes a gradual struggle as we move from our lessor selves to a greater appreciation of the presence of God. In the process, we overcome guilt and inner conflicts as we are confronted by our conscience, wrestle with our soul, and ultimately struggle, as Jacob did, with God. This contention with self and God can be difficult and long lasting. Nor do all of us win our battles. Some of us resign ourselves to our old habits and passions. Some of us carry on the conflict with self and God for months or even years, while we continue to suffer from our inability to accept the blessing of forgiveness by others and by God. Then there are those who, like Jacob, win the argument with the profane side of self, and then go on to experience the cleansing of the soul, and the blessing of God.

This grappling with self and God is aptly put into words by Peter Forsyth.

> Lose the importunity of prayer, reduce it to soliloquy with God . . . lose the real conflict of will and Will, lose the habit of wrestling and the hope of prevailing with God [and] you tend to lose the reality of prayer at last. In principle you make it a mere conversation instead of the soul's great

action. You lose the food of character, the renewal of will. You may have beautiful prayers, [but] in the end you lose the reality of religion. . . .

Resist God in the sense of closing with God, cling to Him with you strength, not your weakness only, with your active and not your passive faith, and He will give you strength.[8]

Our growth in prayer may bring sadness over what we have "lost."

A common characteristic of the deepening prayer experience is that old interests and attachments become less important. For example, our drive for temporal success may be replaced by more appreciation of what we have already. Our urge to get ahead of others may no longer be as pressing as catching up with our own emotional and spiritual development. Our need to control situations may not seem as important as controlling our own prejudices, fears and desires. These insights about spiritual growth and worldly "losses" were described centuries ago in memorable words of Saint Augustine.

> I was sick at heart and in torment. . . . You stood in the secret places of my soul, 0 Lord. . . . The lower condition which had grown habitual was more powerful than the better condition which I had not tried. . . . Those trifles of all trifles, my one-time mistresses, held me back, plucking at my garment and my flesh. "Are you sending us away? . . ." This was the controversy raging in my heart, a controversy about myself against myself.[9]

Our tendency toward self-righteousness may separate us from others.

It is tempting to assume that our new found peace from prayer is a special blessing from God. This may encourage us to feel different from others. Our new satisfied pietism may lead others to look on us as feeling superior, at which times they may leave us for more friendly acquaintances.

To what end is our growth in prayer and spirituality?

If our intent in praying is to become better than others, as fulfilling as that might be, we will actually become less than others because we have introduced the factor of pride. The purpose of prayer is not to make us better than our neighbor so much as it is to make us better than we were yesterday.

Progress in prayer may create a feeling of doubt.

Somewhere along the route of praying we may lose our way. We do not know what lies before us and we become confused with the direction our praying is taking us. We are in uncharted waters of faith. We do not understand new feelings and experiences. We discover that the spiritual trail is unmarked. We do not find familiar signs to point the way. We may begin to wonder if we understand prayer after all. Such doubts and uncertainties may lead us to discouragement and we may even decide to give up our prayers.

Sometimes new spiritual insights may be personally frightening.

Prayer and inner exploration of faith can reveal scary feelings and emotions. We may uncover deep rooted conflicts, disguised doubts, unresolved fears, memories of abuses, or traumas long suppressed. Nor is this discovery a new phenomenon. Centuries ago, writers about prayer were observing the same problem. In 1675, Francois Fenelon, the French spiritual guide to kings, wrote about it:

> As light increases, we see ourselves to be worse
> than we thought. We are amazed at our former
> blindness as we see issuing forth from the depths of

our heart a whole swarm of shameful feelings, like filthy reptiles crawling from a hidden cave. We never could have believed we had harbored such things. But we must be neither amazed nor disheartened. We are not worse than we were, on the contrary, we are better. . . .

Bear in mind for your comfort, that we only perceive the malady when our cure begins.[10]

As a matter of fact, the depth of our prayer experience may be questioned if it is not a troublesome experience, if we do not become involved in a serious struggle even as Jacob knew. If prayer is to penetrate to the foundations our being, then it is going to disturb some of our childlike complacencies, some of our false protections, some of our unknown prejudices, many of our faithless doubts, as well as some of our unrealized ways in which we avoid giving our selves to the love of God. Kenneth Leech, experienced author on prayer and spirituality cries out, "From spiritual smugness and the lifelessness of idols may the fiery troublesome God deliver us." He quotes the Spanish writer Unamuno:

Those who believe they believe in God, but without passion in the heart, without anguish of mind, without uncertainty, without doubt and even at times without despair, believe only in the idea of God, not in God himself.[11]

We may expect some dry periods.

"Why stand so far off, Lord, hiding thyself in time of need," (Psalm 10:3).

"How long , O Lord, wilt thou quite forget me? How long wilt thou hide thy face from me?" (Psalm 13:1).

66

When our God seems to have gone away.

How like the psalmist we all are at times. We cannot find God. God seems to have left us completely. We just want to give up trying to reach God. We are just not up to praying any more. We even wonder why we ever thought prayer was important.

Difficulty in finding enthusiasm for prayer has many causes.

Many of us find ourselves living fractured spiritual lives today. The constant barrage of news and information, the thousands of TV and film images, the multitudes of printed ideas—all assail us. Of course, these might be contributive to a fuller life if they were not so often reflective of a world of violence, of breakdown of family life, of personal insecurity, as well as questions about the stability of our society. It is difficult for many individuals to find inner peace in such a turbulent environment. Everything seems to mitigate against "centering down" in prayer. Indeed, Olive Wyon, the author of the classic book *The School of Prayer*, raises the same concern.

> We cannot indulge in vague, indecisive, excited thoughts about all kinds of things all through the day, and then find our minds, recollected and tranquil when we turn to prayer. . . . All lack of discipline in our daily life, will inevitably tell in our prayer.[12]

One of my correspondents suggests that the experience of social turbulence results in a "wondering mind." He may be speaking for many of us in his testimony about his struggle to "center down."

> I have been greatly helped by reading one of Henry Nouwen's books about his own experiences at

prayer. Nouwen wrote about how easily he became distracted in his prayers, but he doesn't let this fact bother him. Rather, he is certain God is communicating with him even through these distractions. What an immediate relief reading this brought to me. No longer feeling guilty about my distractions, I stopped wasting valuable time and energy getting angry at myself. Prayer has enabled me to realize God's acceptance of me goes much deeper than the wanderings of my mind and heart.

The problem of dryness in prayers.

Sometimes the threats to our inner peace and spiritual strength may result in more than just a wandering mind. We may find ourselves in a time of spiritual dryness. This may have been the experience of the Samaritan woman at the well (Jn. 4:7–30). You recall she admitted to five husbands. Five different loyalties, five contrasting ways of life, five kinds of intimate love. No wonder she reached out for help. She must have been emotional drained, spiritually dry. Her soul was parched. She needed spiritual water. She needed to drink at a different well. She needed to be reminded that dryness could be overcome by drinking living water. "Whoever drinks the water that I shall give him [her] will never suffer thirst anymore," (Jn. 4:14). In like spirit, Saint John of the Cross brings Sixteenth Century spiritual wisdom to modern believers when he says, "My spirit has become dry because it forgets to feed on You."

But what do we do if times of prayer dryness take hold of us?

Don't be dismayed; such unproductive periods are normal. Dry times in prayer are a common experience. Sooner or later, even those most committed to prayer, come to a time when prayer does not seem possible. For example, Saint Teresa, a Sixteenth Century "religious" who knew so much about spirituality that she taught prayer to thousands of her convent sisters, wrote in her journal of faith,

> At times I find myself so arid that I am not able to form any distinct image of God, nor can I put my soul into, any attitude of prayer. My mind at such times is like a born fool. . . . What would those who loved and honour me think if they saw their friend in this dotage?[13]

Friedrich von Hugel, Twentieth Century teacher and spiritual advisor, remembered Father Hocking telling him a story which solved this dilemma quite easily. Hocking described a man who was embarking on a desert journey. Even as he mounted his camel, guides warned him that somewhere along the route there might be sandstorms.

"What shall I do then?" the traveler asked.

"You do what desert travelers always do," he was told. "When the sands begin to blow, you dismount, you cover yourself and the camel with your robes and carpets, and then you just wait out the storm. Sooner or later it will subside. Then the sun will come out again and you can mount your camel and be on your way once more."

Dry periods may serve a purpose.

Although dry periods may be discouraging and upsetting, they may have a function in the life of the Spirit. Perhaps the soul needs rest on occasion even as does the body. Prayer can be exhausting. As we have noted, it can involve an emotional and spiritual struggle. Because prayer is a progressive battle with our selves as well as with God, when we leave lower levels behind and gain higher altitudes we may need time for spiritual renewal. For example, anyone who has hiked up a mountain remembers the level patches that come occasionally on the steep trail, places to rest tired muscles before ascending again. Some campers call them "thank-you-mams." In like manner, dry periods of prayer can afford opportunities for rest and renewal .

Emily Herman, the spiritual writer who shunned publicity and always just signed herself "E. Herman," puts the matter in the larger perspective of spirituality:

> Three fourths of our difficulties about prayer, in its most spiritual aspect would disappear, if we realized the simple truth that prayer is a dying to self and becoming alive to God, and that each stage of a progressive prayer life is a stage in the putting to death of self that God may work and reign.[14]

The Dark Night

Far along the trail of prayer is the experience which mystics, who have delved deeply into spirituality, call the Dark Night of Prayer. The following quotation from the Book of Psalms gives some idea of its despair and seriousness.

> My God, my God why hast thou forsaken me and art so far from saving me, from heeding my groans? O my God, I cry in the day time, but thou dost not answer, in the night I cry but get no respite (Ps. 22:1, 2).

The characteristics of the Dark Night experience.

Because I am not in the class with the mystics and saints who have gone through such spiritual darkness, I rely heavily here on the spiritual understanding and insight of Dr. Georgia Harkness, formerly of the Garrett Biblical Institute. Professor Harkness wrote extensively about all aspects of prayer, including her book *The Dark Night of the Soul*. In it she describes four characteristics of the Dark Night.

1) One who has found in God precious companionship and desires to go on to more spiritual fellowship, finds to his [her] great dismay that he [she] seems to be further from God than before.

2) A second and closely related characteristic is a union of self-distrust and self-condemnation.

3) A third dominant trait is loneliness, which means the bitterness of isolation from God and man. Bereft of divine companionship, the soul cries out for human fellowship.

4) A fourth note . . . is spiritual impotence . . . spiritual weariness and discouragement . . . Almost invariably a soul caught in the "dark night" thinks it will never emerge.[15]

Some comments about the Dark Night.

Is the Dark Night the result of a psychological condition? Some authorities contend that the Dark Night experience is really a description of psychological depression. On the other hand, spiritual life authorities reply that we cannot dismiss the Dark Night as being a mark of emotional disturbance. So many mystics and saints have probed its depths from so many different perspectives and with such critical insights over so many centuries, that it is safe to conclude that the experience lies in the arena of spirituality.

How common is the Dark Night experience?

There are different descriptions of the Dark Night, some more sober than others. For some of us a Dark Night can be an occasion of despair and loss of hope and a night of crying over the kitchen table. For Thomas Merton, his Dark Night caused him to withdraw from life at a retreat center and live as a recluse until he could find himself and his faith again. For most of us, the Dark Night is a more serious alienation from God than we will realize, probably due to the fact that few of us dare to explore the deepest and darkest depths of prayer in our search for God.

Was Jesus' cry about being forsaken a Dark Night experience?

An illustration of the Dark Night which certainly comes to mind is the cry of Jesus, "My God, why hast thou forsaken me?" (Mark 15:35). Although this seems to describe a Dark Night experience, and although such an feeling of abandonment has been described by so many deeply spiritual persons down through history, Professor Harkness observes there is little in the New Testament about the Dark Night. It emphasizes instead, she says, the spirit of "triumphant rejoicing and hope. . . . The prevailing temper of life was certainly not that of divine abandonment, but of divine companionship."

Discussion questions about "Different Aspects of Prayer."

1) The evangelist John Wesley wrote, "I have so much to do that I must spend several hours in prayer before I do it." What do you think of the way he spent his time? Do you feel Wesley would say the same thing today? Why or why not?

2) Your temperament may dictate your style of prayer, but to what extent does your temperament influence your interest in prayer?

3) In your experience, what have been your greatest difficulties in prayer: frustration at slow answers; incomplete or no answers at all; new awareness of places in your soul which prayer

has exposed; or unexpected fears resulting from meeting yourself in the presence of God?

4) A woman observed, "I have been a member of my church for five years, but when I became a part of a prayer group, my faith became more meaningful for me." What do you think she meant?

5) In your experience, how has prayer changed your life? For example, has it helped in your understanding of who you are? Do you have a better insight into the motives of others? Do you have more inner peace? Do you find a greater concern to confront and change the community or system in which you live?

6) Sometimes we find our enthusiasm for prayer waxing and waning. When you have lost interest in praying, how have you responded? Do you have any recommendations for the benefit of others?

"A Prayer When Members of a Faith Group Meet Together" by Saint John Chrysostom, (Fourth Century).

> Almighty God, who has given us grace at this time with one accord to make our common supplications to you; and who promises that where two or three are gathered together in your name, that you will grant their requests; fulfill now, O Lord, the desires and petitions of your servants as may be most expedient for them; granting us in this world knowledge of your truth, and in the world to come, life everlasting, Amen.[15]

THREE PROFOUND BENEFITS OF PRAYER

"If you invoke me and pray to me, I will listen to you; when you seek me you shall find me; if you search with all your heart, I will let you find me, says the Lord," (Jeremiah 29:12–13). This quotation is from Jeremiah's letter to his own people who were captives in Babylon. He is encouraging them to keep the faith and he does so by suggesting what God can do for them if they will trust God and pray.

I must add, however, that Jeremiah would be among the first to affirm that we cannot cajole God, nor tempt God, nor can we bend God's will, by even our most fervent prayers. We should not look to prayer for benefits. Furthermore, prayer is not to be judged by results. We do not pray because of what God can do for us but because we love God without counting the cost or returns. Now, having said that, it can be added that there are benefits to prayer.

Three significant benefits of prayer and the spiritual life.
Evelyn Underhill (1875–1941), an English spiritual life authority, who wrote and lectured widely on topics of mysticism and

spirituality as well as prayer, suggests three benefits of the spiritual life—including, of course, prayer:

> 1) There is a profound sense of security, of being safely held in a cosmos of which, despite all contrary appearance, peace is the very heart. . . . God is Ground of the soul, the Unmoved, our very rest; statements which meet us again and again in spiritual literature.[1]
>
> 2) The relationship is felt rather as the intimate and reciprocal communion of a person with a Person. . . . It is always in a personal and emotional relationship that man finds himself impelled to surrender to God; and this surrender is felt by him to evoke a response.[2]
>
> 3) Spirit is felt as an inflowing power, a veritable accession of vitality, energizing the self or the religious group, impelling it to the fullest and most zealous living out of its existence giving it fresh joy and vigour, and lifting it to fresh levels of life.[3]

We can be inwardly secure amid crises.

The song David sang to the Lord: *"The Lord is my stronghold, my fortress . . . my God, my rock, where I find safety: my shield, my mountain fastness, my strong tower,"* (II Samuel 22:2).

David said it as well as anybody: the Lord is a fortress, a rock, a shield and a strong tower. In those brief references, he expressed the foundation of religious faith which is security in God. Indeed, throughout the scriptures this same theme about the guardianship of God is proclaimed again and again, an example of which is the cry of David to Goliath, "You have come to me with sword and spear and dagger, but I have come against you in the name of the

76

Lord of Hosts," (I Sam. 17:45). Across the generations of faith, the testimony continues; God is a rod and staff, a shield and buckler, those who believe in God cannot be moved. For a modern example of inner spiritual security in the midst of fear-filled uncertainty, consider this example of a man who faced a frightening operation.

I had to go through tests which eventually led to catheterization in which the cardiologist runs wires up through a vein in the groin and then up into the heart while watching the whole thing through a TV monitor. Since I knew that you had to be completely awake while it was being done, I found it very frightening to anticipate.

Going down on the metal stretcher and then waiting I was scared to death. I was not being religious. I was not praying. I was just being scared. Then, unbidden by me, the verses of Psalm 103 flashed through my brain. "Bless the Lord O my soul, and forget not all His benefits, who forgives all your iniquity, who heals all your diseases, and who redeems your life from the Pit."

Well, I did recognize that as God speaking to me. I was so completely relaxed and at peace all through the catheterization that I found it very interesting and actually kind of enjoyable. A physician friend who had been standing by with me told my wife that he expected me to be very tense and found me so much otherwise.

I went on through surgery and the recovery and felt at peace. I do not understand this, why I should be so favored. Certainly goodness has no part in it.

But long ago I learned what God's grace is. I just accept it, praise Him, trust Him, and thank Him quietly with prayer through almost every hour in the day. For if prayer is conversation with God and if we live with Christ, then prayer is not formal speech occasionally and forcibly done, but a day-long sharing of thought with a Friend.

An example of how faith and prayer provided inner strength in the midst of family, personal, and vocational turmoil.

Most of us go through severe trials in our lives. This is an account of what happened to one man, his wife, and his job.

> In recent months, threats to my own self-worth as well as to my job security have brought me anxiety and spiritual pain which I have never experienced. The stress between me and my wife has led me to consider divorce. I have thought of suicide. Needless to say, my job performance has declined.
>
> At the end of four months of such suffering, the threats are still fully present. Yet I have begun to heal. My wife and I are not divorced. I am alive. And some of the foundation of my life and faith is becoming reestablished. I believe that the agony which we two have endured, some of the struggles we have fought, against each other as well as in tandem against outside forces, have been a spiritual exercise akin to prayer.
>
> Some of the recent prayers of my wife and myself have been anguished, some brief, some self-pitying, many unspoken. We didn't know at the depths of our struggling that we were praying. As I look back

at the experiences, I believe that we were. Our lives are changing. We are being saved. We have prayed through.

Several months later, I talked with my friend again and asked, "Has your experience of finding security through prayer held up?" He replied,

As the experience has unfolded, on some Sunday mornings I have been in a very angry mood as I began preparation for worship. Had you or anyone else brought to me a thorny subject, I would have had difficulty in responding in a civil manner. But my usual custom is to arrive at the church several hours before the Service. During that time, I pray and meditate and try to set my spirit for the worship.

At the close of the praying, singing, preaching, with the congregation at worship, I have found myself to be calm, my anger to have been replaced with gentler feelings. I acknowledge that to be God's gift—the activity of the Holy Spirit. Certainly it has not been my agenda, not of my doing. The Holy Spirit has been present.

Perhaps the greatest lesson to be learned from this testimony is that when the storm threatens and then arrives, it is too late to build the foundation. Certainly one of the reasons why this crisis ended as hopefully as it apparently did, was that the man and his wife were familiar with their spiritual resources of faith and prayer. They had prepared and when the winds blew, they were not found wanting.

On finding inner spiritual security amid personal crises

The testimony of a person who found faith and prayer to be supportive in the face of prejudice, hatred, and personal attacks.

The young man of this story, after much prayer and soul searching, took the peace stand of his Mennonite church. It was not surprising then that, when World War II erupted he became a conscientious objector. His assignment was to fight forest fires in the western states.

His train ride West proved to be a dramatic American story. As a CO, without any identifiable uniform, he sat among other non-military civilians until an older woman inquired, "Young man why aren't you fighting for our country?"

He explained his religious reasons for opposing the war but it did little good. The woman was incensed and quickly involved the other passengers in a wild protest, some suggesting that they throw the "coward" off the train. During the melee, the young man dealt with the hostility and explained his principles again and again, relying on his inner prayer security to maintain his patience and courage.

The conductor appeared, decided he could not handle the passengers' anger, and called the authorities who were in command of the last three cars of the train which were filled with troops. An officer heard the complaints of the civilians and listened to the youth's testimony. Then he spoke to the hostile passengers. "This war is being fought for the right of people to be free and have their own opinions, even though they may differ from the majority," he stated. "I do not agree with this man's stand, and you obviously do not either, but we are fighting the war for freedom for others as well as ourselves. This citizen deserves your tolerance, not hatred."

After hearing more complaints from the riders, the officer added, "From this point on, this citizen will ride with us in the troop cars as one of my responsibilities."

It seems safe to conclude that the peace stand which this young man took came about as a result of church and individual religious commitment, supported by personal prayers and a denomination which has a long history of such objection to war. But it is important to note that Christian faith and prayer does not always point to such a non-combatant decision.

The testimony of a man who answered the call of his country.

A close friend, after reading of the above account, had this to say about the role of prayers for those who go to war.

> I believe in the rights of conscientious objectors. I understand the Christian foundation for totally committed pacifists. It is also important to note that those who sign up to defend their country are not callous war lovers.
>
> People in my family have always answered the call because we feel it is our duty. We do it without apology or pride. We believe that freedom is worth fighting for. Does that mean that my brother rejoices that his only son was killed in World War II, or

that Grandpa was happy about his older brother dying in the Wilderness Battle leaving three children fatherless, or that Harold enjoyed picking up the pieces of his blasted and fallen friends.

We all know the horrors of war. Nobody knew better than General Sherman that "War is Hell." There is no one who prays more fervently and sincerely for peace than one who knows military service. My heart is sorrowful in the extreme for the young American men and women who are called to foreign action. I get on my knees and pray that peaceful solutions can be found—a way out of desperate confrontations. We must search for peaceful solutions to our problems. As long as tyrants exist, it won't be easy.

In the two accounts noted above, prayer is seen to be an active agent in two contrasting political and theological positions. In the first, prayer supported the conviction against militarism. In the second, prayer supports persons who are for militarism when necessary.

The difference does not exclude the importance of prayer in either situation. Prayer is not a definer of either political, social or theological attitudes. What prayer does is to keep open the spirit which seeks to follow the Will of God.

For example, I support the objector's position. My correspondent sees the matter otherwise. Nor is this our only difference. I am a liberal, he is more conservative. Obviously we differ in many things. But—and this is significant—we both pray. Because we do, both of us recognize that our convictions are always subject to a greater Truth. I am not saying, nor does he I'm sure, that we depreciate our convictions. Each of us staunchly holds to what we believe with much determination. We do not undervalue our differences but we live with them as members of the community of faith. Because we both find the inner security of prayer, we do not have to resort to the temporary solutions of intolerance, vindictiveness, or hatred. Indeed, because we see a larger picture of life than our differences, we turn our energies to those things about which we can be more cooperative.

Prayer is a process whereby Truth is sought. Prayer is a means to an end; the end being not our own will, but the Will of God.

We can know God in a far more personal way.

> *The word of the Lord came to me: "Before I formed you in the womb . . . I appointed you a prophet to the nations."*
>
> *"Ah, Lord God," I answered, "I do not know how to speak. I am only a child."*
>
> *But the Lord said, "Do not call yourself a child, for you shall go to whatever people I send you and say whatever I tell you to say. Fear none of them, for I am with you and will keep you safe,"* (Jeremiah 1:4–8).

This story of Jeremiah's call is an example of the personal relationship between an individual and God. God talks to Jeremiah. The prophet talks back. God assigns Jeremiah to a prophetic career. The prophet protests that he is human and not capable of such a responsibility. Thus the conversation goes on between a person and a Person (God).

Throughout the Bible, this sense of personal-ness between God and Man is proclaimed.

83

The book of Genesis is careful to present God as communicating with human beings. "God called to the man and said to him, 'Where are you?' The man replied, 'I heard the sound of your footsteps,' " (Gen. 3:9–10). This is more than a primitive concept of God. It is the early conviction that God and persons have a special relationship with each other

Many of the psalmists speak to God in terms we would interpret as personal: "I called to the Lord in my distress and he answered me," (Ps. 120:1). The prophet Isaiah describes his call by God as a personal conversation between the Lord and himself: "Then I heard the Lord saying, 'Whom shall I send?' And I answered, 'Here am I, send me,' " (Is. 6:8). In the New Testament, of course, Jesus is often quoted as speaking directly to God as "Father."

Explanation of the terms "person" and "Person."

When we speak of God as being a Person, we do not mean as men and woman are persons. It is not in the sense that we can see or even feel God as we would other individuals. We mean God is personal because God understands us and is so much a part of our thinking, feeling and praying.

Sometimes we think of God as power, as force, and as first cause. Although such concepts may be helpful, they do not speak to us of forgiveness, confession, or love. Such terms do not call us to care for our neighbor, to walk humbly, or to seek justice. Because we believe God does embody these attributes which are a part of our personal living, we call God *personal.*

We think of God as personal because, as noted in the Bible illustrations above, at special times we can feel that God is talking to us, guiding us, answering us, forgiving us, and loving us. The relationship seems vividly personal. For example, when we pray, our prayers are from a person to a Person who understands, feels,

judges, forgives, knows and loves us better than we know ourselves. Philosopher Friedrich Heiler sums it up this way:

> What does the simple, devout person, undisturbed
> by reflection, think about when he prays? He
> believes that he speaks with God, immediately pre-
> sent and personal, has intercourse with Him, that
> there is between them a vital and spiritual com-
> merce. There are three elements which form the
> inner structure of the prayer: experienced faith in a
> living personal God, faith in His real immediate
> presence, and a realistic fellowship into which man
> enters with God conceived as present.[4]

A testimony about the personal-ness of God .

Dr. Reuben A. Sheares III, formerly Director of Church Life
and Leadership for the United Church of Christ denomination,
traveled throughout the nation visiting churches and talking with
all sorts of believers. People say Dr. Sheares has an intimate sense
of God. I asked how that was for him.

> When I was growing up in North Carolina in a
> hostile environment of racial oppression, I had to
> find in God what I could not find in my environ-
> ment. If I had listened to what the culture was say-
> ing, I would have gotten the impression I was
> worthless. Instead, the mothers and fathers of my
> church pointed me to God. I was given a sense of
> my own self, that I was a child of God. As a result I
> have a very real sense that God is actively present
> in my life and ministry. My self confidence is God
> confidence!

I wanted to follow up with his personal feelings. So, knowing that prayer was very important to him, I asked him why.

> We had the traditional practice of prayer. Out of that, prayer became a routine part of my life. I see a distinction between personal prayer and saying prayers. I have my times of stillness and then there are the rest of times: daily work, meetings, traveling, and the like. Then I pray in all kinds of conditions. For me to pray is to know God, through Jesus Christ. This undergirds me as a person. This awareness of God is the foundation of my life! It counts the most!

For many of us, the answer to the question, "Is God personal?" is answered by our own experiences. In prayer, we become aware that God listens. In confession, we experience forgiveness. In suffering, we find ourselves supported and held together. In temptation, we discover untapped spiritual strengths to confront that which we previously could not resist. In despair, we find hope; in grief, consolation; in service to others, inspiration; and in faith; we find joy and peace.

A Personal testimony concerning the occasion when I felt God took a personal and active interest in my life.

Several years ago, I was fired from a job which I had much enjoyed and held with dedicated passion. In fact, I was so concerned to do well that I went to work early to pray and thus prepare myself as best I could; and I stayed late to pray for the success of the day's work. In spite of my conscientiousness, one Friday I was dismissed without warning.

The lack of any explanation made the dismissal especially painful. It raised doubts about my ability. I hated to tell my wife. It shook my plans for a developing career. It challenged my faith in my prayers. I even considered retaliation. All day Saturday my anger increased. Then a very strange thing happened. Late Saturday night, being unable to sleep, I was deep in my continuing frustration, when the vision of both Jesus and Peter suddenly rose up before me. I saw Jesus saying to a man who had grasped a sword to defend Jesus from attackers, "Peter put up the sword. That will get you nothing."

I was surprised to feel that the message seemed directed at me. The more I thought about it it, the more I felt under its power. I felt it was convicting me of my anger and vengeance. The deeper the biblical image penetrated my feelings, the less I was ruled by my anger and the less I wanted to retaliate. In fact, as the hours passed, my resentment gave way to inner peace and acceptance. When daylight returned, I actually resolved to accept the termination without any bitterness. The biblical image had cleansed my heart in a way I can describe but cannot fully explain; other than to feel that the Spirit had judged my condition and challenged me to a more positive and spiritual solution.

Several days later I accepted my boss's offer to work a few weeks more; during which time I felt many silent prayers of thanksgiving that my destructive plans had been redirected and my faith in myself and in God had been restored.

How many influences are at work in an experience such as this? How can we determine who or what was the active agent which brought about the exceptional change in my attitude and behavior? Perhaps it was my association with Bible stories that allowed me to see a parallel between scripture and my own event.

What is the explanation of the force which literally turned me around? What was the power for good, for forgiveness, and for control over my lesser nature which influenced my mind and heart? What gives me the right to conclude that it was the influence of the Holy Spirit, or Jesus? Or how can I claim it was God?

Is my only resource to authority to say, "I believe, help my unbelief?"

We can have new vitality and energy.

> *He gives vigour to the weary, new strength to the exhausted. . . . those who look to the Lord will win new strength, they will grow wings like eagles; they will run and not be weary, they will march on and never grow faint* (Isaiah 40:29, 31).

Some possible contemporary examples of Isaiah's text.

A) "I stood in a group protesting better labor conditions. I faced the guards daily. I was making a stand for a principle I felt was right. I stood for hours. I rarely ever felt tired."

B) "We were on a mission trip to the poor in Mexico. It was all new to me and I found the experience terribly stimulating. When I came home I was charged up to tell my suburban friends how much I learned. It felt exhilarating to take part in a project for somebody else.

C) "I get tempted, of course. I know I shouldn't be, but when I am, and when I pray, sometimes a strange new spirit comes over me. Whenever I can throw my temptation off in times like that, I feel like a new person."

The vitality of the spiritual life and prayer.

Evelyn Underhill, with her unusual spiritual insight, often emphasized the vitality and spiritual energy which comes from prayer:

There is an unseen energy other than ourselves, and having, in its own right, a range of being and of significance unconditioned by the narrow human world. We do not mean some immaterial energy, the soul of the evolving universe. We mean a substantial reality, which is there first in its absolute perfection and living plenitude, which transcends yet penetrates our world, our activity, our souls.[5]

Sometimes we think of prayer in terms of a request, a confession, or a thanksgiving. But prayer has even additional rewards. By turning our hearts and minds to the spiritual world, very often we experience the unexpected by-product of such prayers in the form of new vitality, new energy, and spiritual effervescence. Spiritually oriented psychologist, Benedict Groeschel, says the spiritual excitement can even be frightening.

As a result of the infused virtue of charity, the individual experiences a force within that includes gratitude, reverence, and inner exaltation which propels our actions and prayers. This force is gradually recognized as the dynamism behind affective prayer. At times it is so strong as to be frightening.[6]

Spiritual life and prayer prove to be a source of vitality for an executive.
A denominational leader, who has the responsibility of consulting with more than one hundred and fifty clergypersons and churches in a large cosmopolitan area and who, like many other executives, is constantly facing the fractured existence as well as the creativeness of inner city life, writes about the energy he receives from spiritual awareness and prayer:

89

I am conscious that the gift of administration is a spiritual gift, and a part of that gift is the capacity to set priorities and make decisions in the light of a vision about the church and its mission. I have been told that some of the church's most gifted administrators were nurtured in the mystical tradition and rooted in the spiritual disciplines of prayer, regular study of scripture, and reflection.

In the midst of a myriad of tasks and urgent requests, they were able to focus their energies on essential priorities and let go of less important items. They were centered people in touch with an energizing vision, and their spiritual authenticity kept them in touch with the needs of the people they served. This certainly provides a model for me to pursue.

Another testimony of the gift of spiritual energy.

One of the common criticisms of spirituality and prayer is that they have no role in the real world. For example, what place do they have in Police or Fire Departments? One clear answer comes from an energetic minister who wanted to support persons in need, as well as make the religious presence visible to the community, but who needed the guidance of the Spirit and the energy of prayer to carry out his effort.

For myself as pastor of a local church, I was the "volunteer" chaplain to the Police and Fire Departments of our town. Often I knew I was needed for an emergency before I was called officially. Frankly there were times I did not want to go because it meant tragedy and pain for someone and

I could never build a wall between their pain and myself. But I knew I had to go and somehow, as helpless and inadequate as I felt in the midst of some of those awful situations, I knew that if I "listened," the Holy Spirit would help us. Somehow my being there, more than what I did or said, was beneficial. While I was called by the Police and Fire Departments, I felt sent by the Holy Spirit. How do you explain that?

On more than one occasion people said I was an answer to their prayers. Is it egotistical to think we are answered prayers? I don't know. What I do know, it takes a lot of courage to answer, "Here am I, send me!" I have not always been as brave as I should have been.

How prayer warmed a cold heart and brought a new spirit.

There are many aspects to a pastor's life. He or she can be responsible for calling, conducting services, administrating the church program, teaching, counseling, financing, missions, and on top of all this, playing a leading role in the community. Is it any wonder that burn-out is often the result? Such was the case with this pastor.

Several years ago I left the church one Sunday aware that my own spiritual journey had come to a final end. My ministry, for example, had been reduced to a casual routine of meaningless activity. I had abandoned all devotional practice whatsoever. And my idea of a loving God who is compassionately concerned for the life of every individual had become, for me, nothing more than a mere theological abstraction. In matters of the heart, I was cold, indifferent and empty.

For many months I tried to pray but nothing came to mind except this single thought which I repeated over and over again: "God, if you are there, reach me in some way."

What happened next is difficult to explain. Because there was no easy way to decline an invitation, I attended a commissioning service for missionaries who were serving a denomination vastly different than my own. And during that service a single line from the story of Blind Bartimaeus recalled in Mark's gospel became a fresh and newly lighted pathway, "Jesus, thou Son of David, have mercy on me."

That prayer pointed me in the direction of a relationship with the living Christ as I realized that healing and renewal, restoration and fulfillment, forgiveness and discipleship, are always available to those who come seeking to know God in their own way.

My dead end spiritual journey is now a growing pilgrimage. And as my relationship with Christ continues to deepen, I often find myself back at the very beginning with that first mantra-like prayer from the inner heart. "Jesus, thou Son of David, have mercy upon me." But today, I now add a second line, "O Lamb of God, I come."

How many months and how many emotions have been compacted into this short description of a major period in this man's life. Indeed, it is necessary to read and reread his brief story to catch the full impact of the change that prayer brought about.

It is significant that his abandonment "of all devotional practice" went hand in hand with his slipping into "a casual routine of meaningless activity." How often the two conditions go hand in hand.

It is important to note, too, how the example of people dedicating themselves to missions recalled this pastor to his own original vows of faith and works in Christ's name. How we forget that we are, as Paul said, living letters known and read by all. We *can* call others to a nobler lifestyle if we have the courage and faith to show the way ourselves..

Prayer is sometimes a long pilgrimage of the mind and heart..

Jim had been "in a state of doubt and confusion. . . . Prayer had seemed to fail." However, he later testifies that "thirteen years of prayer were answered." He became a person who no longer let fear determine his choices but one who chose his future by belief and by faith. New vitality had come to him, in part through prayer. Jim's story as he told it:

> My Christian faith during college years was informed by fundamentalism. Seminary became an experience of shattering that intellectual formulation of faith, leaving me in a state of doubt and confusion.
>
> After an unsuccessful attempt to practice ministry and reformulate my theology simultaneously, I headed for psychiatric help. The loss of fundamentalism's authority revealed personal problems previously covered or unrecognized. A pastoral colleague referred me to a Jewish therapist, who laid out a course of treatment with the words, "We are going to make a Christian out of you." By that he

meant that a Christian is a human being, and I was trying to be God, another way of picturing my perfectionist behavior.

That kind of therapy worked, making me a productive person but leaving a new problem. Prayer had seemed to fail me through the years while psychotherapy helped. I gave up praying for a long time, until it dawned on me one day how easily my life could have been a failure, but seemed to have been led, one step at a time, to healing and success.

I had been pointed to a seminary not of my choosing, where a new way of thinking was offered. I had joined a new denomination where pastoral colleagues offered an atmosphere of spiritual freedom, and referral to real help. I had received calls to ministry in two congregations, and had become a husband and step parent. Had not thirteen years of prayer been answered? I had wanted God to answer my prayer the first time I prayed. Instead God refused to make an exception of life's rule, that we live and learn. God had guided me, step by difficult step. I could identify with Jacob, who woke from his sleep in the wilderness and said, "Surely the Lord is in this place—and I did not know it!" (Gen. 28:16). Life has not become easy but I have been changed from one who let fear determine choices to one who chooses by faith. Can there be any better answer to prayer?

Discussion questions about the "Profound Benefits of Prayer."
1) Originally, Saul was outside of the Christian community. Then he experienced his change to the new life of faith. So many

of the Biblical stories are our stories. Has your spiritual journey been anything like Paul's, or has it followed the life of some other Bible personality?

2) Throughout the Old and the New Testaments, men and women converse with God as if God were personal. Has God ever spoken with you so that you feel God is personal in your life?

3) "And having thee I desire nothing else on earth. Though heart and body fail, yet God is my possession forever," (Ps. 73:25–26). Does such a conviction alleviate the stress of modern life for you, or do you see this as withdrawal from the strain of daily affairs?

4) Please describe a prayer experience which gave you inner security in the face of a crisis.

5) The spiritual leader George Macdonald wrote, "Father, into thy hands I give the heart which left thee but to learn how good thou art." Does this reflect any experience you have had with spirituality or with prayer?

6) It is often said that those who spend time on their knees, stand taller afterwards. If, and when, and where, prayer provides you with new energy and vitality, please share with others how it does so.

"A Morning Prayer," by John Baillie (1886–1960).

> Teach me, O God, so to us all the circumstances of
>   my life today that they bring forth in me the
>   fruits of holiness rather than the fruits of sin.
> Let me use disappointment as material for
>   patience.
> Let me use success as material for thankfulness.
> Let me use suspense as material for perseverance.
> Let me use danger as material for courage.

Let me use reproach as material for longsuffering.
Let me use praise as material for humility.
Let me use pleasures as material for temperance.
Let me use pains as material for endurance.[7]

SILENCE WILL ENHANCE OUR PRAYING

Suddenly the word of the Lord came to him. . . . "Go and stand upon the mount before the Lord." For the Lord was passing by: a great and strong wind came rending mountains and shattering rocks before him; but the Lord was not in the wind and after the wind there was an earthquake, but the Lord was not in the earthquake; and after the earthquake fire, but the Lord was not in the fire; and after the fire a low murmuring sound . . . Then came a voice, and the Lord said to him . . . (I Kings 19:11–13).

The fact that Elijah recognized the presence of God only in the silence following the storm is a good reminder that distractions can prohibit us, too, from hearing God when life is filled with much activity. This is not to deny that God can be experienced in the midst of the animation of the world, but it is to alert ourselves to the importance of quietness to the spiritual life. After the wind and the thunder, then comes the silence and the Voice.

Silence is an inward journey outward.

Inner stillness is a spiritual art. If we spend all our hours keeping up a constant chatter with associates and friends, it takes real effort to suddenly change and be satisfied with periods of personal silence. It takes discipline to switch immediately from our daily life of action to a time when we have quietness. In fact, it is safe to say that we do not receive the rewards of silence and solitude unless we prepare for them. It was after the doors were shut that Jesus appeared to the disciples (Jn. 20:19). That the prizes of prayer often come only after preparation, is affirmed by Emily Herman in *Creative Prayer.*

> The soul that awaits in silence must learn to disentangle the voice of God from the net of other voices—the ghostly whisperings of the subconscious self, the luring voices of the world, the hindering voices of misguided friendship, the clamor of personal ambitions, the murmurs of self will, the song of unbridled imagination and the thrilling note of religious romance. . . . One hour of such listening may give us a greater insight into the mysteries of human nature, and a surer instinct for Divine values, than a year's hard study. . . . That is why the great solitaries surprise us with their acute understanding of life.[1]

Silence is not easy to achieve.

Sometimes we do not want silence. When silence is suggested, we may not know what to expect. We may feel vulnerable. We do not like to lose control. We are not accustomed to having time on our hands with nothing to accomplish. We may also find silence upsetting because we fear such a pursuit will be a waste of time.

Then, too, silence and solitude may be emotionally threatening because we may have to confront ourselves, as one of the Desert Fathers admitted.

> The Abbot Anthony said, "Who sits in solitude and is quiet hath escaped from three wars: hearing, speaking, seeing; yet against one thing shall he continually battle, that is, his own heart."[2]

Silence can be preparation of the Spirit.

God does not expect us to always be doers. God created us to *be* as much as to *do*. It takes as much effort to *be* as to *do*, maybe more. We do not have to be the controller and director of every minute of our lives. If we have been created by God, why not let God continue the process instead of assuming that we have to take over? After all, God is the creator, we are the created, as Saint John of the Cross in his timeless wisdom so valuable to preserve, reminds us,

> A person should take note that although he does not seem to be making any progress in this quietude or doing anything, he is advancing much faster than if he were treading along on foot for God is carrying him. Although he is walking at God's pace, he does not feel this pace. Even though he does not work with his faculties, he achieves much more than if he did, for God is the agent.[3]

When, at the end of a day, I sit in silence next to my wife, although no word may be said, much passes between us. We do not need words to share our feelings of caring and affection. Silence enables each of us to appreciate the other. We move past all outward senses and enter an arena of creative sharing of the Spirit which nourishes us both. Sometimes just watching each other without comment tells us exactly how the day has gone and how we feel. We give each other messages through our silence.

The rewards of silence.

You who have sat alone and pondered and prayed, know that there is a different world when you enter silence or solitude. You know that an early experience of silence may bring to the surface the awareness of many things you should have done but forgot. You find that silence and solitude clear the mind's agenda. You know that silence/solitude results in physical relaxation as your body loses stress and enters a feeling of tranquility. You also discover that calmness of spirit soon pervades your whole being as your mind and heart begin to open to an increased awareness of who you are; as you experience the meaning of the now, i.e. yourself and the things around you. And you know that after a while you feel that there is the strange feeling of not being alone but being in the presence of somebody who is sharing the silence and solitude with you. Yes, you who have entertained silence and solitude recognize the wisdom which is shared with us by Thomas Merton.

> The Christian solitary, in his life of prayer and silence, explores the existential depths and possibilities of his own life. The Christian solitary is left alone with God to fight out the question of who he really is, to get rid of impersonation, if any, that has followed him into the woods. . . . The silence of the woods forces you to make a decision which the tensions and artificialities of society may help you to evade forever.[4]

Silence awakens the spirituality within us.

A life might be filled with frailties of human living, but it is also filled with evidences of God. We are mind and spirit. Although we contain much good as well as evil, there is no human being who is so foul that he or she has no pieces of God within. We cannot forget that we are creations of God; and, being creations, each one of us has within himself or herself many manifestations of the Creator. Through God, our human frailties can be confronted. They no longer need to wander unopposed in the soul. They meet a power, faith reassures us, which is greater than they are. We may be immersed in the evils of life, but once we have heard the song of the Lord, we can hear it anywhere; as I have tried to capture in verse.

> Clatter of trucks, rumble of cars, constant clamor of noisy city streets. High overhead cries an evening nighthawk. A cry reserved only for those who know. How hear the nighthawk, so far above, else we learned it in greener pastures? How know the presence of God in city's din, else we earlier met the Shepherd by still waters?

An example of the Spirit in silence.

A former staff member of a large denomination, shares her awareness of God.

> There was a time a few years back that was perhaps the most difficult I shall ever have to spend. I didn't have time to pray very much, nor did I want to. I was steeped in deep sorrow knowing my husband's life, and our marriage, was nearing the end. Down state was my elderly mother and aunt who

were needing me to come help as often as I could. And on top of that I was still working. When I arose at 5:30 (sometimes earlier) in the morning and there was no laundry to do, no bills to pay, and no letters to write, I did take time to go out under God's heavens and walk. It was inspirational, uplifting, just watching the stars, the constellations and the seasons cross the sky. I knew if God in His greatness could keep everything up there running in its proper course, He could keep me. And He did. I didn't need to get down on my knees and try to think of words to express myself and impress Him. He heard and He knew, and I knew He did.

Prayer silence is listening.

For many of us, prayer is talking to God which seems to be an activity of the mind. We may have a problem so we think it best to tell God about it. As such, prayer becomes a matter of thinking things through. The result is that prayer becomes a "head trip." In reality, prayer is more than talking. Prayer is listening, whether in the middle of a chaotic situation or in the stillness of a tranquil summer afternoon. God as Creator and as Energizer, speaks all of the time, both in the storm and in the silence. Our problem is to know how to listen during either event.

Prayer silence is a practiced art.

Although thinking and reasoning may be helpful in prayer, in actual fact prayer is really a matter of faith, not intellect. Such an understanding of prayer, though contrary to the logic of most of us, has long historic roots. In the Fourteenth Century, an anonymous author wrote a spiritual classic called *The Cloud of Unknowing*. In it he said,

For the love of God, be careful in this work, and do not by any means, work in it with your mind or with your imagination: for I tell you, it cannot be achieved with them. Therefore leave them alone and do not work with them.[5]

The Cloud of Unknowing suggests that we have to be "unknowing" in order to hear God. We have to set aside all recollections, all hopes, all desires, ambitions, guilts, longings and the like so that the mysterious Voice of God can enfold our uninhabited souls. Even memories and traditions are obstacles, he says, to the reception of the Word.

Silence and our desert place.

In many ways, silence and solitude are actualized by withdrawing to a secluded place. The prophet Ezekiel reported that God said to him, "I will entice you into the desert and there I will speak to you in the depths of your heart," (Ez. 20:35). Today, we do not have to live in the desert, as many of our religious forebears chose to do to find solitude, but we do need to have the desert experience.

The value of the desert experience is also revealed by Carlo Carretto who worked for twenty years with the Italian youth movement as well as Catholic Action programs, both before and after World War II. At the age of forty-four, he felt called by a voice which said, "Leave everything, come with me into the desert. I don't want your action any longer. I want your prayer, your love." From that time, Carretto gave his life to prayer and concerns for the poor in North Africa, while living a desert life. His insights about his spiritual renewal have been translated into many languages and sold in millions of copies.

If you cannot go into the desert, you must nonetheless make some desert in your life. Every now and then leaving . . . and looking for solitude to restore in prolonged silence and prayer the stuff of your soul.[6]

The great joy of the Saharan novitiate is the . . . joy of solitude—silence, true silence, which penetrates everywhere and invades one's whole being, speaking to the soul with wonderful new strength unknown to men to whom this silence means nothing. . . . silence at work, interior silence, silence of the soul, God's silence.[7]

An example of the spirit of aloneness and the "desert place."

Words can be left behind when the soul enters the realm of the spirit. At that time, there is no need for explanation, for reasoning, or for doing. It is more than enough to just be, to enter into communion with reality. Such was the experience when this correspondent visited his desert place.

Being alone is not an unusual experience. Some know it from time to time. Some cherish it. To have that time of being alone suddenly filled with great splendor is an unexpected gift. It was in such a moment that I sensed a reaching out to God. Until those long walks on the beach, kicking sand, basking in the warm sunlight, praying and focusing had found a set pattern in my life. As if I had not known any of the ways of silent prayer and contemplation I was embraced by a most healing experience. That experience was beyond the mind's

104

comprehension. Only when the mind and heart joined was there new and full participation in the earth life I have been given along with the searching sense of heaven's readiness to be mine. I felt a belonging as never before. I knew I was part of something beyond the reach of every one of my senses, that the universe in the farthest and darkest corner was available to me. . . . It was something like a birthing moment in which there was no longer a distance between creator and creature.

Additional comments from this writer reveal how the event of that day has remained with him ever since those illuminating moments, which enable him to continually celebrate with the words, "I belong to you and you belong to me." We are all reminded that meditation and prayer in our desert places can have a profound impact on all of life.

A brief look at prayer silence and meditation.
Although this book is about prayer, I define meditation because, for many of us, praying and focusing and meditation seem to be the same thing. They are, however, quite different.

Prayer is the spirit of communication with God which is expressed in such mental and verbal ways as: confession, petition, intercession and adoration.

Meditation is a devotional exercise, or attitude of contemplation, which allows the meditator to get in touch with his or her inner spiritual resources. It is waiting in a contemplative stance for the presence and inspiration of God.

A further description of meditation.
Thomas Merton, the Roman Catholic mystic, wrote extensively about meditation,

One who meditates does not merely think, he also loves. . . . Meditation is not merely a matter of "thinking things through". . . Meditation is more than mere practical thinking. Meditation is for those who are not satisfied with a merely objective and conceptual knowledge about life, about God, about ultimate realities. They want to enter into an intimate contact with truth itself, with God. . . . Meditation is generated not by reasoning but by faith.[8]

The purpose of meditation.

Generally speaking, meditation is the art of giving attention to a selected source and waiting for that source to inspire us with more awareness of ourselves, of others, and of God. We discover our minds and hearts being directed beyond our reasonable choice. Olive Wyon, an authority on matters of prayer and meditation, puts it this way,

Thought is the mind . . . in touch with a problem. Meditation is the soul . . . in touch with a person. Meditation is waiting upon God with thoughtful attention, with an earnest desire to hold communion with God. Or again meditation is thinking about God in the right way and then doing what we are moved to do by our thinking.[9]

Excerpts from a journal.

A pastor who has devoted his life to the fields of spirituality, meditation, as well as pastoral ministry, shares some excerpts from his journal.

June 17: A moment of waking last night (3:45 A.M.) and lingering moments of luxurious thought.

106

I feel a return in meditation to a distant time of meditating but more, in a distant time of life. Self confidence is very much a part of meditation. Being in touch is what it is for me. I'm taking more time and am easier with it. It is a good day.

June 18: Not so much feeling with today's meditation but as much solidness as before. Time goes quickly. It seems I could not have used all the time I allowed. I probably used it in depths much more than I know. As always I began with an expression of love for those I love in particular and special ways.

July 3: The dimensions of each day reach beyond its own beauty as did today. The words "Peace be still" came even to my meditating and I ceased. I felt Oneness. I do not know what waits for me except that I know it will be good.

April 6: "Peace, O God, for our world." That was the meditation focus since last Wednesday. It is a lived experience. To pray without ceasing is not a profusion of words but a lived experience. It is the prayer of the heart that takes a living and moving shape. It is more than a treaty: it is the basis for trust in a relationship. It is declared not by formal signing of documents, rather it is a proclamation that is seen as well as heard. I pray that I might live in prayer knowing peace within and offering it to the world.

Readers will notice several characteristics of meditation and prayer in these journal entries. There is an inner peace, a sense of goodness about life and an expectancy that the future will be touched with grace. There is a continuing mystery, yet a pulling into more depth of meditation. A reader may feel an openness of expression along with a sense of personal relationship with God. He or she may feel the author of this testimony has a confident grip on his personal, spiritual life as well as a continuing concern for the needs of others.

Discussion questions about "Silence and Meditation."

1) Many of us ask, "How can I get more inner peace into my very busy life?" If you have found answers to this common question, please share the processes as well as the difficulties of achieving such a condition.

2) Some religious authorities suggest that we can find God in silence and listening. When you listen, what do you hear? How can you know if it is the Voice of God? How can you protect yourself from inventing an answer as if God was speaking to you?

3) In the 16th Century St. Peter Canisus wrote, "I am not eager, bold or strong. All that is past. I am ready not to do, at last, at last." What do you feel he meant? Does what you think he is saying apply to your life?

4) If you have been on a retreat, please explain the part that silence played in the event. How was silence brought about? Under what circumstances? What happened to you? What change took place, if any, in the group?

5) Is it possible to have inner quietness in the presence of violence or chaos? Would this be a desirable or a dangerous condition? Why?

6) It is claimed by those who practice it, that the practice of inner stillness clarifies the understanding of self as well as of society. Is this true, or is it not true, in your experience?

"A Prayer for Inner Peace," by Henri J. M. Nouwen, (1932–).

Please accept my distractions, my fatigue, my irritations and my faithless wanderings. You know me more deeply than I know myself. You love me with a greater love than I can love myself. You even offer me more than I desire.

Look at me, see me in all my misery and inner confusion, and let me sense your presence in the midst of my turmoil. All I can do is to show myself to you. Yet, I am afraid to do so. I am afraid that you will reject me. But I know—with a knowledge of faith—that you desire to give me your love. The only thing you ask of me is not to hide from you, not to run in despair, not to act as if you were a relentless despot.[10]

Prayer Enriches Sex and Sexuality

Bride:

> I am my beloved's, his longing is all for me. Come my beloved, let us go out into the fields to lie among the henna-bushes. . . . There I will give you my love . . . and all rare fruits are ready at your door.

Bridegroom:

> Under the apricot tree I roused you. Wear me as a seal upon your heart, for love is strong as death. . . . if a man were to offer for love, the whole wealth of his house, it would be utterly scorned. (The Song of Songs, 7:10, 13, 8:6).

In many places of sacred literature, references to sex and sexuality have been used to convey meanings of theology. For example, The Song of Songs in the Old Testament is a series of poems about lovers who are enjoying ecstatic lovemaking, yet in such sacredness that their whole encounter is an appreciation of the wonder and beauty of sex and sexuality.

These lovely and explicit love poems are filled with subtle "doubles entendres" as the author uses the distinctly sexual theme to describe deeper understandings of spiritual beliefs. The poems are a theological allegory of the intimate relationship between God and Israel. They can also be viewed as symbolic of the intimacy between the individual soul and God, as well as humanity's quest for God, and also God's unfailing courtship of us.

The intimacy of our body and soul.

It is obvious that we are sexual creatures. It is, unfortunately, less obvious that we are also soul and spirit. If we exercise our bodies with weights and pulleys, why don't we cultivate our souls and spirits by meditation, prayer and the worship of God?

If we are body and soul, let's not enjoy one without the other. Adequate preparation of spirit is as important as sexual foreplay for the body. To know one of the greatest experiences of being human, we need to employ the whole person, spirit as well as flesh, heart as well as mind, and soul as well as body. To do any less is to defraud the full potential of ourselves as well as the physical and spiritual gifts of God. To think that we can live a full life without the experiences of the Spirit is also a denial of our Creator as well.

Sometimes sexual fantasies appear during prayer.

In as much as we are sexually oriented persons, it is not surprising that sexual thoughts sometimes arise during prayer. In fact, Kenneth Leech in his book *True Prayer*, points out how common this experience may be.

> People who experience strong sexual feelings, lusts
> and fantasies of various kinds during communion,
> or at other times of prayer, are often worried by

this; feeling that they must be guilty of some great sin, and often worry themselves sick with guilt feelings. . . . It is often a relief to know that such feelings are extremely common, and not at all abnormal; and it is important to accept that part of oneself as God-given and redeemable.[1]

Marriage with sex, or marriage with sex and God.

Consider two different marriages. Couple A have what appears to be a "complete" relationship. They cooperate in solving common problems, and they support each other's needs and potentialities. Both are employed and give themselves to making a good home for their children. They see no need for including God in their marriage.

Then there is Couple B. In this marriage, everything is the same as for Couple A except for one additional factor: they are not just husband and wife but live with a third party, their faith. They find the presence of God to be a meaningful part of their relationship. Their decisions are not just theirs alone but are made in the light of spiritual meaning and religious purpose. Their choices are made in the awareness that their lives are responsible, not only to each other, but to God who is greater than either one of them.

Of course, many marriages are a mixture of these two examples, but the illustration may suggest that the relationship which is permeated with an awareness of prayer and God has the added ingredient of faith. The old adage that families that pray together stay together has more truth than poetry .

Religious awareness: a protection against sexual and emotional exploitation.

When the fervent desire for sex as immediate gratification is enhanced by the awareness that we are not just two bodies but two souls, sex becomes far more fulfilling. Sex needs to be complemented by the element of spirituality. It is important to match our sexual concerns with the grace of prayer. By prayer, I do not necessarily mean saying prayers so much as having a continual sense of God's presence. I mean recognition of the sacredness of another, trust in the spiritual feelings of the other person, and recognition that we are not alone but awareness that all we do is done in the sight of God. When such an attitude of reverence and respect is observed, it frees the pray-er from ulterior motives; such as dominance of another, exploitation of a partner, possessiveness for one's own advantage, and abuse of a companion for one's own gain.

The overemphasis upon sex can bring about its own loss.

The whole relationship of man and woman is a union of sex and spirit, of sexuality and spirituality. If we satisfy the body without fulfilling the spirit, we miss the fullness of the human-divine experience. When sex becomes an end in itself it abbreviates what could be a journey of discovery of mind and hearts. Theologian Pierre Teilhard de Chardin observes, "in genital union a short circuit is produced . . . a flash which burns up and deadens a portion of the soul. . . . Physical desire left to its own devices leads to nowhere but to disintegration of self."

So, both Faith and Spirit must be experienced if God's plan for the fulfillment of the whole person is to be appreciated.

Sex and Spirit together give a grace of peace to love.

When the sexual act is understood as more than sex, coitus can be so moving that one feels it to be an otherworldly experience, a mystical event, and a spiritual breakthrough. The deeper the love, the more fulfilling the sex. The greater the respect and caring, the more lasting the experience. The stronger the commitment, the greater the return. The more emphasis upon the

114

spiritual union, the more meaningful the physical union. In fact, intercourse can be sacramental and sexual love can seem to mirror the love and presence of God. As William Johnston, former Director of the Institute of Oriental Religions, describes in *Silent Music*, an important work on meditation.

> Meditation in all great religions leads to remarkable control of sexuality. Not that sexual power diminishes in the depth of meditation. On the contrary, the non-attachment that accompanies such depth penetrates to the subliminal caverns of psychic life, liberating men and women from the unconscious fears and traumatic anxieties that sometimes cause impotency, frigidity, lack of pleasure and reluctance to give oneself physically to another. In this sense, meditation [and prayer] far from weakening, may liberate one's sexual energy, and this is one of the claims of Yoga. But together with this liberation comes a power and self mastery (and this is chastity) which enables people to express their love sexually when it is appropriate to do so and to refrain from physical expression when circumstances so demand.[2]

After sex, what?

A friend wrote me about her wonderful marriage and pointed out that even the most meaningful relationship of human sex may leave an empty spot to be filled only by deeper faith and extended prayer.

> My husband and I had a deeply spiritual, physical, sexual relationship—very healthy and normal too.

115

I loved every moment of it. But (and we sometime discussed this) if couples are really honest with themselves, they will admit (even those who have good, holy, beautiful sex) that when it is over, there is a fleeting sense of sadness. Why? Because deep within us there always remains a void that only God can fill. This is what Jesus meant when he said you must leave mother, father, brother, sister, husband, wife and children, and follow me.

And then she added this insight.

In fiery communion and burning self revelation, lovers open wide the gates of the citadel of self, and for a moment are lost in blissful oblivion. But only for a moment. The satisfaction is not complete. The innermost chamber of the heart remains inviolate, concealed, uncommunicated and incommunicable. The lover and the beloved are still twain. The search for unity and understanding go unrewarded. The self can give all but itself. Itself it cannot give. For itself it does not understand. Thus, all we give or receive is mystery.

In the end, life is a matter of Spirit. We all know that the physical parts of life decay and lose much of their power and attraction. Then, in our maturity, we turn more and more to the Spirit and to prayer. Finally, it is Spirit and prayer which remain. We ask forgiveness for our various indiscretions of the earlier years and throw ourselves on the mercy of God and Life eternal. The rash experiences of former times give way to the soul-comfort of more mature times of the awareness of the presence of God.

116

When prayer is more fulfilling than sex!

For centuries, some men and women of faith have been testifying to the power of religious devotion, as contrasted to the experience of sex. They have found a reward in their faith which has supplanted common ways of sexual activity. They have discovered empowerment through abstinence, strength through self-denial, and fulfillment of their lives through not serving themselves but, caring for those in need. In fact, they have seen sex as a distraction from more sublime goals and states of mind and soul. They have experienced a depth of life which is not dependent upon sex, as Viktor Frankl, the German psychiatrist, describes:

> This, of course, is not to say that love has no desire to "embody" itself. But it is independent of the body to the extent that it does not need the body. Even in love between the sexes, their sexual element is not primary, it is not an end in itself but an expression. True love, in and of itself, needs the body neither for arousal or for fulfillment, though it makes use of the body for both.[3]

Discussion questions about "Sex and Sexuality."

1) What is the difference between sexuality and sex?

2) Do you feel that God is upset if a person has human sexual thoughts which intrude upon prayer?

3) What is your reaction to the statement that sex, when accompanied with an attitude of prayer, is more meaningful than sex for sex itself?

4) How do you feel about expressing theological points of view in sexual terms, such as in the Song of Songs?

5) It is said that sex without Spirit eventually ends in ashes. Do you agree or disagree?

6) In your estimation, can prayer be more fulfilling than sex?

7) It is said that men give affection to receive sex, and women give sex to receive affection. Could prayer bring about a better relationship?

8) In your opinion, how much does prayer and faith in God have to do with a happy sexual life?

9) If men are more threatened by loss of control and power, and women more threatened by a disturbance in their relationships, what role do you feel prayer can play in each condition? Or should it?

"A Prayer," by Temple Gairdner, (1873–1928).

> That I may come to her, draw me nearer to you than to her; that I may know her, make me know you more than her; that I may love her with the love of a perfectly whole heart, cause me to love you more than her and most of all.[4]

POSSIBLE REASONS FOR OUR UNANSWERED PRAYERS

That same day the Lord spoke to Moses and said, "Go up this mount . . . Mount Nebo . . . and look out over the land of Canaan that I am giving to the Israelites. . . . On this mountain you shall die. . . . You shall see the land from a distance, but you may not enter the land," (Deuteronomy 32:49–52).

Moses prayed to enter the Promised Land but died on Mount Nebo without having his ambition accomplished (De. 32:50). King David prayed for the recovery of his child but the infant died anyway (II Sam. 12:19). Is there anyone who has not had an experience with unanswered prayer? Indeed, far too many of us identify with the psalmist. "I cry in the daytime, but thou dost not answer; in the night I cry but get no respite," (Ps. 22:2).

The magnitude of unanswered prayers today.

It is one thing to reflect on the unanswered prayers of the homeless all across America and the prayers of the mothers of starving children in Africa. But we also have to remind ourselves of the unanswered prayers of the neighbor widow who has just lost her husband, the family down the street whose son is on drugs, and the acquaintance who has just learned he has cancer. How many millions cry out for help and rend the air with their appeals: "Where is God?"; "Doesn't God care?" or even, "Is there no God?"

Don't be discouraged.

It is helpful to theorize about why prayers are not answered in the way we want, but every explanation must be seen as mere speculation. Conjectures may prove helpful guidelines for our praying, but they must be seen as educated guesses, touched with intuition as well as faith. Who knows why God does or does not choose to act? Our faith tells us that the Spirit of God is like the wind which, "blows where it wills . . . you do not know where it comes from or where it is going," (Jn. 3:8). It seems that we must wait for understandings of prayer which we do not yet have the faith to accept.

Now, having said there are no provable explanations for unanswered prayers, we can, nevertheless, consider some possible theories.

Are we praying for the wrong objective?

> *Your requests are not granted because you pray from wrong motives, to spend what you get on your pleasures* (James 4:3).

> *The mother of Zebedee's sons then came before him [Jesus]. She bowed low and then begged a favor. "I want you to give orders that in your kingdom my two sons here may sit next to you, one on the right and the other on the left,"* (Matthew 20:20–21).

120

Any claims for special privilege are not good foundations for prayer. Such requests may be met with the same negative response that Jesus gave to the mother of Zebedee's sons, "to sit at my right or left is not mine to grant." Indeed, sometimes it is better that we do not get what we pray for. The family which prays for new things in order to keep up with the Joneses will probably be much better off if they do not get what they want but find, instead, a greater family bonding through sharing what they have with each other.

The right answer to many of our selfish prayers should be no instead of yes.

Don't be discouraged. The Holy Spirit really directs our praying.

Remember the lesson of Elijah. After years of courageous and faithful leadership as a prophet in Israel, Elijah incurred the wrath of Queen Jezebel and was persecuted by her. Despondent and disheartened, he journeyed into the wilderness and prayed to die. "It is enough, now, Lord, take my life," (I Kings 19:4). However, an angel appeared and said, "Arise and eat. The journey is too much for you." It was not long afterwards that, "The Lord said to him, 'Go back by way of the wilderness,' " and then gave him directions on what he was still called to do.

We may pray for the wrong things at times, even for death as did Elijah, but there are greater powers of the Spirit of God at work within our small lives than we realize. Though outwardly and consciously we may ask for things which are negative, subconsciously our whole nature may revolt against such a prayer. The deep influence of a creative, life-giving God within us may have ways of turning us around which are beyond our understanding as happened to Elijah.

121

Could we be lacking in sincerity and persistence?

> There was a judge who cared nothing for God . . .
> and in the same town there was a widow who con-
> stantly came before him demanding justice against her
> opponent. For a long time he refused; but in the end
> he said to himself, "True, I care nothing for God . . .
> but this widow is so great a nuisance that I will see her
> righted before she wears me out with her persistence,"
> (Luke 18:2–6).

To expect an answer to prayer necessitates a determination of heart and sincerity of intent. If our prayers are not answered, it may be that they are not earnest enough. Though such efforts do not guarantee an answer, generally speaking we often get out of prayer what we put into it. As Jeremy Taylor, the author of *The Rule and Exercises of Holy Living*, so aptly suggests:

> Easiness of desire is a great enemy to the success of
> a good man's prayer. It must be an intent, zealous,
> busy, prayer. For consider what an indecency it is
> that a man should speak to God for a thing that he
> values not. Our prayers upbraid our spirits when we
> beg tamely for those things for which we ought to
> die.[1]

How many of us fall into the insincerity of our prayers and resolutions when we are like Saint Augustine, confronted with the need to abandon temptations, "O Lord, make me pure but not yet." We may be concerned about getting over a bad habit but we may not be willing to really address the problem.

On the other hand, some times it is just a matter of more sincerity and dedication. Douglas Steere, American Quaker teacher and author, tells the story of Frederick Libby, a founder of one of the early Prevention of War organizations. In the beginning, Libby took five hundred dollars out of his savings account of one thousand dollars and set out to solicit financial support for his cause. Good responses eluded him. But later, when he committed all of his own savings to the effort, his appeal spoke with such inner personal conviction, that others were impressed and his organization began to grow.

Don't be discouraged. It's not all up to us.

Our sincerity in prayer is important, but it should not lead us to believing that we can determine the value of our praying by more sincerity. On the contrary, God is the determinant of our prayers. God is the author of our prayers. God is the responder to our prayers. God determines whether or not we receive an answer.

Do we need to wait longer for God's reply?

"How long, O Lord, wilt thou quite forget me? How long wilt thou hide thy face from me? How long must I suffer anguish in my soul, grief in my heart, day and night? . . . Look now and answer me, O Lord my God," (Psalm 13:1–3).

This psalmist is in deep emotional turmoil, feeling rejected by God, for he keeps repeating his complaint about being neglected. Of course, we cannot tell how long his trials lasted, but we do know that the time came when he could once again praise God. He had to wait for his own spiritual insight to develop so that he would not blame God but accept God. Finally he does so in a later comment, "I will sing to the Lord, who has granted all my desire," (Ps. 13:6).

Our time is not God's time.

We can't say our prayers are not answered if we do not give them time. We cannot allow our modern tendency of expecting instant gratification to cloud our conclusions about the efficacy of our prayer life. Prayer is not measured by the clock. Some prayers may take years before they are fulfilled, such as happened in the life of St. Teresa, the well known Spanish mystic of the Sixteenth Century. Her journal reveals that she waited many years for her own prayers to be answered:

> On the one side, God was calling me; on the other, I was following the world. All of the things of God gave me great pleasure and I was prisoner to things of the world. It seemed as if I wished to reconcile two contradictions as much at variance with each other as are the life of the Spirit and the joys, pleasures and amusements of sense. "I passed nearly twenty years on this stormy sea, falling and rising but rising to no good purpose seeing that I went and fell again."[2]

Don't be discouraged. Waiting can be important.

The father of the Prodigal Son did not follow after the wild youth and try to bring him back. Instead, he waited until the son had "come to himself." Waiting allowed the youth to mature and make his own decision about what he wanted to do with his life (Lu. 15:11–32).

Or consider how Jesus waited for the disciples to recognize Him when they were walking together on the Road to Emmaus (Lu. 24:13–32). Although Jesus could have told them who He was, He knew it would be better for them if they discovered Him by themselves.

Are we keeping God away by our sinfulness?

> *But they quickly forgot all he had done and would not wait to hear his counsel. Their greed was insatiable in*

124

the wilderness. They tried God's patience in the desert.
He gave them what they asked, but sent a wasting sick-
ness among them (Psalm 106:13–15).

It is your iniquities that raise a barrier between you and
your God. Because of your sins he has hidden his face
so that he does not hear you (Isaiah 59:2).

If the psalmist of these verses spoke in modern slang, he might say, "By your continued drinking you asked for poor health. Well, you got your wasting sickness." He might well have added, "As you sow, so shall you reap."

The prophet Isaiah makes the same point. "Sinfulness raises a barrier between you and God. If you don't live an honest life, you cannot expect to be heard by me when you call." Rev. Harry Emerson Fosdick, the famous New York pastor of the Riverside Church, put it another way, "Many a man's prayers are spoiled by his own shadow."

In like spirit, I have tried to put this wisdom into these couplets.

> If guilt is agitating your mind,
>> how can you recognize peace of soul?
> If you have a storm within your heart,
>> how can you hear the still small voice of God?
> If you are touched with sin,
>> how can you recognize the appearance of virtue?
> If you go to bed with your neighbor,
>> how can you know the love of your spouse?
> If you count your life in terms of dollars and cents,
>> how can you comprehend your true worth?
> If you continually put yourself first,
>> how can you grow in the understanding of

spirituality?

But honesty and righteousness are not always rewarded.

It would be a less complicated world if this concept of cause and effect was as simple as we have suggested above. Of course it is not. The miser reaps the gold, the prostitute marries into royalty, the trusting wife is deceived, the dedicated worker for the poor is murdered in the community she is trying to help. Justice is denied. Righteousness is walked on. Love is overcome. God is disdained.

It is, however, in the face of these apparent denials of the power of God that the believer takes his or her stand for the righteous life, supported by faith in God and Jesus Christ, and by personal and corporate prayer.

The cleansing role of prayer.

Prayer is the tool of the Spirit by which we and God seek to cleanse the mind and soul of the sin which prohibits us from inheriting the benefits and rewards of righteousness. Such a conviction was felt by Nineteenth Century Americans who heard the preaching of the American theologian, Horace Bushnell (1802–1876).

> It requires a very high kind of life, a practiced way of purity . . . to be at all successful in the highest offices of prayer. The motives must be purified and become habitually unselfish, ambition must be taken away, humility must be graded down to meekness, the love must be sweetened by a Christly walk, the vehemence of will and passion must be chastened, and above all, the faith must be so brought up into God's secret as to abide there.

Let us not wonder, my brethren, if our prayers are weak and fruitless; how can they be otherwise, without living a holier life and abiding more closely with God?[3]

Prayer is the alarm clock to awaken us to live for the day instead of the night. It is the voice of our conscience alerting us to the deterioration of character through sin. It is the activity of the spirit calling us to what we know is right and helping us to stand the ground of faith in the pursuit of that righteousness. Prayer is putting our trust in the inviolable law of love of God.

Don't be discouraged. God accepts the sinner if not the sin.
Having claimed that the stain of sin alienates us from God, as well as from the fulfillment of our own potential, it is also necessary to say that though God may hate the sin, God loves the sinner. In the story of the woman taken in adultery, it is significant that Jesus said to her, "Has no one condemned you? Neither do I condemn you," (John 8:3–11). Thus he forgave the woman, but not her adultery. Instead, he gave her a stern rebuke, "You may go; do not sin again."

God may not answer what we pray for, but God will answer us.

> *I was given a sharp physical pain which came as Satan's messenger to bruise me; this was to save me from being unduly elated. Three times I begged the Lord to rid me of it but his answer was, "My grace is all you need, power comes to its full extent in weakness," (II Corinthians 12:7–9).*

127

The apostle Paul was constantly harassed by what he called a "thorn in the flesh," and prayed many times for relief, but spent his entire life suffering from the problem. Nor did he ever define what afflicted him. Could it have been epilepsy, eye trouble, or a stomach ailment? We do not know. What we do know is that he is an example of the power of the grace of God. If God chooses not to answer our prayer as we expect, we may discover the denial is what we need. Through his affliction, Paul discovered a foundation of faith he had not known before. In fact, he was finally able to give thanks for his difficulty. "Be always joyful; pray continually; give thanks whatever happens; for this is what God in Christ wills for you," (I Thes. 5:17).

When our prayers are unanswered but our needs addressed.

Prayer is an activity of the spirit. The spirit reads our souls, not what we say. Though we express a need with our words, the depths of our heart may be saying something quite different. What our mind and logic may consider a denial may, in fact, be an answer our soul needs to experience. An example of such a condition is the famous prayer by Saint Francis of Assisi (1182–1226).

> I asked God for strength, that I might achieve;
> I was made weak, that I might learn to obey.
> I asked for health, that I might do great things;
> I was given infirmity, that I might do better
>   things.
> I asked for riches, that I might be happy;
> I was given poverty, that I might be wise.
> I asked for power, that I might have the praise of
>   men;
> I was given weakness, that I might feel the need
>   of God.

I asked for all things, that I might enjoy life.
  I was given life, that I might enjoy all things.
I received nothing that I had asked for
  Everything I had hoped for.[4]

The power of prayer is not in the result but in the faith to pray.

Dr. Leslie Weatherhead was the pastor of City Temple in London from 1936 and 1960. He saw World War II first hand as the German air attacks sought to reduce that city to rubble. But throughout the Blitz, he stood firm in his faith and was a courageous spiritual bulwark for his parishioners. He knew there were people who prayed for retaliation against the enemy, but he saw prayer in a different light. He did not judge prayer on its material results. Indeed, there were very few, if any. For him and so many others in those days, they saw prayer as a source of courage. He says, "Prayers may not be answered, but pray-ers, persons who pray, will always be answered. . . . There are unanswered prayers, but no unanswered pray-ers." In other words, if God cannot answer the prayer, God may answer the pray-er.

When God says, "No, not at all!"

Our spiritual development may need the discipline of God. God may be saying, "I am not going to help you with your trouble, but I will see you through with your tribulation in order to reveal to you the depth of your resources." If God does say that, the important response is not to question God, but to continue to pray even when no answers seem to be forthcoming. It is not the result of prayer which counts so much as the spirit which is developed by the act of praying.

In summary.

Dr. Perry LeFevre helps us deal with our concerns about prayer in a section titled, "The Pathologies of Prayer," from his book *Radical Prayer.*

Our prayer may fail or be distorted in three different ways: in relation to the one to whom we pray, in relation to our own self understanding, and in relation to the process of prayer itself.

We may for example not be praying to the one who is finally trustworthy. Our real trust may be elsewhere. . . . If we pray for the destruction of our enemies, or for our own triumph at the cost of injuring or exploiting others, we have misunderstood the reality of God. So too if we pray to a God of power rather than a God of love. Our prayer cannot violate either what God is or what God intends. . . .

Then too, we may not recognize our own condition. We may think we are masters of our destiny. We may refuse to recognize our finitude and helplessness. Such falsely grounded prayer fails because it is unable to let new meanings and possibilities emerge. It cannot provide the conditions under which God can change the perceptions of self, world, and other.

Prayer may fail at the level of process too. Our prayer may be only idle chatter. It may not be honest speech. It may not be owned. It may not grow out of our concrete experiencing, our own unique existence situation. Even worse, prayer may be only a speaking, and not a speaking which leads to listening. When this is the case prayer remains the expression of self-centeredness rather than opening the way for the recentering of the self.[5]

Discussion questions about "Unanswered Prayer."

1) The poet Alfred Lord Tennyson, wrote these famous lines: "More things are wrought by prayer than this world dreams of."

Describe some of the prayer situations which might be included in such a description of prayer?

2) If all of your prayers went unanswered, would it still be worthwhile to pray?

3) If a person really makes an offering of his or her life for the noblest of causes, but expresses no words of prayer to God, is that a prayer?

4) There are many reasons for unanswered prayers, some of which we have referred to in this chapter. Can you mention others, from your own experience? Why do you suspect they were not answered?

5) If we do not get answers to our prayers, does that mean here is no God?

6) Please read the prayer of St. Francis again. Which couplet speaks to a particular present condition in your life?

7) If you entertain impure thoughts, such as jealousy, self-pity, sexual uncleanness, or resentfulness, will they have any effect upon your prayer life? If so, why and how?

"A Prayer," by Blase Pascal, (1623–1662).

> Neither discourses, nor books, neither your Sacred Scriptures, nor your Gospel, neither your holiest mysteries, neither alms nor fasts, neither mortification nor miracles, neither the use of the Sacraments nor the sacrifice of your Body can do anything at all to bring about my conversion, unless you accompany all those things with the wholly extraordinary help of your grace.[6]

Part Two:
PRAYING VARIOUS KINDS OF PRAYERS

INTRODUCTION

I cried aloud to God, I cried to God, and he heard me.
In the day of my distress I sought the Lord, and by
night I lifted my outspread hands in prayer. . . . But
then, O Lord, I call to mind Thy deeds. I recall thy
wonderful acts in times gone by (Psalm 77:1, 2, 11.)

Most of us, like the psalmist, cry out when things go against us. When we have exhausted our own emotional or spiritual resources, we seek the help of powers greater than ourselves. We resort to prayer when life becomes too difficult, too burdensome, or too threatening. Such an observation is supported by an Ohio pastor.

> My most important discovery of prayer is that it is a center of truth in the life of an individual. Although there are people who pray lies, I find that for most people, prayer is a time to strip down to the bare essentials, to get at our personal truths and longings.

I find people ask me to pray for the thing they want most: "Pray that the hospital will discharge me before my daughter's wedding"; "Pray that this leg will heal so I can go hiking again before I die"; "I'm sorry for some of the things I've done in this life. Ask God to forgive me."

I suppose you could say that all of these are "self-ish" because they all concern "me," "my problems," but I perceive them as cries from the hearts of people who are in real crisis. Once the cry is made it becomes an opportunity to explore oneself and one's relationship to God. Either in prayer, or in counselling, the agenda becomes: how do we give up a well loved activity gracefully? How can we be assured of our own salvation?

Some of our prayers are petitions for healing, some are confessions, and some are experienced for other reasons. In fact, it may be helpful to the reader to have an overview of the varieties of prayer, so I offer the following list along with scriptural references and biblical illustrations of each. Of course, this is not an exhaustive listing.

Various Kinds of Prayers

Petition: our request to God for help and guidance.
"Give us today our daily bread," (Mt. 6:11). See also: Solomon's petition for personal wisdom (1 Ki. 3:6–9).

Intercession: our appeal for God to intercede on behalf of others.
"Father, forgive them; they do not know what they are doing," (Lk. 23:34). See also: the intercessions of Moses on behalf of his people (Ex. 32:11–13).

Confession: our admission of spiritual weakness.

"Wash away all my guilt and cleanse me from my sin," (Ps. 51:2).

See also: the confessions of Ezra for the sins of Israel (Ez. 9:6–15).

Forgiveness: our plea to be forgiven and accepted.

"Thou, O lord, art kind and forgiving full of true love to all who cry to thee," (Ps. 86:5). See also: Admonitions of Jesus about forgiveness (Mt. 6:4).

Thanksgiving: our appreciation for benefits or for grace received.

"Thou hast turned my laments into dancing. . . . I will confess thee forever, O Lord my God," (Ps. 30:11). See also: Daniel's prayer of thanksgiving (Da. 2:20–23).

Love of God: our expression of our love for God.

"O lord our sovereign, how glorious is thy name in all the earth. I will extol thee, O God my king, and bless thy name, for ever and ever," (Ps. 8:1). See also: Mary's prayer of praise of God (Lu. 1:46–55).

A note concerning this order of prayers.

The above order of prayers suggests that only when we Confess and ask Forgiveness, do we become aware of the love of God. Hence the Adoration of God may be the end result of praying.

On the other hand, there are those who feel that love of God precedes all other prayers. They conclude that if we love God first, then we are moved to Confess and ask Forgiveness.

137

O Lord, I call to thee, come quickly to my aid; listen to my cry when I call to thee. Let my prayer be like incense duly set before thee. . . . Set a guard over my mouth; keep watch at the door of my lips. Turn not my heart to sinful thoughts nor to any pursuit of evil courses (Psalm 141:1–4).

Each sentence of the Psalmist's prayer reveals that he is in touch with the spiritual side of life, with the province of the Spirit, and with God. He is assuming that the world is more than substance and matter. He sees the world as Spirit, as ongoing creation, as the unfolding plan of God. He prays because he believes that the world is being redeemed and that his prayers have some part in that new life. The spiritually minded Emily Herman also writes in this spirit.

As long as we interpret the world . . . merely in terms of science and philosophy, our faith in intercessory prayer must necessarily be at the mercy of the latest scientific or philosophical theory. But if we enter the world of grace—a world redeemed, recreated, and unified by Christ—intercession becomes the most convincing and luminous fact in the world, and every valid result of scientific and philosophical enquiry will ultimately contribute to its right interpretation.[1]

When our prayer becomes a part of the world of the Spirit, we touch deep levels of victorious living. We become a part of the new world being born, the Kingdom coming into being.

Prayer enables us to see God's purpose more clearly.
Miss Herman suggests how prayer helps to clarify our lives and concentrate on the spirit, or spiritual, side of life.

As we become naturalized in the world of prayer, bringing our intellect, as well as our will, to bear upon our communion with God . . . we become conscious of what the mystics have called the "in speaking" of God in the depth of the soul. Gently but surely God reveals Himself. Old things gain a new aspect; the world of men [and women] is seen in a new light. We know ourselves and we know God, as we have never done before. Facts of faith become more real and unassailable than facts of sense.[2]

God is always working. We need to be open to the influence of the Spirit.
Paul Tillich, an influential German-American philosopher and theologian, offered many helpful insights about prayers. He

felt that "the answers to the meaning of . . . existence cannot be grasped abstractly but only through personal faith and decision." Of Tillich's view on prayer, LeFevre writes,

> Tillich holds that a valid interpretation of prayer will not claim that God can or will be persuaded to interfere with existential conditions. Rather it will presuppose that God is always active in and through such conditions. Prayers of supplication or intercession are to be understood as asking God to direct the given situation toward fulfillment. The prayers are themselves an element in the situation. . . . "Every serious prayer contains power," Tillich writes, "not because of the intensity of desire expressed in it, but because of the faith the person has in God's directing activity—a faith which transforms the existential situation."[3]

An illustration of the support of the spirit world in our every day lives.

This director of a church school faced defeating problems but found support from the spirit world and the reality of Jesus, through her faith.

> When I was Director of Children's Ministry, one of my most difficult tasks was filling the classroom teacher roster. One year was particularly trying for me and I was feeling very stressed and very responsible for the whole of the church school. One afternoon, I sat at my desk trying to decide what I could do to recruit more teachers. I felt alone and misunderstood. Then I looked across the room and saw a

141

picture of Jesus that I had on the wall. Suddenly I knew that the burden was not mine alone and that I needed to remember that Jesus was with me. I began to pray. I prayed for help and strength, for patience and for faith. You know what happened. I was given comfort and the realization that this was a ministry shared and powered by the Holy Spirit. A sense of weightlessness came to me and I knew that with the help of Jesus, our ministry would continue. We are not alone.

As this school leader reveals through her own spiritual experience, we have, through faith, deep resources of the spirit. The presence of the spiritual world undergirds us and responds when we call upon it for guidance and support.

The power of the spirit to invade a worldly life.
One of the common characteristics of the spiritual life is its ability to invade our ordinary lives. I well remember when it first happened to me.

As a young man I developed as many youths do, a number of conflicting emotions and feelings about my sexuality. I had urges I could not understand. The problems were intensified as I planned to enter the ministry, a calling which suggested to me that I had better be clear about my own self if I intended to help others search for God.

In the course of my student preparations, I was asked to take part in a summer church service. My assignment was to read a text from Isaiah. I looked at it beforehand but the significance of the words did not strike me until I read them before the congregation, "Though your sins be as scarlet they shall be as white as snow," (Is. 1:18).

I suddenly saw myself admonishing the people for sin of which I myself was guilty. I also had the terrible feeling that the text was revealing my secret sin before all present. When I finished, I groped for my chair and slumped down. My heart was beating at what seemed a wild rate. A feeling of limpness controlled my whole body. I sat in a daze.

Of course, I never heard the other man's sermon, but reflected on the strange occurrence. Suddenly I experienced a great inner relief. My guilt had been known. But I had not been struck down. I felt accepted. I had a sense of being forgiven yet still under the power of one who knew me better than I knew myself.

How do you explain what was going on that morning? Do words of scripture by themselves carry a mysterious weight of conviction? Does our guilt hear from them what we cannot accept from other sources? Was it more than a coincidence that I had been asked to help lead that particular morning, to read a passage which spoke to me so dramatically, and to be in that small chapel where the closeness of the small worshipping group reinforced my sense of being exposed by scripture?

Was it significant that we were gathered for the worship of God with the unexpressed expectancy that worship carries with it?

A chaplain in a large hospital tells how he shared the death experience with a dying patient.

Praying during difficult, somewhat devastating times, may not always be easy. I recall one cancer patient, a young mother of three children saying, "I've a hard time praying when I' m so angry about my disease and the prospect of dying, but I pray anyway. I guess I just need to talk to God about how I really feel."

As chaplain, I found her to be of strong faith, knowing that God would listen, not only to her askings and fears, for she had many unanswered questions. She always welcomed my prayers and would often reach for my hand while I offered to God her special requests and/or those things I sensed she needed. The prayers were simple prayers for strength, patience, peace of mind, and a sense of God's presence. Sometimes she (we) would pray for her husband and children, for she knew how difficult her illness and possible death was for them. What peace of mind and calm came to her through our many prayers.

Eventually, this young mother died, but she never lost faith and never stopped praying (talking) to God. Her death was made easier and became a victory of faith for upon her lips were the words, "The Lord is my shepherd . . ." She then felt the Lord's response, "Peace be unto you . . ." By praying to God in difficult times she received what was needed. She learned that one not only prays for physical healing but for emotional and spiritual healing. For her, neither doctors nor death had the last word.

This chaplain showed his professional training. He discovered early in his visits that the patient was a person of faith. It was important that he should encouraged her to pray for herself, to talk out her feelings, her original anger at God, and her "complaints and fears." (By contrast, some pastors just enter the room, say a prayer and move on to the next bedside). In addition, this chaplain shared prayers with the patient ("sometimes we would pray"), thus identifying himself with her desperate situation and their common faith in God. Also, this chaplain conscientiously stayed with the patient so that in a sense they accepted her death together with faith.

How prayer for self changed a serious church conflict.

Controversy is not uncommon in churches, but this one almost got out of control.

"I have been installed as pastor of this church and I intend to lead it," I declared stubbornly, to which the president of the congregation replied, "I have been elected by the members to make the decisions around here and I'm going to."

That says it all. I and the church president had been locked in a power struggle for months. Our positions had divided the membership. A few life-long friendships were being torn apart. Members were leaving. Attendance was slipping. Very little was getting done.

For myself, I felt I was failing as pastor. What should I do? I suggested negotiation, but it was interpreted as weakness. Charges and counter-charges escalated. I got angrier and angrier at the president as well as at myself. I sought help about managing conflict. And I also prayed. I didn't pray about the problem, but about the man who opposed me as well as myself. My prayers led me to ask what lay behind our differences. What was going on in his life that added to our bitterness? Was he not happy at home, on his

145

job, with his children? Why did I feel I had to be in control? What personal needs was my own anger meeting?

The more I prayed, the more concern I felt for the president as a person. I also felt I could not continue to hate a man for whom I was praying. My prayers seemed to bring an inner peace to me.

Well, after some months, our enmity slowly dis-solved. I did not win him to my point of view but we came to a way of working things out. I felt the skill of conflict management had helped, but more important was my change in attitude brought about by my many prayers.

Reflection has convinced me that when I got control of myself through prayer, the situation changed. Prayer, the process of putting our problem into the hands of a higher authority, gave me a wider perspective on what was happening. The spirit of prayer humbled me and opened the way for new solutions.

Answers to prayer "do not provide total pictures or game plans."

In the following account, notice how the Quaker "Inner light" of the prayer rejects possible estrangement, and creates instead a peaceful understanding, in spite of deep historic, religious and social differences.

> When our college daughter was doing an internship in New York, I prayed that she would make some good friends there. In fact, she met her future husband and now they have two children. But there is more to the story. We are Quakers and this fellow is of Jewish faith. My mother asked if we were going to try to break them up. How could I? I had asked God to make her stay in New York meaningful. God did more than that. Her whole life has been filled with a loving relationship and

we have had the opportunity to widen our awareness and our beliefs. It hasn't always been easy. Some of our basic philosophical and religious differences have caused much uneasiness, but we have all grown because of our interactions, and even though we sometimes have to agree to disagree, we respect and love each other. God has broadened all our horizons.

Every life is confronted with serious problems that seem insurmountable. I know how limited our own ability is, but by giving God's spirit a chance to confront and guide, I am usually able to keep on. Answers to prayer do not provide total pictures or game plans.

Notice the "suppleness of Spirit" in this testimony. The writer finds her daughter making decisions which she, as mother, did not anticipate—decisions which might have brought estrangement to everybody. But the mother remained "open" to the Spirit's leading. Each time a threatening situation developed, she was open to further leading. Such openness enabled her to turn potential alienation to constructive insights, which, in the end, brought the two families to a much more meaningful level in their relationship.

Discussion questions about "Prayer assumes a Spiritual Universe"
1) When we pray to change our own life, are we implying that we know more about how to live than God? Are we impugning God's power, or doubting God's intent, by praying for what we feel is important?

2) When we pray for ourselves, we know a little about that which we should pray for, and what we have to do to help implement our prayers. But when we pray for others, we may know

much less. Do we really know enough about the inner needs of others to pray for them? Do we have to know?

3) Can God's plan for the future be changed by our prayers?

4) If you could count on your prayers being answered, make a list of the things you would you pray about for yourself or for others. Later, as you survey the list, what does it say to you about your values, your interests, and your limitations?

5) Call to mind the name and image of a person you do not like. Over a week's time, pray for that person twice a day. Then evaluate your feelings. Has any change in your attitude taken place?

6) Dr. Gerald May, a spiritually oriented therapist, observes, "My mind plays catch up with my heart. I may like to think I am autonomously charting my own course, but I keep discovering that my little ship has been answering to deeper, hidden currents all along." What is he saying about his (and your) outer and inner life?

7) Someone has said, "There is no home in secularity." Has this been true in your life. If so, what can we do about it?

"A Famous Prayer," by St. Francis, (1182–1226).

> Lord, make me an instrument of Your peace.
> Where hate rules, let me bring love,
> Where malice, forgiveness,
> Where disputes, reconciliation,
> Where error, truth,
> Where doubt, belief,
> Where despair, hope,
> Where darkness, light. Where sorrow, joy.
> O God, let me strive more to comfort others,
> than to be comforted,
> to understand others, than to be understood,
> to love others, than to be loved.[5]

WHEN WE HAVE PRAYERS OF SPECIAL REQUEST

Out of the depths have I called to thee,
O Lord, hear my cry.
Let thy ears be attentive,
to my plea for mercy (Psalm 130:1, 2).

The Lord is near; have no anxiety, but in everything
make your requests known to God in prayer and peti-
tion with thanksgiving (Philippians 4:6).

A petitionary prayer is a request. It is an entreaty to a superior authority. Besides the characteristic quotations above, examples of prayers of petition are numerous in the Bible. The Psalmist asks to know when the Kingdom will come, "How long shall the wicked, O Lord, how long shall the wicked exalt? (Ps. 94:3). In his Letter to the Ephesians, Paul wrote, "Give yourselves wholly to prayer and entreaty, pray on every occasion in the power of the Spirit," (Eph. 6:18). And in his Letter to the Philippians, he observed, "in everything make your requests known to God in prayer and petition," (Ph. 4:6).

The theologian Karl Rahner remarks that petition, along with praise and thanksgiving, is one of the three principle prayers; the primary prayer of petition being, "Lord, have mercy upon us," a prayer which reflects humankind's basic need for assistance and salvation.

Our prayers for help may depend upon other conditions.

In one part of scripture, we are told that all prayers are conditioned by the phrase, "Thy Will be Done." For example, when Jesus petitioned God to "let this cup pass from me," he added a conditioning phrase, "nevertheless not as I will, but as thou wilt," (Mt. 26:39).

On the other hand, in another part of the Bible we are encouraged to pray and are told that we will obtain what we pray for without any condition. "What you pray for in faith you will receive," (Mt. 21:22). A similar counsel comes from the parable about the friend who came at midnight asking for bread for an unexpected guest; about which Jesus observed, "Ask and you will receive, seek and you will find," (Lu. 11:9). No conditions here.

Answers to petitionary prayers may not be the important part.

In striving to reconcile the previous different views of petitionary prayers, we will be missing the main point if we put all our emphasis upon just obtaining answers. If we spend our time telling God how much we expect God to help us, we may get relief from talking our needs out, but we will not be praying. Prayer is the dedication of ourselves to God. Prayer is not just asking. Prayer is listening.

Prayer is not to be judged on its results but rather on the intent and sincerity of trust. We are called to petition with faith, expressed or unexpressed, and then leave the rest to God. In the final analysis, prayer is not a plea for the things of this life but rather it is our submission to the Will of God. On every occasion, we have to guard against using prayers for our own ends. Such was the misunderstanding which Miss Wilson had when she attempted to explain about prayer to young Huck in Huckleberry Finn, the famous American story written by Mark Twain (Samuel Clemens).

> Miss Wilson she took me in the closet and prayed, but nothing come of it. She told me to pray everyday and whatever I asked I would get it. But it warn't so. I tried it. Once I got a fish line, but no hooks. It warn't any good to me without hooks. I tried for the hooks three or four times, but somehow I couldn't make it work. By and by, one day, I asked Miss Wilson to try for me, but she said I was a fool. She never told me why, and I couldn't make it out no way.[1]

Unfortunately, Miss Wilson saw prayer as a device for getting things she wanted. In another misconception about prayer, I recall a friend sharing with me how he bargained with God. He wrote,

> Like most children I was taught to pray at meal and bed time, but since this was taught by my parents as a kind of parental responsibility, I never felt my parents prayed themselves; it never really took root. I do remember, however, somewhere in my thirteenth year, thinking I was going to die from polio. I had almost drowned in a local pool after my parents had specifically cautioned me against swallowing water because of the threat of this disease. So I spent most of one night praying profusely

151

and promising God most anything I thought He might desire of me. I didn't get polio, nor did I keep all those promises about being good.

Perhaps one of the reasons why so many of us become frustrated with prayer is because we incorrectly see prayer as a means of getting something. "All of us are in small boats trying to reach the shore. God is that shore. But somehow we're always trying to pull the shore to us, instead of pulling ourselves to the shore."

A personal prayer of petition.
Prayer can be a process for spiritual development as well as personal discipline. For example, I found petitionary prayer helpful in controlling my own disturbed inner feelings, when I, in the capacity of a pastor, met so many different people. Most were very supportive and cooperative. I felt others were antagonistic and hostile. A few seemed arrogant, vindictive and downright mean. Upon reflection, I composed this prayer.

> O Lord, look with grace upon the people I know.
> Some are more intelligent than I, let me learn from
>   them.
> Some are spiritually dead, help me to awaken
>   them.
> Some are too content, make me challenge them.
> Some are more honest than I, help me to relate to
>   them.
> Some are threatened by circumstance, enable me
>   to support them.
> Some are more mature than I, open me to listen to
>   them.
> Some are satisfied through ignorance, help me to
>   disturb them.

Some are imprisoned by fear, empower me to
    release them.
Some are confused, help me to find clarity with
    them.
Some are strong in their belief in God, let me cele-
    brate with them.

When we pray for ourselves.

It seems obvious that many of us know how to pray for ourselves. But perhaps it is not so obvious, that we fall into times
when we are poor in spirit and really not into prayer. Our hearts
are dry. Hope is at a low ebb. Our spirits dull. When we are in
such spiritual and emotional moods, a simple prayer-discipline of
the French classic mystic, Francois Fenelon, offers a process which
might restore our enthusiasm. It always helps to talk out our
needs.

Tell God your troubles, that God may comfort you;
Tell God your joys, that God may sober them;
Tell God your longings, that God may purify them;
Tell God your dislikes, that God may help you con-
    quor them; Talk to God of our temptations, that
    God may shield you;
Show God the wounds on your heart, that God
    may heal them.
Lay bare your indifference to good . . . your instability.
Tell God how self-love makes you unjust to others,
    how vanity tempts you to be insecure, how pride
    disguises you to yourself as to others.[4]

Prayer can help us find the spiritual resources to meet the problems of life.

Prayer is the link between the world and the Spirit. In fact, we
might not know about the powers of the Spirit unless we open

153

that road from "here" to "there." Prayer can bring about help from the Spirit to meet the anxieties of the world. Prayer can help counteract personal stress. Prayer can be a shield of armor in a time of fear. And prayer can relieve anxiety. In each of these instances, prayer can have a healing affect. Indeed, an acquaintance tells how prayer helped him face a severe period in his life.

> When my wife and I first found out that she had cancer, the whole world crashed down on us. She was in the hospital and I was home alone that night. I prayed as never before for her recovery. But I also found release from my anxiety and I prayed a long time. I got around to thanking God for the gift of my dear wife, even though she might be taken from me soon. I found courage and peace. (She recovered from that cancer for a long while).

The person who prays creates an aura of the spirit.
    A particular ambiance of the Spirit can be read by those who are in touch with the spiritual world. Such was the power at work in the prayer relationships which helped a loving wife through a difficult family period.

> There was a time when my husband was ill— both physically and emotionally. He decided he needed some space. I helped him pack, drove him to the airport and prayed for him and myself. I told very few people about his leaving and wondered how this whole thing would turn out.
>   I look back upon this particularly stressful period of my life and wonder how I ever managed. Then I remember the teacher, whom I did not know well,

who came to me one morning and asked if I believed in prayer. I shared my troubles with her and together we sought God's help. Another friend, also aware of my stressful situation, reached out. A good friend kept giving me food as I was unable to concentrate on cooking. And another person insisted we meet each week for dinner. My daughters were a constant course of comfort and good will. These were answers to my prayers.

I merely did what I could to get through each day. I would try to figure out what was the most important thing I needed to do and then try to do it. I have been told I was courageous. That courage was an answer to prayer. But best of all, the return of my recovering husband again was the ultimate answer to my prayers.

There is a spiritual ambiance about those who pray. They attract others to them who are of the same Spirit. The Spirit makes itself known in ways which only the spiritually sensitive can appreciate. Those of the spirit attract others of the same awareness, even as this person did in the midst of her concern for her husband. Her faith drew others of faith to her.

The Spirit has ways of revealing itself in experiences of which the world is not always aware.

How prayer changed one family's situation.

I asked a friend if and when prayer had changed any conditions in his life. He told me,

As to my actual experience in prayer, I cite this one incident from my high school freshman age.

My elder brother was a university student and had been home for the Christmas break. He was returning to school the morning it happened. My brother wasn't the best steward of money. My father was under the impression my brother had sufficient funds to carry him thru to the end of the semester in January. When my brother revealed to my father, at the last moment before leaving for school, that he needed more money, my father (who did not have much money) became very upset and angry at my brother. Harsh and angry words passed between them. Then I saw my brother get down on his knees before my parents and pray silently. After a short while, he arose and said with a steady confident voice, "I'm all right now." And so ended the episode.

I don't think my father gave my brother any money. But he must have managed all right somehow. But I do know that prayer changed the whole atmosphere very quickly and effectively. They say that prayer changes things. I believe that, and I do know that prayer changes people.

As this testimony reveals, prayer is such a fundamental experience of life that once it has taken hold of us, we rarely forget it. Prayer bypasses many superficial memories and reaches down to where we live. Prayer events are remembered, not because they are unusual, which they often can be, but because they touch us at our deepest roots of life. The author of this event is over eighty years old. While many other events of his high school years were lost, this incident involving prayer came quickly to the surface when his days of youthfulness became a topic of conversation.

When others pray for us.

> *It was about this time that King Herod attacked certain*
> *members of the church. He beheaded James the brother*
> *of John and then proceeded to arrest Peter also. . . .*
> *He put him in prison under a military guard . . . mean-*
> *ing to produce him in public. . . . So Peter was kept . . .*
> *under constant watch, while the church kept praying*
> *fervently for him to God* (Acts 12:1–5).

In the text above, it should not be surprising that the prayers which others made for Peter during his time of imprisonment gave him support and encouragement, as well as strengthened his courage and faith. In the mystery of prayer, it is important to realize that the prayers by others work their unseen powers upon us. Prayer is no less significant if it comes from others instead of originating in ourselves (according to the Spirit.)

The importance of remembering those who are sick, despondent, or lost.

This personal account by a clergyperson helps us to understand what "prayers by others for us" may accomplish.

> A dramatic incident in prayer was the calming
> feelings I experienced when I suffered a critical ill-
> ness and was hospitalized for a month and a half.
> During that time I often felt separated from God.
> I became aware by cards and letters from friends
> and members of my church of the large number of
> people who were praying for my recovery. At the
> same time, the hospital chaplain lifted up the
> quote of Paul from Romans Eight, concerning the

fact that nothing can separate one from the love of God in Jesus Christ.

I read the passage often and remembered the prayers of the folks and I truly felt the presence of God holding, uplifting me. I thank God for my recovery. Prayer for self and others has become even more meaningful in my life! I thank God for the gift.

What a pastor learned when others prayed for his family.

There are times in some of our lives when everything caves in, when all of our supports seem to fail us, and we wonder whether we can go on. Such was the case of a young clergyman who, in the midst of his time of despair, experienced the power of other people's prayers, (their love). He was quite frank as he told his story.

"I'll pray for you" is a term I have often used. It seems to be a natural phrase for a minister to say. But I never realized the power of praying for others until a crisis hit my family, and many people prayed for us.

During the early part of her pregnancy with our second child, it was discovered that my wife had a tumor. A surgeon said he would be able to operate but could not get her on his schedule for nine weeks.

It was during those nine weeks and on the day of surgery that many people prayed for us. The night before the surgery, the surgeon met with my wife and me. His final line to us that night, and unaware at the time that I was a minister, was, "I want you to pray tonight for yourselves and for me."

The day of the surgery, as they wheeled my wife off to the operating room, she said she felt very peaceful. I also felt a special strength and peace throughout the day. The surgery itself took sixteen hours and was the longest day of my life. It is only in hindsight that I realize why we had the strength to make it through that ordeal. I now know that the source of that peace and strength was not from within ourselves, but the result of so many people praying for us. The surgery was a great success, but a few months later my wife developed multiple sclerosis. People continue to pray for us, and again, that is a source of peace and strength.

As a result of this experience I can no longer just casually say, "I'll pray for you." I feel both a sense of obligation to pray for others when I say I will do so, and also an assurance that those prayers are heard and answered in God's own way. I cherish those who pray for me, and now, for me, it is a serious matter when I say to someone, "I'll pray for you."

When others prayed for a minister in trouble.

A conscientious church leader of Ohio says he was deeply affected by, and will long remember, the unexpected prayers of a friend and stranger, at a time when he faced difficulties in a former congregation.

In one of my former churches, a small group were charismatic Christians. They knew I was not charismatic, nevertheless, we respected and learned from each other.

One morning, a member of that group came to

my office. It was during a time when conflict was brewing in the church. She had a friend with her whom she introduced as a well known faith healer who, being on tour, was visiting her. My friend said they would like to pray with me.

With that she got on her knees, prayed silently and then began speaking in tongues. I remained silent; surprised but engaged. Then her guest spoke up. "I'm not sure I understand, but the message I get from God is that the problem in this church is in God's hands. You should not be afraid. Things will turn out all right."

After that my friend rose and again asked God for support. There was another brief time of silence and in it I realized God was speaking to me in love and truth. Soon thereafter my visitors left, explaining they were on their way to a lecture on prayer and healing.

That morning God's spirit touched me in a way I would never have chosen and one I don't understand but, for me, the encounter was truly authentic.

I seek to be disciplined in preserving time for prayer. I need God's love in the midst of my life. Each time I pray I know that relationship is deepened. Each time I pray I feel more complete and whole. Each time I pray I am led again to love with the gifts I have received.

Prayers of concern by others shaped this man's career.
Little do we know what a word of concern or a prayer of caring for a newcomer can do. This friend has cause to remember the

scripture, "when I was a stranger you took me into your home; when I was ill you came to my help," (Mt. 25:35, 36). Such prayers for him, by friends and strangers, redirected his entire life.

> During my university years, a significant experience led me into a call to the ministry. After only two meetings amid young people in a church in another part of town from the university, I had my first experience with illness. The pastor and five of the young people visited me in the hospital. Such personal concern was a new experience for me. I kept going to that church, became active in it, and was moved to enter the ministry. The strength and purpose for life had come to me through the concern for me from people of a vastly different background.
>
> None of this clearly fits what people often think of as prayer—talking to God and asking for something. Rather, it is letting the Eternal Spirit give meaning and purpose so that I could use my experiences in life to help other people. Self-understanding and acceptance could be seen as the fruit of prayer in the quiet sense.

Some might claim that this young man turned toward the Church in response to the sympathetic, friendly support he received from church member strangers at a time when he was away from home, in a new community, sick, and lonely. If that was the case, then let us give credit to the power of religious concern for a stranger. It is also possible that the spirit of God was working in the heart and soul of that young man and that new friends just reaffirmed his change of direction.

Discussion questions about "Prayers with special requests".

1) If natural law determines how things happen, for example, freezing temperature produces snow and ice, what is the use of praying for warm weather? Can prayer change the orderly process of the seasons, of winds, or rainfall?

2) Through prayer, Jesus petitioned God at the time of his crucifixion (Mk. 15:34). Why did not God save him, or did God save him? Please explain.

3) Is there a difference between talking to God and praying?

4) What did the apostle Paul mean when he wrote, "Adapt yourselves no longer to the pattern of this present world, but let your minds be remade and your whole nature thus transformed," (Ro. 12:2). Please rewrite or restate this famous passage in your own words.

5) Some people who "in everything make their requests known to God" seem to be out of touch with the everyday activities. They do not appear to be with it. Are there limitations on how much we should look to God?

6) All of us can experience the material world of things which fill our lives, and we know how to make things work for us. Is there also a spiritual world? If so, how do we get in touch with it. Can we make it work for our benefit, too? If so, how?

"A Prayer," By St. Anselm, (1033–1109).

> O Lord, our God, grant us grace to desire you with
> a whole heart, that so desiring you we may seek
> and find you, and so finding you we may love you,
> and loving you we may hate those sins which sepa-
> rate us from you, for the sake of Jesus Christ,
> Amen.[3]

When We Pray for Others

Simon, take heed . . . I have prayed that your faith may not fail; and when you come to yourself, you must lend strength to your brothers [and sisters], (Luke 22:32).

Love your enemies and pray for your persecutors (Mark 5:44).

The difference between intercession and intervention.

A prayer made in support of someone else is a prayer of intercession. To intercede means to plead on another's behalf, to pray for another. For example, in the first of the preceding scriptures, Jesus prays in the interest of the increased spiritual strength of Simon. In the second quotation, Jesus tells us to pray on behalf of those who persecute us.

By contrast, intercession has to be differentiated from intervention. Intervention means to interfere in the life of another. It means to mediate between two parties.

Prayers on behalf of others are common in scripture.

Prayers on behalf of others are seen throughout the spiritual lives of Old and New Testament personalities. Both Moses (Ex. 32:30–32) and Samuel (I Sam. 7:5) stood before God to intercede for their unfaithful people. Daniel prayed because of the national sin of his country (Da. 9:3–19). Queen Esther interceded with the king on behalf of her people who were being persecuted by Haman (Es. 4:5–17). Jesus prayed to God on behalf of others. "Father, forgive them for they know not what they do," (Lu. 23:34). Paul asked his followers to pray to God for him that he might be saved from unbelievers (Ro. 15:30).

Praying for others can go on in the midst of any day.

The calender of a multi-state conference minister is, of course, crowded with appointments and appearances. Nevertheless, they do not keep this administrator from making prayer, for and with others, a significant part of his official work.

> In my personal life, I find prayer to be the essence of life. I often pray to God for guidance of what to do, what to say. I do this so routinely that it is just a part of my life. I tremendously enjoy praying for other people. I do this when I am in crowds, in small groups, traveling on public transportation, and I am amazed how at times people will turn their heads and look directly at me, and that's the end. I usually simply smile at them, acknowledge their presence, and thank God for them as I have asked God to bless them and to minister to them according to their personal needs. I make it a standard policy to often pray with people when they come into my study to visit with me. There are

164

times when people have gotten on their knees and I have prayed for God to forgive them. These have been very moving experiences and a great blessing to me and my friends.

This person exhibits several significant characteristics of prayer.

1) He sees prayer as an integral part of his work ("essence of life"); not something added on whenever he happens to think of it.

2) In spite of a busy schedule, he finds time to pray. He does not complain that secular work crowds out prayer. In fact, he sees prayer as supporting his administrative duties.

3) Prayer appears to give him a joyful attitude and flavors his relationships—all of which surely cannot be harmonious—with a positive attitude.

4) He does not fear referring to prayer. As a matter of fact, he finds people receptive to his sensitive concern for the deeper issues of their lives.

Intercessory prayers may have an effect on the pray-er.

Prayers in which we pray for others may help us as well as the persons prayed for. Though we do not know whether it is the will of God to intercede, we do know that praying for others does raise our own awareness of their condition. For example, we cannot prove that prayers for Aunt Tillie's better health will help her, but our prayers will probably move us to make a phone call, write a letter, send a card, or make a visit. In this sense, our intercessory prayer for another may also influence ourselves. Such is the testimony of Fr. Anthony de Mello. S. J., author of the modern spiritual classic, *Sadhana, A Way to God*.

If you have been called to the ministry of intercession, there is something else you will discover from the frequent practice of intercessory prayer; that the more you lavish Christ's treasures on others, the more He floods your own heart and life with them. So that, in praying for others, you yourself become enriched.[1]

Praying for others is a foundation of the Church and Community.
As Christians we are called into a holy community, a family of brothers and sisters under God, each of whom has a part to play in the Body of Christ. As Christians we cannot say to any members of the fellowship, "I have no need of thee." We are called to become a part of a blessed communion of believers, bound together, not by the circumstances of time or place, but by a mutual affection for our Lord, we are all partners with God in the continuing creation of the world.

"We are bound together by faith not by experience," says Bonhoeffer, about whose understanding of intercession, LeFevre observes,

> "A Christian fellowship," writes Bonhoeffer, "lives and exists by the intercession of its members for one another, or it collapses. . . . There is no dislike, no personal tension, no estrangement that cannot be overcome by intercession as far as our side of it is concerned." In intercession we bring the other into the presence of God, seeing him [her] as a fellow human being and a fellow sinner who needs grace. To make intercession is "to grant our brother [and sister] the same right that we have received, namely, to stand before Christ and share in his mercy."[2]

166

Praying for others means caring for those who harass us, being open to those who oppose us, and having enough inner peace to return good for the evil others may do us. In his faith, Bonhoeffer followed a disciplined prayer program. "I really enter into the other man, into his guilt and his distress. I am afflicted by his sins and his infirmity."

A congregation joins in prayers of intercession.

On many occasions of suffering or tragedy, we may find ourselves resorting to prayer because of a special need in the lives of others. An experienced pastor tells how individuals of his congregation were emotionally sustained and spiritually supported, during a time of personal crisis, by the intercessory prayers of other members.

> Most rewarding for myself and some others in the congregation was when we were in a sense driven to our knees in response to a crisis. One of our young junior age boys fell off and was stepped on by a horse. He spent several months in a coma and about ten of us gathered each and every week praying specifically for this child and in support of the family. One of our members had a special gift of making our prayers very directed and unified. Miraculously the boy finally responded and with therapy returned home.
>
> We have had another similar case and again the call to prayer has been sounded. I don't know if such prayers are answered. Coming out of such an experience I know that there are those times when one must pray, and being together with several like-minded and spirit directed persons is essential!

What happens when we pray for others.

If we treat other people as they appear to be, we may evaluate them with our own ideals and standards. Indeed, we cannot do otherwise. We can only judge according to our degrees of judgment. If, on the other hand, we pray for them as they could be, that is, see them in the image of God, and pray for them with a faithful spirit, then we tend to bend them to what might be. Such also was a conviction of Bonhoeffer.

> Human love constructs its own image of the other person, of what he is and what he should become. It takes the life of the other person into its own hands. Spiritual love recognizes the true image of the other person, which he has received from Jesus Christ; the image that Jesus Christ himself embodied and would stamp upon all men [and women].[3]

Does God ever anticipate our prayers for others and from others?

A correspondent asks the question, "Does God ever anticipate a prayer without the petitioner even thinking or praying, that is consciously praying?" He then tells of this sad event in the life of his family.

> About twenty-two years ago, our twenty-three year old daughter, newly married and living away with her new mate, was killed by a home invader. This, of course, hit my wife and me very hard, along with my son, who was seventeen at the time. We were strongly supported by family, friends and our church.
>
> Our son had sent applications to a few out-of-state colleges, but when it was time to enroll, he

entered a local college nearby as a commuting student. We wondered why, and when asked he replied, "I just don't want to get too far from the hand that feeds me."

Later, when we thought about his flip reply (typical of his sense of humor) we decided that he did not want to leave us alone at that difficult time. He was, and still is, a great comfort to us.

Was this one of those instances I mentioned above? I sometimes wonder.

Prayers of petition are not ours alone. Certainly they move subtly within our inner beings and influentially among our activities. If such is the case, does God then anticipate our yearnings, before we ever put our needs and longings into words?

Prayer for others changes relationships

When we pray for another individual, we immediately alter our relationship. We become more aware of the other. He or she becomes more a part of our thinking. We are moved to take the other into account, to a greater degree than formerly, as this retreatant reports.

At a retreat, I was asked to pray for another woman who was among the group. It so happened that I knew her. I disliked her very much. I felt she was mean and deceitful. So I resisted the assignment. But the leader urged me to try anyway. After a while, in my stubborn prayers for her, some unexpected things happened.

At first I asked myself again why I hated her. Then I wondered why she acted as she did. Then I

169

reflected that she must have some personal problems. Perhaps some of them were even like mine. To make a long story short, I found myself feeling more sympathetic to the woman and my relationship to her began to change.

The New Testament scholar, Walter Wink, comments on how God becomes a part of the changes which prayer brings about.

> But if we take the biblical understanding seriously, we'd find that intercession changes the world, and it changes what is possible to God. It creates an island of relative freedom in a world gripped by unholy necessity. A new force-field appears that hitherto was only potential, because of a lack of faith. The entire configuration changes as the result of the change in a single part. An aperture opens in the praying person, permitting God to act without violating human freedom. The change in one person thus changes what God can thereby do in the world.[4]

Prayers for others, may raise the level of civic consciousness.
During World War II, Dr. Frank Laubach, the world renowned educational missionary who used the slogan "Each one Teach one" to describe his method of educational as well as spiritual evangelism, held prayer gatherings in large cities across America. At each meeting, he would ask the crowds to raise their arms in prayer for Adolf Hitler, who was then overrunning Europe with his Nazi armies. When Laubach came to Chicago, I was one of those in the Methodist Temple with upraised arms as he led in fervent prayer. Such interceding for an enemy deeply influenced me.

170

It raised my consciousness about my role as a Christian. It moved me to "think peace" and made me question myself about how deeply I meant it. In fact, my participation in that physical and emotional event continues to challenge me; as a Christian I am expected to pray for my enemy. Though the prayer did not seem to change Hitler at that time—he scourged Europe for years thereafter—nevertheless, my witness of Laubach's faith and prayer remains a strong example to me of Christian courage. It has subtly reinforced my own attitude toward prayer.

A larger view of intercession. "History belongs to the intercessors."
Praying on behalf of others is God's way, and hence our way as co-creators with God, of reshaping the future. Intercessors are those, be they secular or religious in outlook, who have a vision of what the future should be like and strive to create such a future. Again I quote from Walter Wink.

> For intercession, to be Christian, must be prayer for God's reign to come on earth. It must be prayer for the victory of God over disease, greed, oppression and death in the concrete circumstances of people's lives, now. In our intercessions we fix our wills on the divine possibility latent in the present moment, and then find ourselves caught up in the whirlwind of God's struggle to actualize it. History belongs to the intercessors who believe the future into being.[5]

Dr. Wink then quotes the same faith/wisdom from the Greek poet, Nikos Kazantzakis, who wrote, "I believe in a world which does not exist, but by believing in it, I create it. We call 'non-existent' whatever we have not desired with sufficient strength."

By praying for, acting for, and living for the vision of the prophets and apostles, we intercede in the moribund forces of today and help recreate a new world. Persons of faith envision a new heaven and a new earth and intercede in today's world to make all things new according to the Will of God.

Intercessory group prayers can produce successful interventions

A Chicago company, whose large plant was in a minority neighborhood on the South Side, only employed white workers. For many months this racial discrimination caused protests, some of which verged on violence.

Different approaches were tried to convince the management to be an equal-opportunity employer but the company stubbornly refused.

Finally, a neighborhood strategy evolved through the efforts of a coalition of local churches. A Prayer Meeting was called, not in a church but on the sidewalk facing the plant, not a one-time meeting but a prayer vigil which was to last until the hiring practices of the plant were changed. Members of the churches and sympathizers stood and moved about various places in front of the building. At first, the uninformed public paid little attention but as the days passed the prayerful discipline kept the protest alive week after week. Soon more and more people began to take an interest in what became a serious racial concern of inequality.

After a short while, other local meetings took place. Editorials critical of management appeared in local papers. Such an increasing flood of publicity finally proved to be too much for the officials and the company agreed to negotiate. After considerable delay, many jobs for minority workers were made available.

Public group prayer and dedicated commitment had brought about what many meetings with company officers had previously failed to accomplish.

Public pressure is often a successful formula for change. When the ingredient of public prayer is added, the movement seems to take on added significance and influence. Protests may be common but protesting in the name of God captures attention, especially of the ethically-minded and religiously-oriented public. Those who campaign with righteous indignation and a sense of moral justice for cleaner lakes, protection of the rain forests, preservation of endangered wild life, or for the elimination of nuclear warheads, have found that the use of vigils and prayer protests have an extraordinarily powerful effect.

Discussion questions about "Praying for Others."

1) Is our active intercession on behalf of world peace, a safer environment, or minority rights, really necessary? Or should we let God work things out. If we don't act, will God?

2) We attribute ultimate power to God, such as the ability to bring about immediate, personal conversions. Does that mean that we, as associates with God, can bring about cures and conversions in his name?

3) The author Oscar Wilde wrote in *An Ideal Husband*, "When the Gods wish to punish us, they answer our prayers." What do you feel Wilde is saying here about prayer? Do you agree or disagree?

4) Our theology tells us that God allows us to make our own decisions, and that we have the privilege of free choice. If we pray for someone, does that mean that we are infringing upon that person's right to make his or her own decisions?

5) Do you believe, or not believe, that if we pray for others, or intercede for others through faith, that we actually bless our own selves in so doing?

6) The inscription on Gandhi's place of cremation at Rajghat reads, "Recall the face of the poorest and most helpless man whom you have seen, and ask yourself if the step you contemplate is going to be of any use to him. Will he be able to gain anything by it? Will it restore him to control over his own life and destiny?" What do Gandhi's words say to you about your life?

"A Prayer," by John Henry Newman, (1801–1890).

> O Lord, support us all day long, until the shadows lengthen and the evening comes, and the busy world is hushed, and the fever of life is over and our work is done. Then in your mercy grant us a safe lodging, and a holy rest, and peace at last.[6]

When We Want, or Need, To Confess

Only you must acknowledge your wrongdoing. Confess your rebellion against the Lord your God. Confess your promiscuous traffic with foreign gods under every spreading tree, confess that you have not obeyed me. This is the very word of the Lord (Jeremiah 3:13).

These dramatic and pain filled words of Jeremiah may remind us of our experience with confession. Confession is an admission of that which bothers us. Confession suggests an awareness of guilt. Confession suggests that we are not right with God. Confession carries with it the hope for forgiveness.

In the Old Testament, Jeremiah, as well as many other prophets, speaks as if God looks for our confession. In like manner, confession is a salient ingredient of the New Testament. If we confess our sins, God is just and may be trusted to forgive our sins and cleanse us from every kind of wrongdoing (I Jn. 1:9).

Three important parts to confession.

The story of the Prodigal Son helps us understand the process of confession. A young man has taken his inheritance and squandered it in wild living. Finally recognizing what he had done, he seeks the security and forgiveness of the home he has rejected. Though his father is ready to forgive him, nevertheless, the son feels it is necessary to make amends to God, to his father and to himself. "I have sinned against God and against you; I am no longer fit to be called your son," (Lu. 15:21).

First: the son *confesses he has sinned against God*. Inasmuch as our primary relationship is to God, we cannot be whole with anyone else or with ourselves until we cleanse our relationship with God, before whom we all are accountable. Confession involves more than an admission of our own individual sins. Confession hopes for our acceptance by God.

Second: the son *confesses he has sinned against his father*. Usually when you or I do what we should not do, we involve someone else. But even if we sin alone, we keep hidden something which would help others to know us. We are cheating what could be fuller relationship.

Third: the son *knows he has sinned against himself*. He is aware of the depth of his own guilt better than anyone else and needs to expunge his personal unworthiness. Until we forgive ourselves, our iniquity still stains us. Until we can erase our guilt from our own souls, it will continue to be a barrier to our acceptance of ourselves and God.

The importance of confession before God.

Prayer is a natural way of confessing. Where we may find it difficult to reveal our secrets to another person, we can speak of them in privacy with God. Prayer allows us to speak freely and reveal as much as we dare without fear of judgment by others. Prayer enables us to talk with ourselves while God listens. A confession in prayer enables us to look at our own feelings. Prayer sometimes enables us to seek solutions to conflicts with people, as well as situations which are problems for us, as a pastor candidly describes.

> After many years of an infrequent and not very meaningful private prayer life, two things occurred to change this for me. One of the two things was finding myself faced with a problem about which I could not talk to either of the two persons with whom I normally talked regarding such matters. The reason I couldn't is because both of these persons were central to the problem. I considered going to someone else to talk to about it, but realized how very long it would take me to tell the entire story and even then perhaps not having it understood. Suddenly the thought struck me, why didn't I take the problem to God? God already knew the story and I wouldn't have to tell it in detail, nor would I need to worry as to whether it would be understood.
>
> So one day, I sat down and unburdened myself in prayer. The relief was great enough that day and on successive days, that I soon found myself sharing other problems as well.
>
> The second thing that happened to me was the realization that I ought to spend a specific amount of time each day in prayer.
>
> I need to explain that I am a person who has always resisted external disciplines. But just the year before, serious illness had led me to begin a discipline of physical exercise. And now spiritual needs were calling for a similar discipline from me.

I decided on fifteen minutes a day of silent meditation and extemporaneous prayer. That amount of
time has continued to seem right for me. One or
two days a week I fail to take the time, and it
seems, at least, as if I often pay for that failure later
in the day in terms of how my other relationships
go.

"Put all your trust in the Lord, and do not rely on your own
understanding" (Pr. 3:5) certainly reflects the writer's feeling. It is
safer to confess to God in prayer than to a friend who, though
helpful in listening, might prove unfaithful. It is also interesting to
note that this pastor who had not been a pray-er, found through
his insights about confession, a new interest in spirituality.

The importance of confession to another person..

Unless we free ourselves from the continuing guilt of our sin,
it will continue to afflict us. A commentator on the value of confession wrote,

> I have done many wrong things during my life.
> Very few of them have I confessed to those con-
> cerned. Some of them bother me to this day. I have
> wondered why it is that some continue to make me
> feel guilty while I do not think of others so often.
> Time and the passing years have made me aware
> that the wrongs I have done which I had finally
> been able to share with others, perhaps as youthful
> indiscretions, have been the ones that I have
> almost forgotten. It is the wrongs I have not been
> able to share with anyone that continue to plague
> me.

It is significant that the "wrongs" he shared with others are the ones he has been able to forget; while "the wrongs I have not been able to share with any one . . . continue to plague me." Tell what is in your heart, on your conscience, or bothering your mind. What holds you in its grip will vanish in the wind. Once, thus blown away, you can move on to more constructive aspects of your life.

While confession is most often related to God, confession can also be made to a friend, neighbor, or even to a stranger; as the Letter of James suggests when he says, "confess your sins to one another," (Ja. 5:16). Of course, James is suggesting that "one another" be those of a fellowship where confession is not abused.

The importance of our own confession about ourself.

Sometimes we have insulated ourselves from those things about which we ought to confess. We may not even be aware of how far we are from where we ought to be. For these reasons it is often helpful to refer to the confessional prayers of others. They reveal areas we may have unconsciously covered up or lost track of through denial. For example, what areas of conscience in your life may be uncovered by this "Ninth Day Evening Prayer," by John Baillie.

> Have I today done anything to fulfill the purpose
>   for which Thou didst cause me to be born?
> Have I accepted such opportunities of service as
>   Thou in Thy wisdom has set before my feet?
> Have I performed without omission the plain
>   duties of the day?
> Give me grace to answer honestly, O God.
>
> Have I done anything to tarnish my Christian ideals?
> Have I been lazy in body or languid in spirit?

Have I wrongfully indulged my bodily appetites?
Have I kept my imagination pure and healthy?
Have I been scrupulously honorable in all my
   business dealings?
Have I been transparently sincere in all I have
   professed to be, to feel. or to do?
Give me grace to answer honestly, O God......

Have I tried today to see myself as others see me?
Have I made more excuses for myself than I have
   been willing to make for others?
Have I, in my own home, been a peace-maker or
   have I stirred up strife?
Have I, while professing noble sentiments for great
   causes and distant objects, failed even in common
   charity and courtesy towards those nearest to me?
Give me grace to answer honestly, O God.[1]

So many of us insulate ourselves against change. We prefer the same old way of thinking. We feel we have it made. Little do we know how much others wish we would grow up emotionally and spiritually. Perhaps Baillie opens a new door for you. Perhaps he is an ambassador of the Spirit calling you to a new understanding of who you are and how much you need to change.

Some additional insights about confession.

Confession is not easy or cheap. Confession is dependent upon sincerity. Confession means throwing oneself upon the mercy of the forgiver. Confession demands a purging of that which demeans a relationship. Dietrich Bonhoeffer reminds us that in confession there is no easy forgiveness. There is, he says, no cheap grace.

That is what we mean by cheap grace: the grace which amounts to the justification of sin without the justification of the repentant sinner who departs from sin and from whom sin departs. Cheap grace is not the kind of forgiveness of sin which frees us from the toils of sin. Cheap grace is the grace we bestow upon ourselves.

Cheap grace is the preaching of forgiveness without requiring repentance . . . communion without confession, absolution without personal confession.[2]

A meaning of grace as an agent in our confession to God.

The grace of God is the undeserved attention or support of God. Grace is the unmerited love of God for us in spite of our virtues as well as our vices. The apostle Paul described grace when he wrote, "It is by his grace you are saved, through trusting him, it is not your own doing. It is God's gift, not a reward for work done," (Eph. 2:8, 9).

Being endowed with free choice, we can resist, or be open to, the love of God, i.e., the grace of God. We all must choose. For many, confession is the process of acknowledging our alienation from God. It is the disclosing of our personal sin with the intent of drawing closer to the will of God.

Discussion questions about "Confession."

1) The apostle Paul says that confession is necessary to salvation (Ro. 10:8–10). Do you believe that, or can salvation be found without confession?

2) Does the phrase, "In God we Trust" really have any meaning in our scientific and materialistic society? Have modern men and women outgrown the belief in God? How important is prayer and God in your life?

3) The great religious leader of the Sixteenth Century, Saint Teresa of Avila, declared, "All that should be sought for in the

exercise of prayer is conformity of our will with the divine will in which consists the highest perfection." What guidelines do you use to help you respond to the will of God?

4) Some authorities say there are three definitions of sin:

(a) unbelief, or lack of trust in God

(b) persons assuming they know better than God

(c) people finding fulfillment through their own gratifications.

Would any of these definitions reveal feelings (or actions) which apply to your life?

5) The writer of the Letter of James says, "Confess your sins to one another, and pray for one another, and then you will be healed," (Ja. 5:16). Can you find your sins forgiven by confessing to a friend?

6) Which of your abilities, talents, or skills, are you now using to change the world to meet God's design? Can you share your strengths and confess the areas where you could be doing more for the common good and for God?

"A Prayer of Confession," from *The Book of Common Prayer*.

Almighty and most merciful God, we have erred and strayed from your ways like lost sheep. We have followed too much the devices and desires of our own hearts. We have offended against your holy laws. We have left undone those things which we ought to have done: and we have done those things we ought not to have done. O Lord, have mercy upon us. Spare those, O God, who confess their faults. Restore those who are penitent; according to your promises declared in Christ Jesus, our Lord. And grant that we may hereafter live a godly, righteous and sober life, to the glory of your holy name, Amen.[3]

When We Need To Forgive, or Be Forgiven

Then Peter came up and asked him, "Lord, how often am I to forgive my brother if he goes on wronging me? As many as seven times?" Jesus replied, "I do not say seven times; I say seventy times seven," (Matthew 18:21, 22).

Jesus certainly emphasized the importance of forgiveness in his answer to Peter, as in the text above. Forgiveness is one of the main doctrines of the Christian Church. ("Forgive us our debts, as we forgive our debtors.") Forgiveness is presented in the Apostles Creed which has been used since the middle of the Second Century. The creed continues to be a basic summary of what Christians believe and is recited in several different forms; such as, "I believe in the forgiveness of sins."

Forgiveness appears in at least two major forms.

A) Forgiveness can be available "on condition that." The Lord's Prayer includes the phrase, "Forgive us the wrong we have done, as we have forgiven those who have wronged us."

Immediately following Jesus' introduction of the Prayer, he makes this comment: "For if you forgive others the wrongs they have done, your heavenly Father will also forgive you. But if you do not forgive others, then the wrongs you have done will not be forgiven by your Father," (Mt. 6:14, 15). It appears to add the condition that if we do not forgive those who forgive us, our wrongs will not be forgiven by God. Indeed, Theologian Karl Barth raises this issue.

> How shall I hope for something for myself if I do not even grant it to my neighbor? . . . How could we, who ourselves are such great debtors, hope to have the divine forgiveness if we did not of ourselves wish to do this small thing, namely, to forgive those who have offended us."[1]

Another slightly different illustration of conditional forgiveness, is the parable of The Unmerciful Servant, in which the servant who had been forgiven did not forgive others and, therefore, was himself condemned (Mt. 18:23–25). In this story, forgiveness depends upon the desire to make amends, upon the definite change in attitude, or upon repentance. None of these were forthcoming, so the servant who did not forgive others as he had been forgiven was censured himself.

B) Forgiveness can be available as a free gift. In the story dealing with the paralytic, Jesus forgave the man apparently without any condition. "Son, be of good cheer your sins are forgiven," (Mt. 9:2). Nor did Jesus ask for any condition of confession of all those involved in his crucifixion, "Father, forgive them for they know not what they do," (Lu. 23:34). In both cases, forgiveness appears as a free gift.

The importance of either kind of forgiveness.

One of the responsibilities of being a Christian is that we are called to forgive others. But this is more than an act of faith; it can be a powerful weapon for change. Forgiveness has the power to shift attention from what has been (perhaps sinful) to what can be. For example, if we forgive a "sinner" (without forgiving the sin), we direct the situation to the future. In setting aside what has been, and anticipating (instead) what can be, we help bring about what may be hoped for. Paul summarized it well when he suggested that we should be "forgetting what is behind me and reaching out for that which is ahead," (Ph. 3:13). Also, notice how the spiritually minded Emily Herman expresses it.

> As we refuse to associate the sinner with his sin, but persist in seeing him as forgiven, and have the faith to treat him as forgiven, the fetters of sin shall drop off him, and the new man shall rise out of the fetters of the old. This does not mean to juggle with the reality of sin. "Thou art Simon," said our Lord; there was no attempt to ignore the imperfect present.[2]

Who has the right to forgive, and to what extent?

According to scripture, Jesus Christ gave the right to forgive to his followers. "Receive the Holy Spirit. If you forgive any man's sin, they stand forgiven; if you pronounce them unforgiven, unforgiven they remain," (Jn. 20:23).

We do not know the depth of forgiveness we can offer to others until that depth has been opened in us. There are those who can forgive much because they themselves have been forgiven much. Most of us, however, can forgive only to the degree that we have been forgiven. A worthwhile illustration from Helen

185

Wadell's insight into the *Desert Fathers,* illuminates the point. "A certain brother had sinned, and the priest commanded him to go out from the church. But Bessarion rose up and went out with him, saying, 'I too am a sinful man.' "[3]

The price of forgiveness.

Else we consider prayer and forgiveness to be an easy process, we should remind ourselves that it is very much otherwise, according to Evelyn Underhill.

> The Christian doctrine of forgiveness is so drastic and so difficult, where there is real and deep injury to forgive that only those living in the Spirit, in union with the Cross, can dare to base their claim on it. It means not only asking to be admitted to the Kingdom of Redeeming Love, but also our willingness to behave . . . under the most difficult conditions; the patriot king forgiving the invaders, the merciful knight forgiving his brother's murderer and sheathing his sword before the crucifix, the parent forgiving his daughter's betrayer . . . the lover of peace forgiving the maker of war. . . . All this is supernatural, and reminds us again that the Lord's Prayer is a supernatural prayer, the prayer of the reborn, the realistic Christian who exists to do God's Will.[4]

As Underhill says, forgiveness is not like passing a wet sponge over a slate. It is a deeply, costly activity which demands the most earnest and faithful prayer. It could be claimed that few persons could forgive to the depth she suggests unless they had the support of prayer.

The blessing which can be received through forgiving and being forgiven.

For our own mental and spiritual health, each of us needs forgiveness and we need to forgive others. Before our own healing can begin, we need to be restored in our relationship to those we have harmed, and to be restored to God. Forgiveness releases the mind and heart from the corrosive influence of bitter feelings and alienation. Prayer can be the catalyst in rehabilitation, as revealed in this account from a friend.

> Years ago I discovered my brother did a terrible thing. I could not believe he could do what he did. I was devastated. I lost my respect for him. Other members of the family said I should forgive him and forget, but I could not. It bothered me so much I actually became so ill I was sent to the hospital. My doctor told me I should confront him. For days I prayed that I could. I finally did. It was a very painful experience I will never forget. But it relieved me. I guess I cannot fully forgive him, but it helped me deal with my rage and bitterness. The doctor was right. It had been making me sick.

An illustration of the extraordinary power of forgiveness.

Two men of the New Testament dramatically remind us of the power of forgiveness: Stephen, a devout Christian (one of the seven prominent disciples in the early church), and Saul of Tarsus, a Jew who boldly persecuted all Christians. They confronted one another directly at a dramatic moment. Stephen lay dying from stoning, while Saul, as a witness, gladly held his clothing. In death, Stephen cried, "Lord do not hold this sin against them," (Ac. 7:60). It was a great act of forgiveness without condition which deeply affected Saul to such an extent that he could not

187

forget the murder, nor Stephen's faith, nor that act of forgiveness. Finally, he broke under the conviction of Stephen and the Spirit and was converted.

You or I might be able to influence others toward the gospel when we have the spiritual courage to initiate the spirit as did Stephen.

Societies and nations need to seek forgiveness, too.

Being imperfect humans, all of us are caught in all sorts of ethical compromises and emotional distortions. Therefore, we need personal forgiveness, but it is important to understand forgiveness on a larger scale than the individual. Forgiveness can assume the stature of a national issue. Nations, too, need to seek forgiveness.

As a patriotic American, I believe we should seek forgiveness for our national sins including: our role of profiteering as arms merchant to the world; our national racism which has become institutionalized; our rape of our environment (with much lost to future generations); our national drug problem which is destroying the lives of youths and families; our failure to solve the problem of the homeless; our unwillingness to recognize the rights of minorities of all kinds; our materialism which undermines the world of the Spirit; our denial of the spiritual life which leads to so much violence; and our rejection of such powers as Honesty, Virtue and Love.

It is not my purpose to appear ungrateful for the greatness of America, which is outstanding and a leader among nations in so many ways. In listing these national sins, I am following in the spiritual footsteps of many Old Testament prophets who pleaded that their lands renounce their national sin(s) and return to God. For example, among the many is Hosea. "Return O Israel, to the Lord your God; for you have stumbled in your evil courses. Come with your words ready, come back to the Lord; say to him, 'Thou dost not endure iniquity,' " (Hosea 14:1, 2).

Discussion questions about "Forgiveness."

1) Is forgiveness a religious experience or a secular happening? Does forgiveness have to involve God?

2) Is repentance necessary for forgiveness?

3) Scripture says, "And when you stand praying, if you have a grievance against anyone, forgive him [her], so that God in heaven may forgive you the wrongs you have done," (Mk. 11:25). Is the forgiveness of your own sin dependent upon your willingness to forgive the sin of others?

4) Jesus says, "Father, forgive them; they do not know what they are doing," (Lu. 23:34). There are many times when people do not know what they do? Does this excuse them from being accountable?

5) How often do you examine your motives in order to identify some secret sin for which you need forgiveness; such as selfishness, prejudice, avarice, envy, or your lack of concern for God?

6) Have you ever experienced the inexpressible joy of being forgiven; by another person, or by God? Would you describe the feeling, if not the reason?

7) What does it take to forgive members of your own family over a long standing family issue? Describe the obstacles and the possible procedures for forgiveness.

"A Prayer For Forgiveness," by William Sloane Coffin, Jr., (1924–).

> We come to you in penitence, confessing our sins; the vows we have forgotten, the opportunities we have let slip, the excuses whereby we have sought to deceive ourselves and you. Forgive us that we talk too much and are silent so seldom, that we are in such constant motion and are so rarely still; that

we depend so implicitly on the effectiveness of our organizations and so little on the power of your Spirit. Teach us to wait upon you, that we may renew our strength, mount up with wings as eagles, run and not be weary, walk and not faint.[5]

When We Are Thankful

Enter his gates with thanksgiving and his courts with praise. Give thanks to him and bless his name; for the Lord is good and his love is everlasting, his constancy endures to all generations (Psalm 100:4–5).

Of all the chapters in this book, perhaps this one has been the hardest to write. Indeed, I have had to leave it to the last because I did not know how to address the topic of giving thanks. Am I so filled with the American spirit of independence ("I can do it myself") that I overlook how my life is really the result of help from others and from God? Oh, I could reread one of the psalms of thanksgiving as quoted above, but that does not seem to be personal enough, nor fully convey the different arenas of thanks which, it seems to me, are called for under the title of, "When we are Thankful." So, I list a number of different reasons why I emphasize giving thanks, both in my own situation and for the life of others.

Ten good reasons for being thankful and giving thanks.

Thank you, God, *for the natural wonders of this world:* the mountains I have seen on vacations; the quiet lakes I have sat beside; the inspiration of sunrises; the sound of the surging sea; the natural beauty of flowers in our back yard or nearby park; and the extraordinary night sky of countless stars. "When I look at up at the heavens . . . the moon and the stars set in place by thee" (Ps. 8:3), I cry out in thanks and appreciation for the world of Creation and say, "Thanks be to God!"

Thank you, God, *for the experience of human love,* for the love by my parents, my spouse, and my children—a love which at times has gone far beyond what I deserve. Thank you for that love which is so deep that I know it must be beyond the creation of the world and must reflect some deeper divine spirit of life, for at times, it penetrates to my soul more fully than I can ever describe.

Thank you, God, *for the abundance of the harvests from the earth,* and our prosperity. Indeed, perhaps no psalm is recited more often on harvest occasions than "A Song for Thanksgiving Day," the Sixty-fifth Psalm. "Thou dost visit the earth and give it abundance as often as thou dost enrich it, with the waters of heaven," (Ps. 65. 9). "Thou dost crown the year with thy good gifts . . . the pastures in the wild are rich with blessing," (Ps. 65:11).

But our thanksgiving cannot end with a harvest dinner. Our lives are filled with all kinds of additional unmerited gifts which insight calls us to recognize. I must give thanks for those who helped me achieve my adult maturity, my life work, and who have supported me in difficult times. Certainly I did not do it all by myself, though I like to think I did.

Thanks *for friends who struggle for justice and peace;* who take as their own the injustices heaped on others. And thanks for the friend who has risen to the heights of managerial power by way of concern for the protection of the rights of employees of great corporations. These and others call me to a nobler vision of what my life could be. In thanking them we lift up ourselves.

Thanks *for persons who have preached sermons to me* from unusual "pulpits" which they did not know they were using: such as the gas station attendant who confided in me about his faithfulness to his sick wife at a time when I secretly knew my own marriage was threatened by my unfaithfulness. And such as the the older librarian who once admonished me when I withdrew a book, "Young man, you should not be reading such a book." And such as the old railroader who, when he died all alone in his transient hotel room, left this note in his pocket: "Thanks for you. I'm through with this." It was a pocket watch he had worn much of his life.

Thanks *for those who have seen more in me than I saw in myself:* for the man who guided me toward ministry long before I found my fulfillment in faith; and for the parishioners who bent my young innocence heart, when I first came to their church, toward the problems of race and poverty.

Thanks *for those who give the world meaning by their professional dedication:* for my doctor, banker and lawyer who are guided by standards of integrity, honor and and skill, upon whom I depend with trust; for the mail person who brings my mail with daily personal attention; and for the garbage man who righteously throws my unboxed refuse back on the lawn so that I will put it in the right receptacle the next time.

Thanks *for the recurring ways in which we all can see examples of "Yes" to life:* the small flower growing the the middle of the highway;

my five year old granddaughter packing her doll suitcase for a trip the family will make in three months; and the determination of an eighty year old to dance after a hip operation.

Thanks *for forgiveness by others and by God:* for the woman who, with forgiveness, guided me through the labyrinth of my sexuality; for the friend who continued to respect me when in my youth I could not hear his encouragement to change destructive personal habits; for the people I served who needed a deeper awareness of the Spirit than I could share with them. Certainly the One Hundred and Third Psalm (probably the best known of all the psalms of Thanksgiving) gathers unto itself such feelings of thanks by a person who has been forgiven. "He has not treated us as our sins deserve, or requited us for our misdeeds. For as the heaven stands high above the earth . . . so far has he put our offenses away from us," (Ps. 103:10, 11).

Thanks *for the spiritual mysteries which have touched my soul,* inspired my spirit, warmed my heart, supported my visions, opened new insights of unexpected joy and led me on a thankful journey from limited Self to the sublime freedom of trust in that which I call God. Perhaps no psalm expresses this spirit of new life than the Song of the Redeemed of the Lord, (Psalm 107).

> Some [people] lost their way in desert wastes; they found no road to a city to live in. . . . their spirit sank within them. So they cried to the Lord in their trouble, and he rescued them from their distress (Ps.107:3–6).

A variety of motives for giving thanks.

194

Thanksgiving sometimes must be "Thanks for hope."

Few people have had such an impact on our understanding of the role of God in our lives as Paul the evangelist, who, in the course of his life of testimony, was beaten, shipwrecked, and experienced dangers of all sorts. He tells how he often went to sleep hungry while suffering from cold and exposure. Yet Paul is among those who proclaim a deep sense of thanksgiving. "Be always joyful, pray continually, give thanks whatever happens, for this is what God in Christ wills for you," (I Thes. 5:16–18).

Paul gives thanks, not so much because of his escape from dangers, but because he sees beyond his difficulties to the design of God, the hope offered by God, and his own trust in the Will of God. True thanksgiving is founded on faith rather than on the beneficial results of circumstances.

The experience of "the joy of the Lord" leads to thanksgiving.

We give thanks because our soul and spirit sometimes feel at one with the indescribable, mysterious presence of God; an example of which is this letter from a woman in Illinois.

> Prayer is usually thought of as a spoken word directed to our Lord. In the Sermon on the Mount, Jesus tells his listeners to enter into a closet and pray. Literally, I couldn't make it; I have but two closets and they're full. So there must be other ways. Sometimes I can hardly contain myself because of happiness, and I simply want to jump into the arms of God and give him a tremendous hug.

Gratitude in the form of partnership with God.

A correspondent describes his pattern of thanksgiving as a

"Continual Conversation." He says his prayers go on all the time, even in his larger family where prayer is not the common activity.

> Whatever formal habits of prayer I developed across the years tended to eddy around the pastoral prayer. Private prayer was really not separated from such preparations. But I am quite conscious that for me any kind of prayer has grown out of a Continuing Conversation in which I am engaged most of the time I'm awake—and maybe when I'm asleep. I am content to speak of God, with whom I am engaged in this Continuing Conversation, a Mystery. But the mystery is a congenial Mystery.
>
> Some of my relatives are trained in science and describe prayer as an attempt to turn over to God what we ought to be doing ourselves. My posture toward these people whom, after all, I love, is evasive; neither they nor I want to argue about religious faith. Their attitudes do, however, affect the Continuing Conversation; I do the religious arguing with God.
>
> The subject of the conversation is often along the lines of a Colloquy, about what religious faith is, what is unique about it, what power it has in a culture so completely devoted to mechanistic and violent forces as ours is. The Continuing Conversation goes best when the subject is gratitude. I find healing and even progress in the conversation when I begin with being grateful to my Partner.

This writer deals with a situation which could be very destructive as he recognizes differences which might destroy his family relationships. His prayers seek to heal the family conflicts in several ways. He prays for those in his wider family who even attack his religious beliefs. He prays for the ability to accept those who differ from him. But even more than this, the Continuing Conversation proves to be a constant inner source of strength and comfort even when the family differences threaten.

Some scriptural references about thanksgiving.

Thanksgiving for forgiveness. "Happy is the person whose disobedience is forgiven, whose sin is put away," (Ps. 32:1).

Thanksgiving for God's righteousness. "At midnight I rise to give thee thanks for the justice of thy decrees," (Ps. 119:62).

Thanksgiving for the victory of Jesus Christ. "The sting of death is sin . . . but God be praised, he gives us victory through our Lord Jesus Christ," (I Co. 15:57).

Two memorable Thanksgiving prayers contrasted.

The following pulpit prayer, from a pastor, is a significant example of how prayer can move beyond the usual summary or obvious listing of needs. It lifts up the connection between individual faith and God's action. It connects the responsibility of the pray-er and the work of God. It reveals the theological stance of the prayer, which helps the congregation in the understanding how the pray-er can relate to our understanding of God.

> O God, Giver of Healing and Source of Life, this
>   world which you have created by love anticipates
>   Your fullness of life.
> Enable us to enter into this prayer that calls to you
>   in spite of our own withholding.
> We need to pray, for we speak only in part with
>   each other.

197

The sources of enmity which plague this world, are
a recognition of our need for one another, and for
wholeness to which we are called.

We thank you for every sign and messenger of
meaning (among the mighty or powerful and
poor or broken), that reveal to us your creative
plan and purpose, which are never still in spite of
our uncooperative response.

We thank you for your activity in seen and unseen
ways, which informs us that we are fully known
and fully forgiven.

O God, enable us to share in all of your creation,
and to experience your glory that waits to be
completely revealed.

We give thanks for our struggles which give way to
peace, and for our sufferings which lead us to
understanding.

Teach us to be unafraid of our human losses, which
set us free to serve you.

Help us to love enough, that destructiveness cannot
prevail within us.

You did not love us into life in order to deceive us,
O God, keep our hearts open so that we do not
deceive ourselves.

O God, defend us by your loving mercies, and lead
us unto that yielded living, which needs defense
no more.

The second memorable Thanksgiving prayer is that of Rev. Walter Rauschenbusch, noted American disciple of the Spirit as well as spiritual social activist. His prayer does not attempt to carry on a dialogue with God. Instead, it is like many of our prayers. It is a listing of that for which we feel thankful.

O God, we thank you for this earth, our home,
    for the wide sky and blessed sun,
    for the salt sea and the running water,
    for the everlasting hills,
    and the never resting winds, for trees
    and the common grass underfoot.
We thank you for our senses,
    by which we hear the songs of birds,
    and see the splendor of the summer fields,
    and taste the autumn fruits,
    and rejoice in the feel of the snow,
    and smell the breath of Spring.
Grant us a heart wide open to all this beauty,
    and save our souls from being so blind that we
    pass unseeing when even the common thornbush
    is aflame with your glory, O God, our Creator,
    who lives and reigns for ever and ever, Amen.[1]

The contrast between the two prayers suggests that Thanksgiving is more than lists, as important as they are. Thanksgiving calls us to a deeper appreciation of our relationship and responsibility to God.

Discussion questions about giving thanks.

1) Do we really need to thank God for our prosperity and ease of modern living, or is our life better because of the achievements of scientists? Would it be more reasonable to give thanks to them?

2) Each of us is endowed with different talents, insights and abilities. In what ways do you express your thanks and your "yes" to life?

3) Take a look at the journey you have been on since childhood. Make a list of the incidents in which a person has played an

important part in your development. Do these memories raise feelings of thankfulness? How can you express your gratitude?

4) The theologian Henry Nouwen, who gives much of his time to retarded people, says, "It's more important to spend an evening with someone who can't speak than to speak to thousands of people." What does this viewpoint mean to you? Is it relevant to your life?

5) In Paul's Letter to the Colossians, he says, "give thanks to God who has made you fit to share the heritage of God's people in the realm of light," (Col. 1:12). Please say the same thing in your own words.

"A Prayer," by James Martineau, English philosopher and minister, (1805–1900).

> Eternal God, who committest to us the swift and solemn trust of life; since we know not what a day may bring forth, but only the hour for serving thee is always present, may we wake to the instant claim of thy holy will, not waiting for tomorrow but yielding today. Consecrate with thy presence the way our feet may go and the humblest work may shine, and the roughest places be made smooth. Lift us above unrighteous anger and mistrust into faith, and hope, and charity, by a simple and steadfast reliance upon thy holy will. In all things draw us to the mind of Christ, that thy lost image may be traced again, and thou mayest own us at one with him, and thee, to the glory of thy great name. Amen.[2]

WHEN WE WANT TO LOVE . . . GOD

"Hear, O Israel, the Lord is our God, one Lord, and you must love the Lord your God with all your heart and soul and strength," (Deuteronomy 6:4–6).

This text is often called the greatest expression of love to God in the Old Testament, and it's also the basic message of the New Testament: " 'Love the Lord your God, with all your heart, with all you soul, with all your mind.' And the second command-ment is 'Love your neighbor as yourself,' " (Matthew 22:37).

These two quotations suggest that there is nothing in all of life which is more important than loving God. Some would say there is nothing more important in life than love itself. Before I get into a chapter about love, I want to define what I mean by "love," as well as point out why I think prayer is a significant part of love.

A spiritual understanding of love.

The greatest living example of human love is Jesus Christ. He spent his days, caring, forgiving, praying, healing, and living a sac-rificial life. He taught that the love of others is the most impor-tant aspect of human relationships. But of even more significance is the fact that he pointed to one whom he said was even greater than he. He called him "Father." In claiming such a relationship, Jesus Christ becomes our clearest revelation of what the Father is like. Furthermore, Jesus is quoted as saying that he and the Father were one (John 10:30). We call the Father *God*. Because Christ loved compassionately, forgave through love, saved through love, we know what God's love is like.

This revelation of the New Testament agrees in large measure with the historic wisdom and long developed faith of the prophets in the Old Testament.

Three traditional definitions of love.

When we say God is love, we are talking about whole, complete, unending, inexplicable widths and depths of perfect love. But when we try to define love in human terms, we find various limitations of love.

Eros: is a sexual love, such as a relationship which has erotic overtones. Eros is that kind of love in which a person loves another in order to possess that person and enjoy him or her for selfish satisfaction. (Of course, the love of God supercedes this carnal love.)

Philia: is a love such as the affection between friends. It is the desire to help another person without wanting to possess him or her. (It is obvious that the love of God surpasses friendly love.)

Agape: is a love that loves another person to the depth of one's soul without any thought of return. It is selfless commitment to another for love's sake only as in the 13th chapter of I Corinthians. (Agape is the closest description of the love of God.)

Four levels of love.

I am indebted to the French spiritual leader, Bernard of Clairvaux, for his classic and basic definitions of the various levels of love and spirituality. However, I have taken the liberty of changing them slightly. I suggest the following four levels of love and prayer.

1) The love of the self.
2) The love for others without acknowledging God.
3) The love for others in the spirit of God.
4) The love of God without any awareness of self.

The Love of self.

Love of self does not have to mean love of self in the selfish sense; quite the contrary. There is an admirable side to loving oneself. It is based on the belief that God created all things and when all was finished God looked around and, "saw all that he had made and it was very good," (Ge. 1:31). We are part of that creation, that goodness. Therefore, we are responsible to care for that goodness, which includes being concerned about ourselves. Love of self is the desire to be good stewards of God's gift of an individual life. Here is how one correspondent's described his care for himself.

> I am very conscious of my soul and body. I try to eat the right things. I exercise regularly. I make sure to get the proper sleep. I try to read the right things to make the best use of my mind. I have a discipline of spiritual prayer and mediation for the nourishment of my soul. I do this because I am a creation of God. God loved me and I feel I should love what God gave me, my soul and body. If I should hate myself, it would be an affront to God. If I don't take care of myself for God who will? If I am not true to myself, certainly I will not be true to anyone else.

This kind of love is not selfish. It is not selfishness. The writer is not thinking of himself only, as his last sentence affirms. He is loving himself so that, in turn, he can be of worth to others. It is also significant that he bulwarks his spiritual discipline with prayers.

The love of others, without acknowledging God.

Many people are turned off by the institution of the Church because they feel the Church is more interested in having people support the program of the Church than it is concerned about reaching out and serving the needs of the people. In fact, among such critics was one of the most conscientious believers in God, Dietrich Bonhoeffer, who said we ought to have a "religionless Christianity," meaning that there should be more faith and less organization. A similar message, was preached by the prophet Amos. "I spurn your pilgrim-feasts; I will not delight in your sacred ceremonies. When you present your sacrifices, I will not accept them. . . . Let justice roll down like a mighty stream," (Am. 5:21ff). Both Bonhoeffer and Amos are saying let love be genuine. Love in all sincerity. Don't go to church for show. Don't pretend to be religious. Let love be authentic.

Several years ago I visited and interviewed a man who, like many people, was an example of love, without dependence upon God or prayer.

Michael and Marie were a loving married couple for more than thirty years. He was a conscientious salesman and she taught at the Kindergarten level. They raised three boys who became successful in their respective fields. After the boys left, life changed for them. Marie was afflicted with a series of strokes which finally forced her to be bedridden.

"I took care of her for more than three years," Michael told me. "At first, she could help herself a little but for the last two years I had to feed, bathe and care for her total needs. My children are far away. I had no help."

So I asked my friend, "If you were all alone with Marie, and I understand her strokes left her unable to talk or move in bed, what kept you going during those years?"

"I did it myself, though it was hard. No, I don't believe in God and I didn't find prayer much help, though I do go to church when I can get a ride. I did it because I loved her. And I don't regret a minute of it."

Michael has always been an independent man. In spite of the handicaps of many years, he continues to see life as good. He still claims that he can take care of himself, and is used to the phrase "I can do it myself," the hallmark of so many Americans. He does not acknowledge God or prayer as part of his sacrificial love for his invalid wife. He is not unlike people who live by strong moral standards, and find their lives meaningful even though God and prayer may play no role. They seem guided by reason, individual insight, personal courage to overcome difficulties, and high ethical decisions.

The love of others, in the spirit of God.

In contrast to those who do not acknowledge God, there are people who feel that life is relatively empty without the support of spiritual values such as faith, prayer and the Presence. For example, I feel the man in my poem epitomizes such a person of faith and Spirit.

205

I am to have dinner with the woman I love. It will be prepared by her hands and heart. Although she will make the meal, how it is planned and what it will be is not important to me. I'm not going for the meat and potatoes. Our dinner looms large in my sight, because of a different kind of nourishment. What will my love prepare for my mind? What will she choose to nourish my heart? How will she give sustenance to my spirit?

As we share, I will bring some things too. I must add a course of good conversation. I will bring a bottle full of dreams. I can flavor the meal with memories. I will offer myself and my spirit. I shall make a toast of faith.

So our dinner will be changed from food to communion. God will be present through our love.

This man wanted to move beyond mutual trust to a common acceptance that there are spiritual forces at work, blessing life more than we can bless each other. He apparently felt that a deeper friendship results when we are bound in faith to love each other in the sight of God.

The love of God, without any awareness of self.

I doubt if any of us are ever able to forget ourselves enough, and to adore God enough, to be able to love God with our whole heart and soul and strength. Indeed, such a union with God, so sought after by the mystics and others, will always elude all of us. God is complete and perfect love; God is beyond our human capacity to understand.

But we can always reach out, and we do have ways of telling ourselves what it could be like to love completely, as revealed in this personal story.

A neighbor whom I can see, because he is just outside my window, has been picking vegetables from his garden. He has just carried away an armful of cucumbers and tomatoes. I watch as he disappears into his home.

"What kind of a person is he?" I ask myself, for he looks strange and rarely speaks. "Does he really deserve those cucumbers and tomatoes?"

But the tomatoes never ask those questions. They present their nourishment and joy to anyone who will plant, cultivate, and harvest. They are ready to feed a rich woman, a poor man, a farmer, or a poacher. God is like a tomato. A tomato knows the importance of giving oneself away. A lesson I have yet to learn.

Obstacles to loving . . . God.

We need to overcome hidden destructive inner passions. The purpose of prayer is to love God, in all the very best ways that love can be offered. A Fourteenth Century story can serve to remind us how single-minded we must be in our love of God. No ulterior motives are allowable.

> One afternoon an old peasant woman was seen walking the streets of Strasburg all alone. In one hand she carried a bucket of water. In the other, she held a lighted torch. Needless to say, she aroused the curiosity of everyone.
>
> Finally, an old man asked her, "Why are you carrying the bucket?"
>
> "To put out the fires of Hell!" she replied.
>
> While the old man went away grumbling because he thought it a very strange answer, another passerby stopped her to inquire, "Why are you carrying the torch?"

At that, the peasant woman held up the torch with such vigor that all those who were watching began to feel her inspired passion.

"I'm carrying the torch to burn down the mansions of heaven," she explained, and with a great flourish she added, "I'll give my life to see to it that people seek God without any fear of the punishments of Hell or the rewards of Heaven!

Prayer is the process whereby, with the help of God, we seek to understand ourselves more fully. Through prayer we throw light upon the dark areas of our minds and souls which have hitherto confined and limited us. Through Confession and Forgiveness we move closer to our Salvation, when we become able to fully open our souls to ourselves, to others and to God.

I wanted to give myself to my wife when I married her. But I did not know enough about myself to do so. Since that day, over more than fifteen years, I have sought to understand myself enough in order to open more and more of my heart and mind so that she can know, at least in part, who I am. In our early married life, we only related to each other on relatively few things. Now, as the years have passed, we see ourselves more and more face to face. However, we will never know each other completely. We will never be able to fully give ourselves to each other. But the hunger for ever more complete union is always before us and incremental achievements fill us with hope.

One of our spiritual guides in many of the previous pages has been Peter Forsyth. Again he helps us to understand this need to throw off those things that deceive us and keep us from being more open to the presence of God. He writes,

> If you may not come to God with the occasions of
> your private life and affairs, then there is some

unreality in the relation between you and Him. If some private crisis absorbs you—some business or family anxiety of little importance to others but of much to you—and if you cannot bring that to God in prayer, then one of two things: Either it is not you, in your actual reality, that came to God, but it is you in a pose—you in some role which you are trying with poor success to play before Him. You are trying to pray as another person than you are. You are praying in court dress.[1]

We need to discard any thought that God needs our love.

Our human understanding of Love allows us the following insights.

None of us can search for God on the belief that God needs our love. If we believe God is love, we know that Love does not seek itself. And if we believe that through creation Love is imbedded in our lives, then we love because of the love in us and not because we think people need our love. Nor should we love God because God is righteous. We love God for love's sake only. And we should not assume that God will love us if we are righteous. God may, but not because of our life. God loves as God loves.

We need to appreciate the presence of God in all those who love their worlds, just as God, through love, loves his own creations.

There is a danger in concluding that love is confined to some kind of a spiritually oriented relationship. We need to remember that "God so loved the world . . ." (John 3:16). Consider the depth of love of the people who likewise love the world: the architect who is designing a new building; a steel worker who is rolling steel flat plate; a surgeon who is repairing a body; a business man who is creating a new product; and a teacher who is loving children into the next grade. All of these, and so many like

209

them, are in love with their chosen world. Each is giving his or her life in creation of a new "world" with which he or she is in love.

God loves every part of creation. God's purpose and plan will not be fulfilled just through Old or New Testament kings and prophets but through those who live and move and have their being today. The Word of Love must become flesh and dwell among us to recreate us according to God's plan for a new kingdom. Concerning his mission, Jesus explained to his disciples that "the field is the world," (Mt 13:38).

If God is loving the world into a renewed creation and if we, as Paul says, are partners with God, then we are called to love the world and bring it, through the power of Love in a thousand different ways, to its salvation.

Discussion questions about, 'When we want to love.....God."

1) If you believe that God's love is an active agent in all things in this world, will you give an illustration of where and how you see this activity going on in your life, or in the lives of people you know.

2) Our faith tells us to love God for God's sake only. What do you feel must be done in your life to move toward more fully loving God?

3) Can a person fully love without thinking of God?

4) Does your love of God help to give prayer validity, or doesn't it?

5) Sometimes we just feel so loved that we can not explain the heightened emotion of warmth and peace and joy and exhilaration. How do you interpret this mysterious experience? Is it, or is it not, an evidence of the love of God?

"A Prayer of Adoration," (Gelasian Sacramentary, Seventh Century).

Eternal God, the light of the minds that know you, the life of the souls that love you, the strength of the wills that serve you, help us to know you, that we may truly love you, so to love you, that we may fully serve you, whom to serve is perfect freedom.[2]

Part Three:
HOW PRAYER MEETS SOME OF LIFE'S CRISES

How Prayer Encourages Personal Salvation

"The Lord is my light and my salvation; whom should I fear?"
(Ps. 27:1).

"God sent His Son into the world . . . that through him the world might be saved," (John 3:17).

Salvation means liberation from present or impending evil.

Salvation is concerned with both the personal and social areas of life.

Salvation is a term which has been used to define deliverance from: captivity (Ex.14:30); terror (Ps. 91:5); enemies (Ps. 98: 1–3); disease (Mt. 9:2–22); physical death (Mt. 8:28–32); guilt (Eph. 1:7); or from evil perils of every kind.

The problem of Salvation: the need to recognize our sin.

Many of us do not appreciate salvation. We say we are not murderers; we have not held up a bank; we have not plotted to kill anyone; and we feel we live respectable lives with our neighbors. But the fact is we have not looked into ourselves deeply enough. We need to look more closely at our motives, our feelings and our sense of God. We need to acknowledge our self-conceit, our selfishness, our personal greed, our lack of concern for others, and our indifference to God's presence and love.

In his book *Whatever Became of Sin,* psychiatrist Karl Menninger helps us look at our inner selves by asking a number of probing personal questions.

> What have you done this week to hurt your neighbor, your sister, or your wife?
> What have you done to hurt yourself?
> What have you done to hurt this church or the ideals for which its stands?
> What have you done to hurt this city, this land on which you live?
> What have you done this week against the interests of the next generation?
> What have you left undone for the suffering, damaged, polluted earth and its hungry, miserable exploited population?[1]

Because we are part of the imperfect communities of family, village or nation, all of us find ourselves, by our involvement, stained with imperfections. The famous New York preacher, Harry Emerson Fosdick, put it this way:

> Each man is socially guilty by deed or consent. His individual transgression comes from the climate of the times, and flows back like a rivulet into the broad river of public wrong. His private angers swell mob violence; his private greeds feed gross commercialism. The shame of city streets and the shadow of city slums make every man accountable, and no man is in sound health until he has made joint confession with his neighbors.[2]

We become entangled in conflicts, maladjustments, repressions, and unnamed dark areas, which prohibit us from emotional and spiritual wholeness. As Paul says, our alienations from God hold us prisoner within ourselves. An Anglican priest named Richard Baxter, took up the claim in the Seventeenth Century when he wrote that we have "hidden enemies in our houses" and "depths of deceitfulness." Even if we want to be good, "conscience has, at a time of temptation, such a low voice that it can be drowned out by the clamor of conflicting passions."

Our entanglements are called sin.

When our lives are filled with the fear that others will discover what we keep hidden, that is sin. When we feel alienated from our friends or acquaintances because there is something about us we don't dare let them know, we are sinners. Paul Tillich defines sin as "everything that separates us from God and from each other. Separation may be from one's fellow men, or from our true self, or from God."

If we do not do something about our sin, God may.

Tillich, warns that unless we seek salvation for our sin, God will press it upon us. "God shakes the complacency of those who consider themselves healthy, by hurling them, both externally and internally into darkness and despair. . . . God reveals to them what they are by splitting their blindness towards themselves."[3]

How can we escape the destructive consequences of sin?

Like Paul we may cry out, "Miserable creature that I am, who is there to rescue me out of this body doomed to death?" (Ro. 7:24). Or, we may feel like John Bunyan who, at the beginning of *Pilgrim's Progress,* cried, "Who will save me from the City of Destruction?" When we remember either Paul or Bunyan and look at our own lives, we recognize that it is our personal city of destruction from which we must flee.

How can we find salvation from the sin we may not know about? How can we find liberation from the consequences of our past willful unrighteous choices?

We are more than sinful creatures.

Although we may be caught in sin, we are not sin. Human nature is not sinful in itself, rather we have made it so by the self-centered motives we have added to the original gift of God. We have been created in the image of God. We are not children of darkness but of light. Our selves are more than chaos and sin. In the economy of God, we have a relationship with the eternal. We are related to God through the love of God. We are a little lower than the angels. Our need is to retrieve the fullness of this basic communion. Our need is to cast off the old self and recover the true self.

So we have the spiritual power to cultivate our salvation.

When it comes to redirecting our lives toward more faith-filled lifestyles, there is no end to those who would tell us what to do. Many self-renewing motivational programs abound. They emphasize a clearer understanding of self, an awareness of who we are, a better control of our inner lives, and other methods of knowing our history and our present condition. Unfortunately, many of these programs deal with the adjustment of self to society, whereas the real problem is the adjustment of self to God. It may be helpful to adjust to the social scene but, unfortunately, the social milieu is sinful itself. It is much more important to measure ourselves to the highest we know, to the noblest vision we can have, to what could be instead of what is, and to God. Our fundamental relationship is not with society, not with the changing social customs of the world, but with the unchanging will of God. In short, the saved life involves more than the salvation of our minds, but rather the redemption of our souls and the soul of society.

Three means of salvation from sin.

Prayer is the opening expression of need. Prayer is a port-of-entry for personal salvation. Prayer helps us to probe deeply within our psyche, as well as our soul and discover more about the good and evil of our selves. Prayer is a type of communication needed to reach out to God and Christ in order to seek forgiveness for our rebellion and to plead for acceptance. Prayer is the conversation between the sinner and God, and the eradication of our estrangement and isolation. Prayer can be at the root of the various avenues of salvation:

a) salvation through confession to others
b) salvation through the grace of God
c) salvation through faith in Jesus Christ

a) *Salvation through confession to others.* "Therefore confess your sins to one another, and pray for one another, and then you will be healed," (Ja. 5:16).

Revealing our sin to a brother or sister in the sight of God is one avenue toward salvation. Both the Letter of James (above) and the advice of Bonhoeffer (below) encourage us to such confessions.

> A man who confesses his sins in the presence of a brother knows that he is no longer alone with himself. He experiences the presence of God in the the reality of the other person. . . . Does this mean that confession to a brother is a divine law? No, confession is not a law, it is an offer of divine help for the

219

sinner. It is possible that a person may by God's grace break through to certainty, new life, the Cross, and fellowship with confession to a brother.[4]

Confessing our sins to others, even trusted members of our spiritual community as James suggests, may be difficult if not psychologically impossible. Thus the time may come, as it did for me, when there seems to be no alternative than to reach out to God.

I had been through a drinking habit which, although it did not keep me from work, nevertheless, was becoming more and more personally troublesome. What is more, I was too embarrassed to reach out to any of my friends for help in spite of the fact that my enemy was getting more dominant.

One morning, I lay in bed and can recall very clearly crying out to God in desperation, "God, help me, help me. I cannot beat this myself."

Nothing particular happened then except for the comfort that I had told my problem. I did feel better for that. However, for days afterwards, my cry stung my heart and it carried a strange power. I knew two things. One, I was ready to change. Two, I had been heard and was not alone in my battle. Both of these motivated me to do more than I had previously done to break free.

It seems to me several things were going on here. I was in trouble. Without doubt, longer than I realized. I did, however finally face the problem. When I cried out to God, it was out of an awareness that God's support was available to me—the same support that I as a pastor had shared with others. I jumped on the salvation wagon and it was off. There was no need to know if it would go.

The person who has already known the journey of faith can move more quickly toward the New Day than those who have to first convince themselves that the Promise of Salvation is valid and true.

b) *Salvation through the grace of God.* "For it is by His grace that you are saved, through trusting Him; it is not your own doing. It's God's gift, not a reward for work done," (Eph. 2:8–9).

Part of the sublime, exhilarating, and inspiring aspect of belief in God is the occasion when faith leads to salvation by grace and/or the unmerited gift of God. Such is the testimony of a navy chaplain who was attached to a navy hospital of almost three thousand beds. As such, he had been granted permission to have his family with him before being assigned overseas.

> My wife was just twenty years old. I was a navy chaplain. My wife had had a very difficult pregnancy and within a month her kidneys malfunctioned, her physical condition disintegrated, and she became a patient at the same naval hospital to which I was assigned.
>
> On a certain Thursday, I was called to meet the captain who was the head urologist. He told me that due to the organic disorders and being unable to control the uremic poisoning, my wife would probably die. I went to my wife's bedside and took her in my arms and spoke of great plans and dreams of a wonderful future. As a navy chaplain, I had stood in the presence of death many times but this was my own wife. How terribly hard it was.
>
> I left her bed but when I stepped outside in the hall, I put my arms against the wall and buried my head as deeply as I could. I remember I told this great God of mine how much I loved this lady and how much I loved Him. I told Him I knew how helpless we were and that He was in charge. We had used all our resources and now He was in total

221

command. I let Him know that whatever happened would be acceptable for it was within His will and I could trust Him. I donned my cap and went out into the night.

I awaited that night for a final call from the hospital but none came. When, in the morning I got to my wife's room the door was closed. I heard voices and went in. A nurse and my wife's doctors were around the bed. There was my wife in a clean hospital gown, sitting up with the help of pillows, holding a red rose, and smiling. Here I was positioning my soul for death and I was surprised by life. The doctors told me that when the fever had broken, the kidney output returned to normal. One doctor hastened out to find a flower to give to his favorite patient.

The doctors and nursing staff of that hospital have never taken the credit for the curing or the return to health of my wife.

At the end of his story the chaplain adds:

As for me, the past many years I have feared no evil. I do the best I know how to do. I fail Him; I deny and give poor measure for what I receive, but, never, never has His love failed me. You see I have learned to talk with the Creator. Some call it prayer.

c) *Salvation through faith in Jesus Christ.* "We believe that it is by the grace of the Lord Jesus that we are saved," (Acts 15:11).

Jesus Christ calls us to have faith in Him. We are to accept Christ without reservation, to acknowledge Him to be in control of our lives, and to confess Christ as our personal saviour. Any generalization about Jesus being the greatest prophet, the ideal for living, or the best human being, is certainly not enough, as this friend testifies.

I was reading a magazine about faith when Jack stopped by my dorm room. He saw I was interested in religion and talked with me about my beliefs. I had always believed in God and that Jesus died for our sins but I didn't take my conviction very seriously. I rarely went to church.

Over the next few months, Jack and I talked and prayed. During that time, I accepted Christ. No flashing lights. I just knew that Christ was my Lord and Savior. But I was still a lukewarm Christian, neither hot nor cold, like the people in the church of the Laodiceans. I had no group to support my new conviction about Christ.

During the next year or so, I got into an active Christian fellowship. Still I felt that if I sinned, Jesus would leave me. Sometimes I felt badly about what I did. Then Jack helped me see that when Jesus was real in me, I had the assurance that he would not leave me. As I have grown in the faith, I know I have forgiveness even though I've blown it at times. Jack reminded me that Jesus wants us to turn over our whole life to Him. But I know, too, that I can't rely on the promise of forgiveness. I must do something about my acceptance. I must let Christ be in complete control of my life. I know I have eternal life and I know I want to live a life pleasing to Him. The Christian life is accepting Jesus as Lord and Savior, and being saved from the sins of the world. It also means being saved from our selves.

Discussion questions about "Prayer and Personal Salvation."

1) There are many questions which revolve around the experience of being saved. For example: What does it mean to be saved? Who are we saved by? Is salvation a one time event or do we need to be saved over and over? Do any of these questions raise a response in you?

2) Do your friends know what you really think about Jesus Christ as Saviour? Should they know, or is it none of their business?

3) A church member observed, "The difficulty of faith is that too often we expect members to live before they are born." What is this church member saying?

4) Paul wrote, "I delight in the law of God, but I perceive there is in my members a different law," (Ro. 7:22). What was he referring to? Where do you experience the two different laws in your life?

5) Dietrich Bonhoeffer says, "Jesus calls men not to a new religion but to a new life." Is this a fair evaluation of the work of the church?

6) A German proverb observes, "Not to be ashamed of sin is to sin double." Is this comment true?

7) Are we responsible to God if we know our neighbor sins, and we do nothing about it?

"A Famous Testimony," by Hannah Whithall Smith, (1832–1905).

Lord, Jesus, I believe that thou art able and willing to deliver me from all the care and unrest and bondage of my Christian life. . . . I believe thou art stronger than sin, and thou canst keep me, even me, in my extreme of weakness, from falling into its snares or yielding obedience to its commands. . . . I have tried keeping myself and have failed most grievously. I am absolutely helpless. So now I will trust thee. . . . I give myself to thee. I hold back no reserves. . . . I believe thou dost accept that which I present to thee. . . . I believe that thou has even at this present moment begun to work in me to will and to do thy good pleasure. I trust thee utterly and I trust thee now.[5]

How Prayer Facilitates Social Change

> My brother and sisters, what use is it for a man or
> woman to say he or she has faith when they do nothing
> to show it. Can that faith save them? Suppose a brother
> or sister is in rags with not enough food for the day, and
> one of you says, "Good Luck to you, keep yourselves
> warm, and have plenty to eat," but does nothing to
> supply their bodily needs, what is the good of that? So
> with faith; if it does not lead to action, it is in itself a
> lifeless thing (James 2:14–17).

Whereas in the previous pages we have been concerned about
prayer and the salvation of the individual, in this chapter we turn
to the needs of the society around us. None of us lives entirely
alone but rather in community with others. As prayer deals with
individual salvation, it also plays an important role in the salvation of society. Indeed, we see this in the above quotation from
James, in which he suggests that prayer must be matched with
works for others. If faith and prayer do not lead to action for the
community, they are lifeless things.

The scriptural relationship between prayer and action.

The Bible is replete with examples of how spiritually motivated leaders understood salvation, not only in terms of individual piety but also in terms of salvation for the whole society. The prophet Amos campaigned against those "who oppress the poor and crush the destitute," (Am. 4:1). Dorcas, the benevolent seamstress, "filled her days with acts of kindness and charity," (Ac. 9:36). Lydia, one of Paul's first converts in Europe, labored faithfully with him in carrying the gospel into difficult communities (Ph. 4:12). Jesus said his commission was, "to proclaim release to the prisoners and recovery of sight to the blind," (Lu. 4:18). All of these references reflect the admonition of the voice which Saul heard on the road to Damascus: "I am Jesus whom you are persecuting. But get up and go into the city and you will be told what to do," (Ac. 9:5, 6). More of us need to get up and go. We will find there the needs to be met.

Though, of course, none of these have specifically referred to prayer in these quotations, we know from other references that all these persons were people of deep prayer convictions and practice.

Authorities in our time stress the importance of prayer and action.

The French religious philosopher, Jacques Ellul, is among those who emphatically suggest following prayer with social commitment. What is more, he reminds us (I believe correctly) that prayer is strenuous, difficult, exhausting, and always demanding zeal for the cause.

> If a person thinks of prayer as a way of not getting
> involved, of not acting, of avoiding risk; if he sup-
> poses that prayer lets him escape fatigue and dan-
> ger, assures him of tranquility and a good con-
> science, gives him all around protection, then we

can say not only that he has not understood the reality of prayer, but also that he is stepping into the most dangerous enterprise of all, for that is the point of the prophecy of Amos (ch. 5:18–29): "Woe to you who desire the day of the Lord."[1]

Ellul goes on to say that if we pray for peace, we should act for peace; if we pray for a sick friend, we should call or visit or otherwise help that friend; if we pray for strength to fight a bad habit, we should confront that temptation in every additional way we can. He adds, "Prayer requires that we do ourselves what we ask God to do. If we ask for us (and not for *me*) our daily bread, I shall myself give this bread to those around me who lack it."

We are all part of the family of God and expected to be accountable family members.

None of us can look upon prayer as an avoidance of our responsibilities to God. If we are, as Paul rightly says, fellow citizens (Eph. 2:19), joint-heirs (Eph. 3:6), and fellow-workers (I Th. 3:2), then we are parts of the family of God. We are called to be participants in the creation of God's Kingdom. In fact, how intimately each of us must be personally accountable is a theme of the Danish theologian, Soren Kierkegaard, who speaks out of a background of deep involvement in the meaning of prayer. He says that each person,

> as an individual, should render his account to a God. No third person dares venture to intrude upon this accounting between God and the individual. . . . The most ruinous evasion of all is to be hidden in the crowd in an attempt to escape God's supervision of him as an individual. . . . Long ago,

229

Adam attempted the same thing when his evil conscience led him to imagine he could hide. The king shall render an account as an individual, and the most wretched beggar as an individual.[2]

If we claim to be faithful to the example and spirit of Jesus Christ, then we are also accountable to him. We cannot ask to be members of a club without recognizing there are obligations to membership. As enlightened persons, we are responsible for our own morality and our ethical behavior.

This means we are called to strive for justice and mercy for others. We cannot avoid the fact that sexism permeates everything, that the right to be educated is denied to minorities, and that we are wasting the environment which our children and grandchildren must inherit. Moral accountability means moral activity. Of course, previous generations have also faced great social problems. In their day and since, they have been guided by the inspiration of Saint Teresa of Avila (1515–1582):

> Christ has no body now on earth, but yours, yours are the only hands, with which he can do his work, yours are the only feet, with which he can go about the world, yours are the only eyes, through which his compassion can shine forth upon a troubled world. Christ has no body now on earth but yours.[3]

Prayer gives direction and support to social activism.

For many social activists there is no place for prayer. They often feel it constitutes a withdrawal from life or a subjective stance which does not recognize the evils of the real world. On the other hand, there are many who see prayer as the very root and foundation for social change. For them, prayer is the originator and sustainer of social concern. Prayer is the spiritual source which gives social action strength and sustains it when it meets opposition. Again, Jacques Ellul explains this understanding of prayer.

> Action really receives its character from prayer. Prayer is what attests the finitude of action and frees it from its dramatic and tragic aspect. Since it shows that the action is not final, it brings to it humor and reserve. Otherwise we would be tempted to take it with dreadful seriousness. But in so doing prayer bestows upon action its greatest authenticity. It rescues action from activism, and its rescues the individual from bewilderment and despair in his action. It prevents his being engulfed in panic when his action fails, and from being drawn into activism, when he is incited to more and more activity in pursuit of success, to the point of losing himself. Prayer, because it is the warrant, the expression of my finitude, always teaches me that I must be more than my action, that I must live with my action. . . . Thanks to prayer I can see that truth about myself and my action in hope and not in despair.[4]

Prayer and politics.

Does prayer have a role in politics? Most certainly, says spiritually minded Evelyn Underhill. She reminds us that spirituality, which suggests prayer expressed or unexpressed, is really the root of all political action.

> The prevalent notion that spirituality and politics have nothing to do with each other is the exact

opposite of truth. Once it is accepted in a realistic sense, the Spiritual Life has everything to do with politics. It means that certain convictions about God and the world become the moral and spiritual imperatives of our life; and this must be decisive for the way we choose to behave about that bit of the world on which we have been given limited control.[5]

Mrs. Underhill's concern for action following prayer is founded on two principles.

First, prayer and meditation often make us more sensitive to our own selves. Knowing ourselves can lead to a deeper appreciation of others. Familiarity leads to concern. Concern calls us to care. Thus the more we pray, the more we identify with others, the more we appreciate what others are facing, the more our familiarity encourages us to help.

Second, prayer touches us with the presence of God. The love of God moves us to love our brother and sister as ourselves. Or, to put it another way, once we commit ourselves to God, the Spirit moves within us to love others as God loves us. Thus we discover it is not only fulfilling an obligation to pour out our lives for others, it is a personal responsibility.

Of course, whenever we suggest that prayer plays a part in solving social problems, we are also saying that it does so according to the will of God as we understand it. Prayer for social change, like all spiritual forces, needs to have the guidance of the Holy Spirit. Prayer and social action are expected to reflect the teachings of Jesus Christ.

The role of prayer in social change.

Prayer was an important element in the Civil Rights Movement of the 1960s, when African-Americans broke out of the long years in which they suffered so much prejudice. Their campaign was largely founded on the religious conviction (previously nurtured by their commitment to religion and church attendance) that God wants every individual to be free. Minority hope and expectations were nourished by the preaching of the Word. Later, when the new movement became widespread and the marchers began to be threatened by reactionary powers, they were called back to the churches for prayers. The preachers retold the story of Moses and others who testified to the power of God to come to the aid of the oppressed. With such spiritual encouragement, the struggle was renewed. Finally, even the racist politicians and prejudiced citizenry were moved, and the historic national Right to Vote legislation was enacted.

Theologian Perry LeFevre summarizes the observation of the contemporary author, James Cone, about this concern for racial understanding.

> Black prayer has served to define identity, to give courage to survive and to sustain hope in the face of a culture which denied identity, thwarted survival, and pressed the black community toward despair. Prayer, perhaps more than anything else, maintained and nurtured the sense that black persons and black communities were not alone, that they were not totally abandoned in a culture of suffering and oppression. Not being alone meant more than having someone to turn to for help and sustaining power; it made possible the recognition and maintenance of human dignity in the face of a culture bent on denying it. The intimate relation with God and Jesus in prayer carried with them, implicitly even when not explicitly articulated, the meaning, "I am somebody."[6]

Few of us would deny the supporting role which faith and prayer have played in the long, long effort toward recognition of the minority population as an equal part of America. In the midst of the years of servitude, faith supported by the Word and prayer, kept alive a religious vision of freedom, not unlike Moses' vision of the Promised Land. Indeed, the anticipation of a time when "the wolf and the lamb shall feed together" (Is. 65:25), calls subjected people of all races to the fulfillment of the undeniable Will of God.

Faith and works must together fulfill the Gospel!

> *Martha . . . had a sister, Mary, who seated herself at the Lord's feet and stayed there listening to his words. Now Martha was distracted by many tasks so she came to him and said, "Lord, do you not care that my sister has left me to get on with the work by myself? Tell her to come and lend a hand." But the Lord answered, "Martha . . . you are fretting . . . about so many things; but one thing is necessary. The part that Mary has chosen is best; and it shall not be taken from her,"* (Luke. 10: 39–42).

The story of Martha and Mary is often used to illustrate the need for both doing and listening, and to point out that social activism and personal piety are parts of the whole Gospel. Of course, both *participation in social change* and *individual salvation* are necessary. Each commitment must supplement the other. The parishes which emphasize collective social action and the parishes which stress the cure of soul, need each other. The social activist who puts social change before anything else, and the person who puts personal piety above everything, need to work together.

Furthermore, individual salvation as well as social concern should be combined in the mind and heart of the same person; as the writer Alan Hunter says, "Those who picket should also pray, and those who pray should also picket." Obviously, this idea of piety and activity is not new. In the Thirteenth Century, Meister Eckhart, who continues to be read as an authority on mystical thought, said,

> The active life is contemplation. One must root himself in this soil of contemplation to make himself fruitful in works. The object of contemplation is then achieved. God's purpose in contemplation is to lead one to the accomplishment of fruitful works whereby many are saved in love.[7]

Faith, as well as funds, is needed for the ghetto and barrio.

Dramatic examples of the need for combining faith and works are the city neighborhoods of the underclass where whole blocks of buildings are gutted by fire or vandalism; where souls are ravaged by misuse, exploitation, drugs, poverty and hopelessness; where family structures as well as community institutions are blighted; and where individuals are caught in endless hopelessness. Society may spend millions on urban renewal of housing and infrastructure, but that is not enough. What good is a new house, or neighborhood, if there is no will to respect it, no spirit to give it vitality, no faith to give it meaning and purpose?

A street youth needs a job, but he also needs renewed inner will to achieve. An addict requires medical care, but he or she also needs personal loving support. A fatherless family should have adequate health services, but it also needs a community which can help make life whole for the mother and children. A person in poverty needs much more than bread; he or she needs spiritual friendship which can help to reestablish hope. In short, we should not only liberate persons from economic want, but should meet their deeper spiritual needs for the rehabilitation of their souls and spirits.

It is not enough to cure the body and neglect the soul.

Thomas Merton, whom we have quoted often because he was among the most insightful and practical spiritual leaders of our day, reminds us of the importance of the role of spirit in good works.

> He who attempts to act and do things for others . . .
> without deepening his own self understanding of
> freedom, integrity, and capacity to love, will not
> have anything to give others. He will communicate
> to them nothing but the contagion of his own
> obsessions.[8]

In a personal poem, I have sought to catch the spirit of faith and works together.

> Faith is of a holy innocence. It needs the practicality
> of worldly Works to keep it germane.
> Works often loses its spirit. It needs the sustaining
> power of faith to provide it with endurance.
> Faith needs the everyday experience of Works to
> keep it relevant.
> Works needs the spiritual foundation of Faith to
> keep its vision alive.
> Faith must be validated by work.
> Works must be validated by faith.

Discussion questions about "Prayer and Social Change."

1) In your view, what is the connection, if any, between prayers made in the secrecy of one's own closet (Mt. 6:6), and the style of life we live out in the world?

2) In the Lord's Prayer, we are taught to pray, "Thy Kingdom Come." Do you think the time of peace and justice will arrive even if nobody prays?

3) We often hear it said that the Church should not be involved in politics. Others say it should be. What is your opinion, and on what is your conviction based?

4) The philosopher, Friedrich Nietzche, observed, "From people who merely pray, we must become people who bless." Please consider what you feel he meant by this statement.

5) Can you see any relationship between the final purpose of God and what is going on in the world at the present time? What do you feel is God's final objective? What part, if any, does prayer play in bringing it about?

6) A contemporary religious leader says that today's emphasis upon activism has secularized the gospel. Would you agree or disagree.?

7) In your concern for racial understanding, the rights of minorities, the role of women, a better environment, and the struggle for peace and justice, has prayer played any part. If so, how?

"The Work of Peace, A Prayer," by Alan Paton, (1903–1989).

> Give us courage, O Lord, to stand up and be
>   counted, to stand up for those who cannot stand
>   for themselves, to stand up for ourselves, when it
>   is needful for us to do so.
> Let us fear nothing more than we fear you.

Let us love nothing more than we love you, for
thus we shall fear nothing also.

Let us have no other Gods before you, whether
nation or party or state or church.

Let us seek no other peace, but the peace which is
yours, and make us its instruments, opening our
eyes and our ears and our hearts, so that we
should know always, what work of peace we may
do for you.[9]

How Prayer Resists Temptation

"Finally then, find your strength in the Lord . . . for our fight is not against human foes, but against cosmic powers, against the authorities . . . of this dark world, against the super human forces of evil in the heavens," (Ephesians 6:11–13).

The Bible is replete with persons who have struggled with temptation. Jacob was tempted by jealousy to deceive his father Isaac (Ge. 25:29–34); Delilah was tempted by others to betray Samson (Ju. 16:5); King David was tempted by his desires for Bathsheba (II Sam. 11); Job's wife was tempted by doubt to renounce God (Job 2:9); King Ahab was tempted by greed to take Naboth's vineyard (1 Ki. 21); Pilate was tempted by political expediency to condemn Jesus (Jn. 18:29–31); and Peter was tempted by cowardice to renounce Christ (Mk. 14:66–72); to name only some well known examples.

How to recognize temptation.

Temptation implies some enticement. To tempt someone or be tempted by someone, is to be involved in an unwise or immoral act. That which tempts us is often not good for us. The very things that call us away from a clear conscience, from what we believe is right, from maintaining moral standards—these are temptations. In fact, temptation is of such significance that it is emphasized in the Lord's Prayer: "Lead us not into temptation."

Temptation is a lifelong trial.

Temptations will never leave us as long as we live. We will always be tempted to our dying day. There will be no relief from the voice of the tempter. As with Adam and Eve, so shall we be plagued by profane attractions of the flesh and self.

If we think we have overcome temptation today, there will be new enticements tomorrow. In every age of life there are new songs of the Sirens. In early youth, we are tempted to cheat in school and steal at the store to test life. In our teens, we are sexually tempted into escapades we smile about or regret later. In our young adult years we are tempted to accumulate much stuff, which afterward we find we do not need. In midlife we are tempted by power and affluence to believe we are more than we are. In our senior time, we are tempted to resist giving our lives over to God. A writer from a bygone age concluded that, "Temptation hath a music for all ears."

Our temptation may be a good warning to change.

Without temptation we might not know the areas of our lives that need repair. Disastrous bouts with alcohol can prove corrective warnings to the drinker to seek help. Abnormal sexual fantasies may suggest professional attention before more serious problems arise. The common excuse, "The devil made me do it," may really be a cry for help and might suggest that more personal discipline is necessary. Perhaps we should give thanks for our temptations because they open the door to our inner natures and, though sometimes very painfully, reveal us more fully.

Seven ways by which our prayer may confront temptation.

1) Confronting temptation by saying "No."

For some, the answer to temptation is to command more moral courage and more individual resistance. As Saint Francis suggests, "Maids can never be married as long as they say No." In like manner, we see public advertisements in America today, "Say No to Drugs." Indeed, this resolve simply to resist has been a traditional response to temptation, but as one Desert Father explained, saying no is not easy.

> A brother came to the abbot pastor and said to him, "Many thoughts come into my mind, and I am in peril from them."
> And the old man pushed him out under the sky, and said to him, "Expand thy chest and catch the wind."
> And he answered, "I cannot do it."
> And the old man said to him, "If thou canst not do this, neither canst thou prevent the wind."[1]

The answer to temptation is far more complicated than just saying "No!"

2) Regular prayer is an effective defense.

Temptation usually catches us unaware. Our resistances may not be ready. When a house is empty invaders walk in. When we leave our morals unprotected, temptation may gain a foothold in us. All of which underlines the importance of constant vigilance and prayer. An active dependence upon the presence of God is a moral bulwark. Perhaps such a continual awareness was what motivated our Lord to advise, "Stay awake and pray that you may be spared the test. The spirit is willing but the flesh is weak," (Mt. 26:41). The Serenity Prayer has helped an untold number of persons.

"God grant me the serenity to accept the things I cannot change, courage to change the things I can, and the wisdom to know the difference."[2]

3) Counting the cost helps to overcome temptation.

One of the most effective counter attacks to temptation is the practice of counting its cost, as I have had to do. As a young man, I had the opportunity to manage a student store. The job also included sorting and dispensing, not mail, but incoming mail packages. Because I like to read, I was sometimes attracted to parcels which obviously contained books. More than once I stole one, (a Federal offense?).

But I paid a high price. My conscience afflicted me and loudly protested. I felt cheap. I could not face the rightful recipients. Although stealing became easier, I was never easy about it. Finally the price of being a dishonest man became too great and I broke off the practice.

Ever since that time, I have discovered that, for me at least, counting the cost has been a helpful defense against temptation. The spiritual pain and emotional uncomfortableness which more adult temptations have cost me, have helped me avoid more serious involvements. When I have longed for the extra curricula of wine, women, and song, I have found strength to resist by asking myself, "Am I willing to pay the price of guilt again? What will a new secrecy cost me?" Then, when I think of the possible damage, including loss of character, risk to health, compromising my estimation of myself, and lowering my standards in the eyes of my friends, I am able to overcome my desires more often than not. I guess you could say that fear of the consequences of exposure has protected me. Perhaps, in a more subtle sense, it is also my fear of God.

4) It helps to know that temptation is greater when we are alone.

Many of us do things alone that we would never be tempted to do if we were with others. Temptation needs an ally, namely aloneness, in order to seduce us; which may be one reason why temptations are more powerful at night. Bonhoeffer writes that sin stunts our emotional and spiritual development with others because sin demands that a part of our life be lived in separation.

> Sin demands to have a man be himself. It with-draws him from the community. The more isolated a person is the more destructive will be the power of sin over him. . . . Sin wants to remain unknown. . . . In the darkness of the unexpressed, it poisons the whole being of a person. This can happen even in the midst of a pious community. The sin must be brought to light. . . . It is a hard struggle until sin is openly admitted. "But God breaks gates of brass and bars of iron," (Ps. 107:16).[3]

Of course, it may also be true that we fall into temptation when introduced to it by bad friends or when we are carried away by being with an evil crowd.

5) The importance of exposing our temptations to the light.

Identifying our temptations can weaken their power. "Naming the demons" has been a traditional protection against being tempted. For example, discussing allurements may help us gain control over them. Confessing them and bringing them out into the light of day, removes much of their attraction, as Ignatius Loyola, in his *Spiritual Exercises*, said long ago.

The enemy also acts like a false lover who wishes to be hidden and does not want to be known. For when this deceitful man pays court, with evil intentions, to the daughter of some good man or the wife of a good husband, he wants his words and suggestions to be kept secret. He is greatly upset if the girl tells her father, or the wife her husband, for he sees clearly that his plans will fail.

When the enemy of our human nature tempts a just soul with his tricks and deceits, he wants and desires that they be received and kept secret. When they are revealed to a confessor or some other spiritual person, who understands his deceits and evil designs, the enemy is greatly displeased for he knows he cannot win in his evil plan.[4]

Talking our problem over with a trusted friend often helps. Sharing our temptation in prayer with a prayer group is an effective counter attack. Discussing our temptations with a pastor or therapist will help. Sometimes, even admitting our weakness to a total stranger whom we will never see again, will help bring our problem into better focus.

6) Overcoming our temptations by minimizing them.

Frederich von Hugel, who has counselled many about their prayer life, recognizes that sometimes we can attack our temptations by actually minimizing them.

The error lies in our lurking suspicion that, for such trials to purify us, we must feel them fully in their tryingness—that is, we must face and fathom them directly and completely. It ignores the experience of God's saints across the ages, that, precisely in proportion as we get away from direct occupation with our troubles to the thought and love of God, to the presence of Him who permits all this, in the same proportion do and will these trials purify our souls.[5]

7) Meeting temptation with the spirit of God.

Of course, as if often the case, we cannot overcome our temptations by ourselves. All too often they have become too important a part of our life pattern. Though they are hazardous, we may not really want to find better alternatives. We admit they are not good for us but we keep repeating them again and again because we have a subtle need for them.

When we have resisted to the extent of our strength, there is God to turn to. A soul touched by temptations is also a soul touched by God. None of us is at the mercy of temptation alone. We have a counter force within us, as Paul wrote to the Corinthians.

> So far you have faced no trial beyond what man [and woman] can bear. God keeps faith and God will not allow you to be tested above your powers, but when the test comes, God will at the same time provide a way out, by enabling you to sustain it (I Co. 10:13).

It helps to remember that temptations may be only temporary tenants.

Temptations may inhabit our bodies, minds and spirits, and they may be difficult tenants who cause us all sorts of troubles, but they are only tenants. They do not own us, though they may think they do. We have another tenant, one who is far more powerful, and who will help us confine the tenant called Temptation when we pray. Or, to put it another way, our minds are composed of many parts. Temptation may control one or even a few parts. Isolating those areas and confronting them through prayers can be a method to control temptations. Rev. Harry Emerson Fosdick said it well.

> When Ulysses passed the Isle of Sirens, he had himself tied to the mast and had his ears stopped with wax, that he might not hear the sirens singing—a picture of many a man's pitiful attempts after negative goodness. But when Orpheus passed the Isle of Sirens, he sat on the deck, indifferent, for he too was a musician and could make melody so much more beautiful than the sirens, that their alluring songs were to him discords.[6]

We can be surprised at the weakness of temptation and the power of prayer.

A friend wrote me this reassuring story about his temptation experience.

> It was cold turkey. I had quit smoking of my own volition, but the strong temptation to resume kept nagging me. No ifs, ands or buts, I was determined to snuff out this problem! Resistance to the urge to smoke became a periodic and even painful ordeal. Then I remembered to appropriate the power of prayer.
>
> As a nicotine fit would come over me I would pray for deliverance. An amazing sensation would come over me—like a giant divine piston moving

246

downward through my body driving the filthy exhaust of desire out of me. I almost expected to see smoke coming out at the end of my toes! After some time of periodic urges being lifted up in prayer then beaten down by my imaginary "piston," I was free at last from the habit of smoking. Many months later I tried taking a few puffs, became ill, and knew then that I was indeed free.

Perhaps not all of us can throw off a tempting habit as easily as this smoker. Temptation and ingrained habits gain their control over us and prove very, very difficult to eradicate. Nevertheless, it is helpful to know that some of our temptations have a weaker hold on us than we imagine. Such a release from temptation can come unexpectedly and quickly.

It is not impossible. It does happen. Have we become so persuaded by the world that we overlook the spiritual aspects of our existence? Faith has removed mountains, sometimes instantaneously, and will continue to do so.

A proven discipline to combat the temptation of addiction.

An addiction is any thought which will prohibit us from fully living our life and relating to others around us in a whole manner. An addiction is a tragedy because it cuts us off from others who can contribute to our wholeness.

The Twelve Steps program of Alcoholics Anonymous reflects many spiritual and prayerful concerns: "admitted we were powerless"; "came to believe a Power could restore us"; "made a decision to turn our lives over to the care of God"; "Admitted to God . . . the nature of our wrongs"; "Sought through prayer . . . to improve our contact with God."

Although addiction is usually incurred in community, and therefor combatted through community, it is also apparent that addiction can be a tragedy which some people fight alone. For the individual who seeks the help of prayer and God in his or her personal struggle against addiction, I include the following paraphrase of the usual way the uncopyrighted Twelve Steps are presented.

The Twelve Steps: a personal petitionary prayer.

1) I admit I am powerless over _____, that my life has become unmanageable.

2) I come to believe that a Power greater than myself can restore me to sanity.

3) I make a decision to turn my will and my life over to the care of God as I understand God.

4) I make a searching and fearless moral inventory of myself.

5) I admit to God, to myself, and to another human being, the exact nature of my wrong.

6) I am entirely ready to have God remove all these defects of character.

7) I humbly ask God to remove my shortcomings.

8) I make a list of all persons I have harmed, and am willing to make amends to them all.

9) I make direct amends to such people wherever possible, except when to do so would injure them or others.

10) I continue to take personal inventory and when I am wrong promptly admit it.

11) I seek through prayer and meditation to improve my conscious contact with God as I understand God, praying only for knowledge of God's will for me and the power to carry that out.

12) Having had a spiritual awakening as a result of these steps, I try to carry this message to _____ and to practice these principles in all my affairs.[7]

The power of the Twelve Step Program.

The following is an anonymous experience of how both prayer and the Twelve Steps were instrumental in bringing about recovery and a new life.

My name is Bill. I'm an alcoholic with diabetes, and heart disease, and high blood pressure. I came into the program and was physically, morally and spiritually bankrupt. My doctor used a tape recorder when we had an appointment. I was taking eighteen pills a day, seeing six doctors every six months, that's one a month.

Since then I found the A. A. program and my higher power, who I call God. And I believe in Jesus Christ. Jesus Christ is my friend because I have had a complete turn around in my health and life. When I started praying and meditating, things started happening. I had the courage to change myself in many ways, like starting a diet, taking cooking lessons, and getting off all my pills. My health is returning; my finances are getting better. I can do things I used to have to drink to do. Like acting in a skit and getting up and singing in front of two hundred people.

I have more feelings for my fellow Man and Woman. Today I give thanks to God every time I give of my time and my talents. I used to hate anything and everything. I used to say God damn, another damn day. Now I think every day is beautiful; it's just some days are more beautiful than others. I have that peace of mind that God promised to all who believed in him—even a wretch like me.

Discussion questions about "Temptation."

1) Someone has said, "Where there is no temptation, there can be no claim to virtue." Perhaps a similar quote is, "Whoever has not experienced temptation cannot inherit the Kingdom of God." How do you feel about this?

2) There are many classic excuses for giving in to temptation. "It was the woman who gave me the fruit." "The serpent tempted me." Are such excuses justified? Have you used better ones?

3) Do you believe that temptation is a device which God uses to test our morals or our faith? Would a loving God resort to temptation or testing for our own good, or for another reason?

4) We have all struggled with temptation. Will you share some of the ways in which you have confronted temptation? Was your effort based on common sense resistance, help of others, your own prayer life, or what?

"A Prayer," by Saint Patrick, (389–461).

> Christ be with me, Christ before me,
> Christ behind me, Christ in me,
> Christ beneath me, Christ above me,
> Christ on my right, Christ on my left,
> Christ where I lie, Christ where I sit,
> Christ where I arise,
> Christ in everyone who thinks of me,
> Christ in every eye that sees me,
> Christ in every ear that hears me.
> Salvation is of The Lord.
> Salvation is of the Lord,
> Salvation is of Christ,
> May your salvation, O Lord, be ever with us.[8]

How Prayer Encounters Suffering

Lord, hear my prayer . . . for my days vanish like smoke, my body is burnt up as in an oven. . . . I cannot find the strength to eat. Thin and meagre, I wail in solitude, like a bird that flutters on the roof top. . . . My days decline as the shadows lengthen, and like grass I wither away (Psalm 102:1, 3, 4, 7, 11).

The Psalms were used in family gatherings, in village meetings, and in the synagogue in early Hebrew life. They reflect the varieties of daily living, the times of thanksgiving and the times of suffering. In his commentary on the Psalms in 1563, the Genevan theologian John Calvin wrote, "All the sorrows, troubles, fears, doubts, hopes, pains, perplexities, stormy outbreaks by which the hearts of men [and women] are tossed, have been depicted here."

Four ways of facing suffering.
How we pray when we suffer reveals a lot about how we may encounter suffering. 1) We may pray to obtain distance from our suffering. 2) We may find in our prayers that suffering has

revealed faith we never knew we had. 3) We may pray to accept our suffering and even honor it. 4) We may pray in thanks for what suffering teaches us.

1) *We may pray to obtain distance from our suffering.*

Prayer helps to direct us away from focusing on our pain. Our prayers enable us to lessen our suffering by expressing and venting our feelings. Prayer helps us to direct our attention to the fact that God is present and that God helps and heals. The prayers of others also can remind us we do not suffer alone. The concern of friends through prayers, cards, and visits help us gain temporary distance from our pain and fear, as this former patient experienced.

> When I was in the hospital, I kept the cards on the table beside my bed and window sill. Sometimes the nurses put the humorous ones on the wall. They helped me forgot my troubles if but for a moment. The funny ones made me laugh and relaxed my body. The personal messages were food for my soul. When I was suffering I needed to know that I was loved. It felt good to be loved.

2) *We may pray in recognition that suffering reveals faith we never knew we had.*

Sometimes, suffering or sickness introduce us to new appreciations of faith. A hospitalization with visits by a chaplain, along with prayers of friends, and time to read the scriptures, may introduce us anew to the importance of faith. Indeed, suffering can force us to confront significant religious questions, such as, "Why did this happen to me?" or "Is God saying something to me in this suffering?"

Our experience of suffering can move us to deeper thought. Instead of asking why, we may move to being concerned about what we are going to do about what has happened to us. We may ask, "What is the role of faith in my recovery?" or "God wants me to be well. How can I put more trust in the power of God to see me through my suffering?" or "What can I do about what has happened to me?" Many a new life has been born again out of the days of suffering which also allowed time for reflection and meditation on what is valuable about life. In fact, the famous *Spiritual Exercises* of Ignatius Loyola, which are spiritual disciplines that have been a point of departure for many modern systems for the direction of the soul, were created in the Sixteenth Century during Loyola's long enforced recuperation after a battle injury.

3) *Prayer helps is accept our suffering and even honor it.*

"False prayer asks relief from suffering. True prayer asks the strength to bear it." Such is the counsel of Professor Perry LeFevre, author of an analysis of the prayer life of the Danish theologian Soren Kiekegaard, *The Prayers of Kierkegaard*.

> Ordinarily prayer is thought of as a consolation in relation to suffering because men prayed to be relieved of the suffering. For Kierkegaard it is otherwise. The consolation which is available to a witness for the truth is that of being able to ask God to strengthen him in order to bear all suffering.
>
> Thus by prayer he digs down always more to the heart of suffering; the nearer he approaches God in intimacy, the more he anchors himself in suffering. . . . Each time he prays in this way, he strengthens himself, and anchors himself in the conviction that he will know how to sustain suffering.[1]

All of us are composed of body and soul. The one upon which we concentrate the most will probably influence us the most. If we pray only to be relieved of physical pain and suffering, we may become aware of it all the more. On the other hand, if we pray for the support of the Spirit, that different perspective may ease our mental anxiety and help relax our tensions, as well as give strength to our soul.

A prominent clergyperson who, while anticipating a successful career in journalism and the Church, suddenly found himself afflicted with an eye disease which threatened him with blindness. In telling his story of how he was able to adjust to such an affliction at a most promising time of his life, he says, "I grew worse and worse as I lamented what I had lost; but when I became thankful for what I had, I became better."

This understanding of suffering is raised to an even more significant level in the writings of P. T. Forsyth in *The Soul of Prayer*.

> We pray for the removal of pain . . . but there is a higher prayer than that. It is a greater thing to pray for pain's conversion than for its removal. It is more of grace to pray that God make a sacrament of it. The sacrament of pain! That we say, or try to say, with resignation, "Thy will be done." It is not always easy for the sufferer . . . to see that it is God's will. It may have been caused by an evil mind, or a light fool, or some stupid greed. But now that it is there, a certain treatment of it is God's will; and that is to capture and exploit it for Him. It is to make it serve the soul and glorify God. . . . It is to convert it into prayer.[2]

4) *We may pray in thanks for what suffering teaches us.*

Suffering changes our usual patterns of living and introduces us to new insights. We learn from our own suffering. Very often we learn from the suffering of others. In this sense, we should appreciate suffering because it teaches us what we would not ordinarily experience. Wisdom such as this was contained in a letter by Frederich von Hugel when he wrote to his niece,

> Suffering is the greatest teacher; the consecrated suffering of one soul teaches another. I think we have got all our values wrong, and suffering is the crown of life. Suffering and expansion, what a rich combination. . . . Religion has never made me comfy. I have been in the deserts ten years. All deepened life is deepened suffering, deepened dreariness, deepened joy. Suffering and joy. The final note of religion is joy. . . . Suffering teaches: life teaches. Be very humble, it is the only thing. Don't weaken, love.[3]

Suffering can certainly be teaching; an example of which might be the young man who struggled through the rigors of military service, only to say afterward, "I suffered in those days but I'm thankful for what I went through. It toughened me for later life." Or note the experience of the couple who struggled to understand each other through the painful discoveries of marriage therapy, only to say afterwards, that the suffering taught them to appreciate and love each other all the more. Another example would be the word of a friend who submitted the following experience in a personal letter after he had proofread this book.

> My high blood pressure should have warned me that my life was out of balance. But I didn't listen til the attacks began. They immobilized me. But I've learned so much from my suffering. I've

learned to respect the needs and limits of my body and to pay attention to the signals. Sometimes I still want to complain but maybe that's the only way I would have learned.

Perhaps this man has read the comment by Erich Fromm concerning the value of suffering: "The beginning of liberation lies in man's capacity to suffer. . . . The suffering moves him to act."

It is unfortunate that suffering is always seen in a villainous light where, in truth, it may come as a concerned lover.

Suffering voluntarily can bring change.

For most of the world, victory is based on the power to overcome, to win, to dominate, to control and to rule. Not so for the Christian, who sees in the suffering Christ the ultimate power. In Him, we find that the real power is the willingness to suffer for another. Indeed, prophets across the centuries have often used voluntary suffering as a powerful tool for change. Those who willingly lay down their lives for a cause, draw us to that cause by the dedication and sincerity of their example. The words and example of Jesus Christ, that he gave his life for us that we might know, call us to follow him.

In our day, among many prophets, Rev. Martin Luther King, Jr., knew the power of sacrifice for others. He claimed suffering had to be the medium and the cost of reform.

> We will match your capacity to inflict suffering with our capacity to endure suffering. We will meet your physical force with soul force. We will not hate you, but we cannot in good conscience obey your unjust laws. . . . And in winning our freedom, we will win you in the process.[4]

Christ suffered the passion of the cross for us. His capacity to suffer found strength through his prayer(s). "Father, if it be thy will take this cup from me. Yet not my will but thine be done," (Lu. 22:42). He voluntarily suffered that we might have life and have it abundantly.

Prayers in suffering reflect courage, constitute hope.

It took a battle with cancer to help me discover more about the spiritual strengths which lie within myself, and, of course, others also.

I did not pray to live. In fact, I prayed to die and I did so with all the strength I had, which was very little. Repeated amounts of radiation for prostate cancer had taken away all my emotional security. Pain and loss of strength had weakened my interest in living. Death seemed preferable to more suffering. Often in my aloneness, I hoped that I would die. But my prayer was not answered. The painful time lasted for weeks. Then one particular night I felt I could not go on. I hung over the kitchen sink and in utter desperation cried to God, "Help me, God, help me."

No sooner had I uttered the words than a strange calm came over me. My whole body, heretofore so tense and rigid, was enveloped in an unusual relaxation. I felt an inner quietness surrounded with an experience of peace and even spent-joy. My aloneness left me and I felt a new sense of being cared for and supported.

Although the following days were still filled with pain and difficulty, I began to hear and accept the constant words of encouragement of my wife and children I began to sense the prayers of friends. My body seemed to seek its own recovery. My mind reached out for tapes of meditation and inspiration. Prayer, so long obstructed by suffering, became real again. More and more I wanted to help myself.

257

Now, many months later, I find my cancer is in remission, but it has left me with a handicap. It reminds me of Paul and his thorn in the flesh whose example is helpful because it encourages me to try to make my thorn serve me as he did his. Of course, my cancer may attack again or I will die in some other way. Whichever it is, I will never forget that night at the sink. Today, I know more about the fragileness of my body, but I also know the superior, strengthening power of the Spirit, hope, and prayer.

This account raises significant questions.

Like people in similar situations, my pain was so great I had no interest in prayer. Then, when the pain became unbearable, I was forced to cry out. Who is there to appeal to but God? Even the unbeliever will often do the same.

I don't know what I expected to happen. Just some, any relief. Even the crying out might be a help. What happened, however, was a complete surprise. The inner peace was totally unexpected and so real. Certainly, I had been heard. There was no doubt I got help. I knew immediately, as I continue to know, there is Someone out there who hears prayer.

Discussion questions about Suffering.

1) The Greek philosopher, Aeschylus (525–456 B.C.), wrote, "Wisdom comes by suffering." Please describe what you feel he meant. Has this been your experience?

2) Can suffering be creative or educational? If so, how?

3) Some people say that spiritual suffering can be more painful than physical suffering. In your experience, what makes you agree or disagree with this point of view?

4) Paul was a man who suffered many difficulties, such as shipwrecks, imprisonment, and the thorn in his flesh. Yet he said, "In all my troubles my cup is full of consolation, and overflows with

joy," (II Co. 7:4). What did Paul mean by this remark? Have you ever been able to say that you rejoice in your suffering?

5) Why, in your opinion, did Jesus suffer? Or did he?

6) How has suffering (your own or others) affected your relationship with God? Strengthened it; shaken it; or destroyed it? What part did prayer play, if any, in the situation(s)?

7) In his book, *When Bad Things Happen to Good People*, Rabbi Harold S. Kushner writes, "We may not ever understand why we suffer . . . but we can have a lot to say about what suffering does to us, and what sort of people we become because of it." What do you think?

"A Prayer," by Walter Russell Bowie.

> O Christ, my Master, let me keep very close to thee. When I am tempted to be undisciplined or self indulgent, let me remember thy forty days of prayer and fasting. When the fires of my spirit burn low, let me remember thee continuing all night in prayer. When I flinch from hardship, let me go with thee to thy Gethsemane. When I am lonely, let me turn to thee, my risen Lord. Whatever the outer facts may be, grant me thy gift of inner joy, in thy name and through thy grace. Amen.[5]

How Prayer Confronts Evil

Hide me from the factions of the wicked, from the tur-
bulent mob of evil doers. . . . They hatch their secret
plans with skill and cunning, with evil purpose and deep
design. But God with his arrow shoots them down, and
sudden is their overthrow (Psalm 64:2, 6, 8).

The faith that evil can be confronted.

The psalmist quoted here shares the faith that evil can be confronted. However, he is not naive about it for he details the seriousness of the threats. He is also saying that by faith the arrows of
God will overcome the evil which threatens him.

Unfortunately, the evil we experience and in which we
become involved, is not dispatched as easily as we might hope.
Evil seems to take on a very pervasive and stubborn power of its
own. The wickedness, the sin, all that is destructive of the common good are so powerful and aggressive at times.

Recognizing our personal evil and evil in society.

One has only to keep up with the media to see the activity of evil in our day. Unscrupulous corporations rape the environment; selfish individuals cheat on their faithful spouses; violent governments engage in ethnic cleansing; perverted adults abuse children; dishonest business people deceive consumers; conniving public officials practice fraud; and organized mobs undermine society through crime and drugs. Indeed, crooks are everywhere. Evil is structural and systematic as well as individual.

Evil has always been such a pernicious, terrible, and perennial threat, it is a major concern in the greatest prayer of the Christian faith: "Deliver us from evil."

We can seek spiritual support to confront evil.

When God creates us, God gives us the freedom to act and to decide how we want to live. But because of inexperience, ignorance, rebellion or selfishness, we make decisions which limit ourselves; we curtail our full relationship with others, and we deny our oneness with God. When we complicate our lives by choices which are destructive of wholeness, we become confused about ourselves, our society, and God. This alienation constitutes evil.

We are likely to continue in this state of confusion until some power helps us to change. Sometimes the very pain of being involved in evil will cause us to seek our salvation. For example, the apostle Paul cried out, "who will deliver me from this condition of sinfulness," knowing that faith would be the answer. Like Paul, religious believers are of the conviction that the redemption (release) of the person infected with evil is through faith.

Six helpful ways by which prayer can confront evil.

1) *We can meet evil with good.*

In writing to the Romans, Paul urged, "Love in all sincerity, loathing evil and clinging to the good," (Ro. 12:9). Later he added, "Do not let evil conquer you, but use good to defeat evil," (Ro. 12:21). This method of confronting evil is epitomized by the Christian leader, Methodist Bishop Muzorewa of Zimbabwe. His prayer reveals the depth of his faith.

> People are unreasonable and self-centered.
> Love them anyway.
> If you do good, people will accuse you of selfish, ulterior motives.
> Love them anyway.
> The biggest man with the biggest ideas can be shot down by the smallest man with the smallest ideas.
> Think big anyway.
> What you spend years of building, may be destroyed overnight.
> Build anyway.
> People really need help but may attack you if you help them,
> Help them anyway.
> Give the world the best you have and you will be kicked in the teeth.
> Give the world the best you have anyway.[1]

What is Bishop Muzorewa really saying? In spite of the evil he experiences, he is taking a stand for the fact that this is a good world. He is claiming trust in God whose will for good must be fulfilled. He is setting himself up as an example to others to take the shield of faith in the ultimate victory of God and therefore stand fast. He is calling to you and to me to follow in his footsteps in confronting the common evils of selfishness, and violence, with faith.

2) *We can refuse to meet evil with evil of our own.*

All of us become enmeshed in evil. By association, if not by intent, we can become evil. If we meet hatred with hatred, we become the evil we condemn. If we confront war with war, the sin of war is ours as well. If we meet slander with slander, we become the slander we espouse. In our personal dealings with each other, we are sometimes tempted to meet bad temper with bad temper, resentment with resentment, and anger with anger. When we fight evil with more evil, we become the evil, too.

The Christian faith advises us differently. Jesus calls us to break the vicious circle of an eye for an eye which was an Old Testament concept. Jesus asks the crucial question, "How can Satan cast out Satan?" (Mk. 3:24). How can evil be the cure of evil? How can two wrongs make a right? Jesus calls us to a new way of confronting evil. "If someone slaps you on the right cheek, turn and offer him your left," (Mt. 5:39). Do not meet evil with evil.

In the Twelfth Century there appeared a book entitled *The Little Flowers of Saint Francis*. Because it is filled with examples of living the spiritual way, it has been a favorite of pray-ers ever since. One of the many stories and parables is of particular significance. Brother Leo asks Saint Francis to describe "perfect joy." In response, Saint Francis relates the following incident.

> "Brother Leo, consider that we were traveling on a cold winter day and, for comfort, went to a near-by monastery. When the door was opened, the insider reproved us, criticizing us for being out in such weather, kept us waiting for hours, and then closed the door in our faces.
>
> "Brother Leo consider that later that evening we knocked at the door again. Again we were met

with hostility even greater than before. We were threatened and vilified with all sorts of unkind accusations. And again the door was slammed shut.

"Brother Leo, consider that we knocked a third time. We were met with clubs and beaten, rolled in the snow and covered with mud. We were cast away and the door was closed."

Then Saint Francis turned to Brother Leo and said, "If you can accept all these rebuffs and still love the brother at the door, that is perfect joy."[2]

People often dismiss this parable as being utterly unrealistic and impracticable. But it is necessary to look again.

There is an important parable here. Saint Francis is describing how we should respond to evil. Does our Lord not knock at the doors of our imperfect and evil lives? Do we not deny him entrance? Does he not knock again? Do we not then turn him away with antagonism, hatred, and sometimes violence? But does not Christ keep coming back? Does he ever forsake the effort to come into us? Does he ever reject us as we reject him?

(Granted that Saint Francis is also saying that we should meet evil with love, but he is also making the point that we should not return evil for evil.)

3) *We can confront evil with vision.*

There are those who take a position against evil knowing full well that they will not succeed. Nevertheless, they persist in the struggle. They know the outcome, as martyrs have known the outcome for those who have battled against power and greed for centuries. Martin Luther King, Jr., knew by the number of threats to his life that his personal struggle against evil might be short lived. In the crusade against the forces of prejudice he took the high ground. His prayer-built faith enabled him to see beyond the evil of the times. He gave America a vision. He prophesied a coming certainty. "I refuse to accept the idea that the 'is-ness' of our present nature makes us morally incapable of reaching up for the 'ought-ness' that forever confronts us."

4) *We can minimize evil's attraction and weaken its influence.*

Absence does not always make the heart grow fonder. In fact, absence can often help us forget. The same can be said about evil. The less we think about evil's presence, the less hold it may have upon our passions. Professor Perry LeFevre summarizes the claim.

> For example, if one's mind is filled with evil thoughts, the best prayer is not to linger over these as a problem. The longer and more fearful such a prayer becomes, the more one cultivates the evil thoughts he would be rid of. In this case, one must learn to acquire in all haste the most intensive trust in God. There is not time to add another word to the prayer, for then I am reminded of what I should forget.[3]

LeFevre is not caught in denial here. He is warning that accepting evil is the first step toward believing in it. Do not let evil gain a foothold against our faith that evil can be overcome. Very often a thought entertained can turn out to be a prophecy fulfilled.

5) *We can cultivate the moral courage to stand up to evil.*

Women are repeatedly referred to in the scriptures as great models of extraordinary faith and moral courage in confronting evil. Women's role in the birth of Moses is a memorable example.

266

It was a woman, the mother of Moses, who overlooked the threatened violence of the Pharaoh if she gave birth to a son. They were two Israelite women, Shiphrah and Puah, who courageously agreed to be midwives and disobeyed the vicious king to deliver the boy (Ex. 1, 15). It was the Levite mother, in constant fear of persecution, who hid the child for three months and then sought to save him by placing him in the reeds. It was the infants older sister, through faith in God, who stood guard and thus risked her life as an accessory to the crime of saving a male. It was the mother again who defied the Pharaoh's continuing persecution and nursed the child until he was older. It was Pharaoh's daughter who courageously adopted the Israelite child and even took him into the palace of her violent father who was known for his abuse of children. Such were women who celebrated their faith in God with historic acts of courage.

6) *When facing evil, we sometimes have to throw ourselves on the mercy of God.*

Perhaps few know the power of prayer as those in the military who have been under enemy fire. In fact, a person who intimately experienced many such prayers was this chaplain who shared months of perilous, fatal fighting in World War II.

> I found courage, spiritual strength and great help from prayer during combat while in the front lines in World War II in Europe. Perhaps the power of prayer kept me from "cracking up," having battle fatigue, or combat exhaustion.
>
> When enemy planes would strafe our column, my men would hit the ditch. I would pull my steel helmet as far over my head as possible getting the sensation that my entire body was inside. At such a

267

time, I would repeat the Lord's Prayer, the 23rd Psalm, and pray my own prayers. We were often attacked at night, sometimes while in foxholes. Death was immanent. I prayed for protection and deliverance from the terrible danger.

As a front line infantry chaplain, I would attend to as many as two hundred wounded/dying soldiers each day. Prayers were always said and God's blessing invoked over the men of whatever condition. Added to our prayers were acts of kindness and physical comfort. Sometimes a wounded soldier had no use of his arms and needed water and a smoke. I could light a cig and put it into the man's mouth long enough for a drag. Didn't seem very spiritual, but hopefully the prayers and whatever else we did, helped more than we could imagine. We did what we could, spiritually and materially.

All of the above tended to be emotionally and psychologically draining. I am grateful that my faith in God and in the power of prayer sustained me during eleven months in combat. Some outfits in our forward positions sustained a turnover of four hundred percent. Every day in combat seemed like a month. Each month seemed like a year. But prayer is timeless, a part of our "eternal faith" in an eternal God, and we were sustained!

I wrote hundreds of letters of condolences to families of the dead, wounded, prisoners, and men missing in action. Each letter was like a prayer, hopefully bringing comfort.

We cannot evaluate the efficacy of our prayers of supplication for ourselves or of our intercession for others because of our human weakness and imperfection, but I trust God to answer every prayer, either in the way we expect or in the way God knows is best for us.

Discussion Questions about Evil.

1) Many people claim that God does not do anything about evil. For example, why did not God stop the Holocaust? Why didn't God do away with Hitler when the dictator was causing so many millions of people such misery and death? What is your opinion.

2) How do we handle the evil spirits which lie within our own hearts; such as mistrust, lying, resentment, jealousy, self-righteousness, and others?

3) If evil is a part of our lives, do we ever actually overcome evil, do we just confront it, or do we only delay it?

4) In your opinion, is there actually an Evil Force, an Evil One, a Satan, or a Devil?

5) The apostle Paul claimed that "everything works together for good for those who love the Lord?" Is this a realistic observation for today's world? Do you believe what he says?

6) In *Table Talk*, Martin Luther reflected, "For where God built a church, there the devil would also build a chapel." What did he mean? How does such wisdom apply to our lives today?

"A Prayer for General Use," by Thomas a Kempis, (1379–1471).

Grant me, O Lord to know what I ought to know,
to love what I ought to love,
to praise what delights You most,
to value what is precious in Your sight,

to hate what is offensive to You.

Do not allow me to judge according to the sight of
my eyes,

nor to pass sentence according to the hearing of
the ears of ignorant men;

but to discern with a true judgement between
things visible and spiritual,

and above all, always to enquire what is the good
pleasure of Your will.[4]

How Prayer Heals

Is one of you ill? He should send for the elders
of the congregation to pray over him and anoint
him with oil in the name of the Lord. The prayer
offered in faith will save the sick man. . . . Therefore,
confess your sins to one another, and pray for one
another, and then you will be healed (James 5:14–16).

James was not an apostle but he held, authorities agree, a position of authority in the early church. The fact that his letter was incorporated in the sacred scriptures gives much credence and substance to what he says.

James understood the relationship between body and soul. He had the Old Hebrew perspective that, "humans are beings who are souls rather than bodies that have souls."

Three basic spiritual methods to enhance healing.

In accepting some of James' approaches to sickness, it is important to see that he saw body and soul as one whole. Hence, he concluded, and I believe rightly, that if the soul could be addressed, many of the afflictions of the body might be alleviated. With this approach in mind, James offers the following specific directions about spiritual care in times of sickness of either body or soul.

1) *Sick persons need friendly, human support.*

When a person is sick, he or she needs the presence of a friend. No one likes to face illness alone. Thus, James suggests that the elders be called as the first response to sickness. But the issue is larger than that. Sickness raises all sorts of fears and worries. Emotional and spiritual reactions can set the stage for either speedy or slow recovery, or even none at all. A sick person may begin to wonder about the cost, about the type of cure, about the competency of the doctor, about the possibility of hospitalization, and so much more. James has the insight to see how important first concerns really are. No wonder he said to send someone who understands life; not the bellboy, but an elder person of experience.

2) *Sickness of any kind may raise significant spiritual problems whose solutions are important to the healing process.*

When a person faces an illness or surgery, very often the occasion brings into clearer focus some of the fundamental issues of a life. Why has this happened to me? Doesn't God care? Is God punishing me for my guilt? Will God help me? Have I even the right to ask for God's support? If I don't live, what will become of me? Is there life hereafter? Such questions may reveal how anxiety and fear can begin to eat away at a person's body and soul.

James knew what he was doing when he advised prayer with sick persons. Send in an elder who is able to deal with matters of faith. As a matter of fact, we follow the same procedure today. Hospitals call in the chaplain before the operation hour. Clergy pray with individuals when they make their sick calls, as well as with the patient's family in times of crises. Thus, the religious community, like that of James, meets the threat of illness with the sustaining power of prayer and the comforting presence of God.

3) *Patients often need some obvious signs of spiritual support, along with the directions of the physician.* .

Words of faith-filled encouragement are important, but there is also a place for more material symbols of the Presence of God. Roman Catholic institutions feature the crucifix in halls and rooms. Clergy may use their hands as agents of the spirit for actual touching and hand holding during prayers. Clergy may use the Bible or prayer book as an obvious sign of spiritual values being present. Pastors may offer the Sacrament of bread and wine. "Do this in remembrance of me." The use of oil is another symbol of blessing.

For many persons of faith these sacraments and symbols are vitally important. They are evidences of the love of God—for some believers the actual love of God. When the clergyperson has gone, the memory and impact of these symbols of faith may be like the continuing, sustaining arms of God.

Sickness and healing of the soul.

There are many biblical references to healing of the spirit. The psalmist needed healing of his soul and prayed, "Lord be gracious to me, heal me, for I have sinned against thee," (Ps. 41:4). The prophet Jeremiah prayed that God would heal his backsliding: "Come back to me, wayward sons; I will heal your apostasy," (Je. 3:22). When Jesus announced the purpose of his life, he said, "The spirit of the Lord is upon me . . . to heal the broken hearted," (Lu. 4:18, KJV).

Thus, healing prayer may well be directed toward a person's attitude, toward a person's sense of faith, toward a person's awareness

273

of God, as well as a person's understanding of death. Healing may mean the healing of fear, loneliness, guilt, or other realities of the broken or sick spirit.

Sickness and healing of the body.

Jesus often directed his spiritual powers of faith to healings of the body. He healed the man who suffered from palsy (Mt. 4:23); the individual with leprosy (Mt. 8:3); the individual with the withered hand (Mt. 12:11); the diseased person (Mt.14:36); and the lame, dumb and blind persons (Mt. 15:30). There are numerous other references to healings by Jesus (Mt. 8:16). Each seems to be contingent upon the sick person's belief or faith that the spiritual authority represented in Jesus could bring about a cure.

Healing by faith not limited to a professional few.

Healing may be within the power of more of us than we imagine, as the insight of the well known writer Kenneth Leech points out.

> Healing is an important aspect of the life of prayer
> and a spiritual gift. Not all possess the gift of heal-
> ing in the specific sense, although it needs to be
> remembered that in Christian use *therapeuein*, to
> heal, means far more than the removal of symp-
> toms; it means therapeutic . . . and all Christians
> are involved in healing work.[1]

What some authorities say about spirit, faith, and healing.

How prayer heals the soul and thus the body is described by many writers on spirituality, including Kenneth Leech and Father Francis MacNutt; the latter is the author of the classic book *Healing*. Both authorities suggest several levels of prayer for healing.

First, prayer for repentance—

> "where there is a personal sin causing the sickness.
> Forgiveness of sin is intimately connected with
> physical and spiritual health, and a good deal of
> sickness is due to, or affected by, the fact that we are
> not right with God. . . . The refusal to forgive is one of
> the most serious barriers to prayer and health.[2]

Second, prayer for inner healing.

> Prayer "operates at the level of deep emotional
> wounds, which prevent us from making progress in
> the Christian life. . . . If healing is to take place,
> these wounds and painful memories from the past
> must be healed.[3]

Both Leech and MacNutt are saying at least three things.
Alienation from God (sin) creates an alienation from the wholeness of our bodies. The disturbance calls for forgiveness—of ourselves as well as of others. Such forgiveness may necessitate confession, as James suggested in the text. And confession may be
necessary to dig out and illuminate (before ourselves and God)
the deep wounds of the spirit. Finally, after forgiveness and confession, physical rehabilitation may come.

Norman Cousins, who did research concerning the connection between physical sickness (cancer) and attitude, states that,

> Emotions and health are closely related. It has
> been known for many years that negative emotions
> and experiences can have a deleterious effect on
> health and can complicate medical treatment. Not

as well known is the connection between positive attitudes and the possible enhancement of the body's healing system.[4]

Bend the soul and you bend the body. Purify the soul and you release the body to act naturally. Go and sin no more, warned Jesus. Make peace with your neighbor before you present yourself to the altar for healing. The condition of the soul is often reflected in the condition of the body.

Additional authorities of the spirit subscribe to the importance of faith-attitude and healing. In his book *Head First*, Norman Cousins, who has done research about cancer and the attitudes of cancer patients, says, "Belief becomes biology." What we believe we tend to fulfill. "People tend to move along the lines of their expectation, whether on the up-side or on the down-side." Cousins suggests that we should respect the doctor's diagnosis but not necessarily the doctor's verdict. He notes that the physician has more medical knowledge than the time to share personal hope with his or her patients. Patients have to supply the positive factor of hope themselves. They have to create the constructive belief.

In a similar plea that belief matters more than we may suspect, Kenneth R. Pelletier, a well known author on spiritual and health matters, observes in *Mind as Healer Mind as Slayer*, that how we believe suggests how we live. He encouragingly claims that belief, and hence prayer, has a definite influence upon the outcome of what happens to us.

> Perhaps the most essential feature of holistic systems of healing is the profound alteration required in an individual's belief system. Once an individual adopts the concept that he is an active and responsible participant in the process of self-healing, he is

no longer the passive victim of disease or the passive recipient of a cure. . . . It has become evident that the structure of personal belief systems concerning the nature of self and the universe govern experience. Inherent in any system of belief is the self-fulfilling prophecy: what is expected is what is observed, and what is observed confirms the expectations.[5]

Testimonies of healing by prayer and faith.

Let us turn to a number of actual incidents of healing by faith and by prayer, as related by a number of contributors to this book. 1) Healing of a physical ailment by faith. 2) When prayer healed a broken family relationship. 3) When prayer healed a despondent soul. 4) The healing of a person in fear of death.

1) An instance of spiritual healing in the parish.

The story of a pastor of a parish in a western state.

In a church I served we held a healing service one Sunday night each month. There were many people who felt this was extremely inappropriate because "we have never done it before." Nevertheless, we usually had 25 to 50 people attend. For each service I would have a central focus and on this particular evening it was forgiveness. We would begin with hymns and then a brief message focusing on a scriptural passage followed by prayer with the laying on of hands.

On this night, I spoke about the need for us to forgive people who were close to us and whom we felt had mistreated us at some point. One church

277

member (among several) came forward and shared with me that her primary concern was that she had a shoulder that was locked from acute arthritis to the degree that she was not able to dress herself completely or even comb her hair. As she was making her brief statement to me, she also said that she needed to forgive her father and that she was going to him at the conclusion of the service and forgive him. I prayed that God would simply bless her, that her father would receive her forgiveness, and I prayed for the healing of her shoulder.

The service ended and people began chatting. I looked through the windows leading into the narthex and I saw an arm twirling in the air, moving around like an airplane propeller. I said to those with me let's go to the narthex because I truly believe there has been a significant healing. By the time I got there this arthritic shoulder had been completely freed of pain and she was spinning her arm freely. Her father accepted her forgiveness and a blessed reunion occurred in their lives.

I felt confident that had she not reached a point in her life where she could forgive her father that this healing would not have occurred at the time it did. It may have occurred later but not then.

The above healing appears to be the result of several factors. a) The program of healing was initiated because of the faith of the pastor, who was not willing to accept the negativism of others. b) He believed that God could heal. c) It was done publicly. d) It was part of the process of forgiveness. e) It was the result of spiritual forces which none of those present could fully explain. f) It produced a new family relationship. g) It lifted up faith-healing as part of the religious acts of people of that congregation.

2) *What healing role did prayer play in a basement full of water?*

We make a mistake if we conclude that healing has to take place within the confines of "religion." God is at work everywhere and can reveal healing powers in unexpected places, as a friend described:

> My son and I had never been able to establish a warm style of communication. I had always wanted the best for him and being the wise adult, knew exactly what thoughts and actions it required of him to achieve the best results. Naturally he resisted my style and often our conversations ended in shouting conflict. The relationship troubled me deeply. I thought and prayed about it often but no improvement was forthcoming. Then a strange thing happened.
>
> My son returned home from college on a particularly rainy weekend. On Saturday night, before leaving to join his friends, by chance he discovered our basement was filling with water. We both changed our clothes, slogged through the mess to discover the problem. As the water grew deeper, we two worked side by side trying different solutions, sump pump, drain pipe, clogged sewer, whatever. Although we had a severe situation on our hands, I was somewhat enjoying the whole process because my son and I were working together and communicating as a real team.
>
> At around 9 P.M., seeing that we were finally getting the water to recede, I asked him what plans he

had for the evening. He replied that his friends were meeting at his girlfriend's about 7:30 and would likely go to a movie. I urged him to join them but he chose to stay.

During the next hour we talked as I had always hoped we'd be able to talk. We discussed his progress in college, his aspirations and accomplishments. I asked his opinions and he asked mine. My eyes fogged over at times as I realized something incredibly special was taking place, something I wouldn't have believed.

You know, most people who have basement water problems probably seldom want to think about them. I love my basement. It carries an ongoing spiritual value in our home.

For discussion:

a) Was the flooding planned by the Holy Spirit to occur when the son was home, or was the time of the flood just a coincidence?

b) The father wanted a rapprochement with his son but did not know how to bring it about. Did prayer help? If so, how?

c) Did the son experience a new sensitivity in the father? Could the father's prayers have influenced the son?

d) Was prayer important in bringing them together or was it just the common struggle with the sump-pump and sewer-drain?

3) *The role of faith in healing.*

A pastor reveals the importance of prayer and faith in the counseling/healing process. Notice how he first builds trust and then participates himself in the pain and tears—which ultimately opens the door to acceptance and recovery.

I have had a lot of opportunities to counsel people and while I have not prayed with all of them, I have found it helpful in specific situations.

A prime example of its effectiveness is that of a young woman who came to see me one day. She revealed that she had a little girl, but was divorced and troubled about something. It took a couple of hours of getting to know one another before trust and desperation allowed the secret to be spoken.

Previous to her marriage she had a brief relationship with a young man she met at college which led to a pregnancy she could not in any way afford, either financially or emotionally. She was able to have a safe abortion through some contacts with friends of the family. Even though she considered herself a feminist and had held to a stance of prochoice, she now experienced a sense of grief, guilt and sadness she had never addressed.

She expressed the desire to tell the unborn fetus that she loved it and was distressed over the choice she felt she was compelled to make, but felt it was too late. I suggested to her that perhaps it was not too late. We could pray together, and I would help her image this child and she could speak to it of her love and sorrow. She did this as tears came down her face. I then suggested that she image Christ coming to her, laying his hands upon her and telling her that she was loved and forgiven.

I then put my clerical robe on and together we went into the chapel alone and there she knelt and, as I knelt beside her, we prayed together for reconciliation and wholeness. More tears were shed by both of us. She was unable to speak but later wrote me a letter saying that it had been a healing time for her and she had a sense of gratitude that ours was a loving God.

Several helpful things can be said about this account.

a) The pastor, sensing that the client had a story to unfold but was afraid to reveal, took the time necessary for the client to develop trust.

b) When the woman doubted that she could become reconciled with the dead fetus, he took her over that barrier with professional assurance.

c) He introduced prayer and joined with her in its use. Then he added the authoritative but caring image of Christ.

d) He moved from the counselors chair to the powerful imagery of the chapel where he joined her tears with his own. She knew he helped carry her burden. He did not absolve her himself but let the Spirit of the sharing release her.

4) *A hospital chaplain describes a relationship between prayer and healing.*

Those who serve to heal the body and restore the soul deserve honors of recognition, places of rest, and the rewards of peace among the gods. Their touch of caring is so well symbolized by the work and spirit of this chaplain.

My chaplaincy is at a veterans hospital. I make many calls a day, ten or twelve of which will be extended conversations about life and death. When I visit, I am frequently asked, Why me? Has God taken a vacation? What have I done to deserve this? Does God really care?

I meet men who say they haven't prayed for a long time, but when they are sick, they want me to pray for them. Mr. B., a new patient, told me right off he didn't want me to preach to him. Later he become very sick and called for me. He was very fearful and anxious. We prayed together, and shortly he died. But he prayed *with* me. Healing takes place when a person prays with the chaplain. The spirit needs to be healed first and then the body often follows. In this case, Mr. B. was ready to die and wanted his relationship with God healed. Healing prayer is a surrender to God. In surrendering, one experiences strength and courage and peace—a peace which those who are battling disease need (or search for). The nurse told me Mr. B. died peacefully and that's what he had asked for in his prayer.

When I listen for a patient's spiritual needs, I may give him a spiritual prescription, such as the 23rd Psalm, or the 46th, 91st, or 121st. A ninety year old heart patient asked, "Please get me a prayer book. It gives me strength to face another day." Prayer is the source of the grounding of all healing because persons feel the touch of a power beyond themselves.

The writer is an officially recognized Protestant chaplain with full credentials for her work. I asked her what keeps her going week after week as she faces some of life's most serious terminal situations. She replied,

To the patients, I as a chaplain represent hope. When I visit they brighten up. I bring light and peace and love into dark places. That is tremendously rewarding. As for my own self, I pray constantly during my work day. My prayers energize me to do God's work. And often I feel the healing touch of God's love. The words of Jesus ring true, "If you have the faith of a grain of mustard seed . . ." mountains can be moved, and healing happens in impossible places.

Discussion questions about "Prayer and Healing."

1) Paul prayed repeatedly to be relieved of his thorn in the flesh, but the affliction did not leave him (II Co. 12:7). Would he have been better off if his prayer had been answered?

2) In his book, *The Wounded Healer*, author Henri J. M. Nouwen says, "A Christian community is . . . a healing community, not because wounds are cured and pains alleviated, but because wounds and pains become openings or occasions for a new vision." Is this interpretation of healing helpful to you? Yes? No?

3) In a recent survey of over one thousand people, researchers claim that persons who do not attend church have a lower percentage of good health. They say that religious people have a social network for coping and support. They add that faith helps people to make sense of their lives, and enables them to face stress. Do you, or do you not, find that faith produces good health?

4) Have you ever been "worried sick" because of something you have done, or said, or thought? What is the significance of those two words appearing together? Have you seen illustrations of that meaning?

5) Do you believe, or not agree, that it is possible to make matters worse by giving too much attention to physical afflictions or infirmities?

6) Some people claim that by yielding our body and mind to the Peace of God through prayer, we can allow "the healing waters of the Spirit" to flow through our ailing life? What is your opinion of the role of faith and belief in healing?

A healing scripture for prayer and meditation.

> Jesus, armed with the power of the Spirit . . . came to Nazareth and went to the Synagogue . . . and stood up to read, "The Spirit of the Lord is upon me because he has anointed me; he has sent me to announce good news to the poor, to proclaim release for prisoners and recovery of sight for the blind; to let the broken hearted go free, to proclaim the year of the Lord's favor."[7]

SUMMARY AND CONCLUSIONS

A. The number of participants:

Approximate number of interviews initiated	90
Persons who submitted prayer experiences	49
Persons who asked to remain anonymous	4
Total number of respondents	53

B. The number of prayer experiences recorded:

Number of individual experiences submitted	49
Additional accounts from those individuals	8
Experiences included from my own life	11
Experiences of persons who wished anonymity	4
Total number of prayer experiences recorded	72

C. Types of contributors

Of the 53 persons who submitted experiences:
laypersons: 15 (7 women, 8 men).
clergy: 38 (4 women, 34 men).
(An effort was made to have equal representation from men and women.)

D. Some reasons offered by those who did not participate:

Approximately twenty persons offered specific reasons for not taking part. Among their personal explanations were the following: I am not into prayer; The denomination never gives prayer a chance; I'm too busy, sorry; My prayer life consists in reading the Daily Devotional Guide which does it for me; I will not be able to contribute anything now because of the pressure of the church work here; My congregation is not much interested; I let the prayer-people take care of such matters; I've too many meetings and responsibilities, I can't center down on spiritual things; I get along without prayer OK; To tell the truth, I have not had a significant prayer incident, either in my own life or that of another persons; My contribution would only be church stuff; I've had a lot of experiences but not of the prayer sort; I fell battles for justice and peace must come before anything else.

E. Sixteen additional participants acted in a support capacity.

Both professional and lay persons (who do not appear in the text) appraised the whole book, or sections thereof, at various stages in the project's development. Their names appear in the note of Appreciation. Not all were personally known to the author.

Conclusions

1. The conclusion that prayer is not so much a search to satisfy immediate, individual needs, as a life long commitment to a closer union with the Will of God.

Rereading all the preceding prayers suggests that for many of us, prayer is a means of addressing personal problems. We may pray for specific reasons, such as recovery from sickness, consolation after loss, or support in a time of crisis. Unfortunately, such prayers can become agents of our own reasoning rather than efforts to place our needs in God's hands. When we pray only to satisfy our own concerns, prayer can become a distortion.

Prayer is the way of asking for the presence of God to act as God wills, rather than directing God to ease our pain, bring back our loss, or give us support. True prayer must be oriented more to God than to self. It must deal with God and the Spirit first, with the faith that God will meet our personal needs as God wishes.

2. The conclusion that we always need to see our personal prayers in relation to the larger arena and creative activity of the Spiritual Life.

The prayer accounts which I have recorded must be appraised against a larger spiritual background. Although for most of the respondents prayer has resulted in positive outcomes, we must acknowledge that many times prayer does not seem to produce anything at all, or creates situations which we cannot understand.

It is unwise to assume from our analysis in these pages that all immersions in the spiritual life produce a desired or hoped for result. This is not to deny the activity of the Spirit, but rather to remind ourselves that prayer is a part of the Spirit and must not be judged only on results. It should be seen as an opportunity to align ourselves with the esoteric spiritual arena where the Will of God decides what happens and makes the final decisions.

3. The conclusion that prayer should be seen as a process and movement for continual growth and development, always under the guidance of the Holy Spirit.

As I review how the various degrees and depths of prayer reward some with spiritual insights and leave others in the shoals of shallow spirituality, I become increasingly concerned about the matter of prayer growth and spiritual development. While it is important to discuss the roles of forgiveness and sinfulness as we have, it seems to me that our greatest concern should be how we grow in prayer and how we experience more of the fullness of the spiritual life.

To that end, I devoted special sections to the means of spiritual development. They were: 1) the importance of a *prayer cell;* 2) the value of *retreat;* 3) the significance of *literature of the Spirit.* Each of these is vitally important for prayer growth. Each has been and can be a proven path to spiritual development.

Through small prayer groups people learn how to practice the techniques of faith. Through retreats everyone can temporarily leave the restricting machinery of temporal life and open their souls to God. Through literature of the Spirit, all of us can grow by the insights of previous travelers.

No church should ever be without such programs. No congregation should be denied these established avenues to spirituality. All three are fundamental to evangelism and the spiritual life. All three reflect salient aspects of the life of Our Lord, Jesus Christ.

4. The conclusion that there is a spiritual world, a spiritual arena, and a life in the Spirit, which is revealed through prayer.

Reviewing the previous different ways by which people can leave the rational world and engage the world of the spirit through prayer, I am reminded that prayer is a movement from one kind of living to another. Prayer carries us into the different world of the Spirit. Once there we must recognize that all the rules are different. As we become citizens of the spiritual Way, we discover how much unnecessary baggage we have been carrying and how filled with possibilities our new way can become. Whereas the temporal world may be guided by expediency, the world of the spirit, to which all of us are called by God, may be directed by the love of God.

5. The conclusion that pray-ers live for the future as it is prophesied by the prophets and by God. By dedication, pray-ers bend the world of today into tomorrow's Kingdom of Heaven.

When we look again at the reasons of those who declined to participate in this book, we are reminded of the many ways by which people denigrate prayer. For some, prayer has little credibility because it does not seem to deal with the real issues of a sin-filled world. For others, prayer is seen as the peculiar interest of a few religious-minded believers who do their thing apart from everyday life. Fortunately, a moment of reflection reveals how inaccurate such opinions about prayer really are.

A pray-er prays, not so much because he or she may despair of a situation but because he or she is aware, through faith, of the creative potential of the circumstance. A pray-er has a foundation of faith which suggests new possibilities. A pray-er is not unaware of how the world is. He or she is more concerned with how it will be.

Such is the meaning and value of all those who pray and in so doing, actively reveal and anticipate the constant coming of the Kingdom of Heaven.

Friend, let this be enough.
If thou wouldst go on reading,
Go, and thyself become the writing,
and the blessing.
                              Angelus Silesius
                              (1624–1677)

APPRECIATION

Sincere appreciation is extended to the following individuals who have shared their prayer experiences.

"Bill," Rev. Gene Birmingham, Rev. Richard Barbour, Rev. Philip Desinis, Chaplain Marjorie Ferrell, Rev. Robert Frederick, Rev. Porter French, Rev. Edward Goltz, Mr. Cliff Gower, Mrs. Roberta Hainer, Rev. Alexander Harper, Rev. Edward Hoeffer, Rev. Clarence Higgins, Rev. Donald Hobbs, Rev. John Hubner, Rev. Karl Kirkman, Rev. George Knapp, Rev. Robert Laaser, Mrs. Lillian McKesson, Mrs. Ardyce Mons, Rev. Lawrence Olson, Rev. Truman Parker, Mrs. John Pyle, Rev. Paul Rawley, Mrs. Gerald Rees, Rev. Lawrence Rezash, Rev. Joel Reif, Rev. Jack Robinson, Rev. Theodore Roos, Mr. William Sailor, Rev. Sally Scheib, Rev. Donald Schmidt, Rev. Delbert Schrag, the late Rev. Reuben Sheares, Rev. Paul Stiffler, Rev. Michael Smith, Rev. Arthur Stratemeyer, Mrs. Barbara Schwarting, Rev. Frederick Traut, Mr. Joseph Vance, Rev. William Voelkel, Chaplain Clifford Voll, Mr. Ed Weiss, Mrs. Jane West, the late Mr. Thomas West, Rev. David Wheeler, Mr. Harry White, and Rev. Joseph Wilcox.

Besides the contributors mentioned above, I also want to express my thanks to many persons who offered helpful criticism of this book, or parts thereof, as it has developed over the past four years; who, I pray, will approve its publication but are relieved of accountability for its final form: Rev. Phyllis Carter, Mrs. David Egbert, Rev. Rob Hatfield, Dr. William Hoglund, Rev. Rowland Koch, Dr. Perry LeFevre, Dr. James Marcum, Miss Helen Olson, Dr. Robert Randall, Dr. Robert Sandman, Mr. Don Segraves, Rev. Warren Seyfert, Rev. Joel Tibbets, Professor Barbara Troxell, Rev. Richard Williams, and Miss Judith Welles.

INVENTORY OF PRAYERS

First line or identifying phrase, author, page.

AUTHORS QUOTED AND PAGE NUMBER

RECOMMENDED BOOKS

Andrews, Lancelot, *Private Prayers of Lancelot Andrews*, 1957.

Baillie, John, *A Diary of Private Prayer*, 1936.*

Bloesch, Donald, *The Struggle of Prayer*, 1980.

Boyd, Malcolm, *Are You Running with me, Jesus?* 1966.*

Buttrick, George A, *Prayer*, 1942.

Casteel, John Lawrence, *Rediscovering Prayer*, 1955.

Coburn, John, *Prayer and Personal Religion*, 1957.

Day, Albert Edward, *An Autobiography of Prayer*, 1952.

deSales, Francis, *Introduction to the Devout Life*, 1952.

Ellul, Jaques, *Prayer and Modern Man*, 1970.*

Forsyth, Peter T., *The Soul of Prayer*, 1916.*

Fosdick, Harry Emerson, *The Meaning of Prayer*, 1929.*

Freer, Harold, *Growing in the Life of Prayer*, 1962.*

Harkness, Georgia, *Prayer and the Common Life*, 1948.*

Heard, Gerald, *A Preface to Prayer*, 1962.

Heiler, Friedrich, *Prayer*, 1958.*

Herman, Emily, *Prayer*, 1934.*

Hugel, Friedrich von, *The Life of Prayer*, 1960.*

Leech, Kenneth, *True Prayer*, 1980.*

LeFevre, Perry D., *The Prayers of Kierkegaard*, 1956.*

LeFevre, Perry D., *Radical Prayer*, 1989.*

LeFevre, Perry D., *Understandings of Prayer*, 1981.*

Merton, Thomas, *Contemplative Prayer*, 1971.*

Merton, Thomas, *Spiritual Direction and Meditation*, 1960.*

Nouwen, Henri, J. M., *With Open Hands*, 1979.*

Oxford Book of Prayer, ed. by George Appleton, 1986.

Quoist, Michael, *Prayers*, 1963.*

Rahner, Karl, *Prayers for Meditation*, 1977.

Rauschenbusch, Walter, *Prayers of the Social Awakening*, 1910.*

Sponheim, Paul R., *A Primer on Prayer*, 1988.
Steere, Douglas, *Prayer and Worship*, 1938.*
Wyon, Olive, *The School of Prayer*, 1947.*

(*Denotes references found in this book.)

FOOTNOTES

INTRODUCTION   XVII

[1]Soren Kierkegaard, *The Journal of Kierkegaard*, ed. and trans. by Alexander Dru (Collins, Fontana Books, 1958), p. 97.

[2]Perry LeFevre, *Radical Prayer* (Exploration Press, Chicago, 1982), p. 75.

[3]P. T. Forsyth, *The Soul of Prayer* (Independent Press Ltd., London, 1949), p. 46.

PART ONE

SOME PLAIN DIRECTIONS FOR ALL PRAYERS   1

[1]Bernard of Clairvaux, *On Consideration*, tr. G. Lewis (Oxford University Press, 1908).

[7]Dag Hammerskjold, *Markings*, tr. W. H. Auden and Leif Sjoberg (Alfred A. Knopf Inc., New York, 1965), p. 118.

[3]Thomas Kelly, *A Testament of Devotion* (Harper and Brothers, New York, 1941), p. 45.

[4]William Law, *A Serious Call to a Devout Life*, ed. John W. Meister (Westminster Press, Philadelphia, 1975), p. 92.

[5]Kelly, op. cit., p. 60.

[6]Forsyth, op. cit., p. 64.

[7]Jeremy Taylor, *The Rule and Exercises of Holy Living* (World, Cleveland, 1956), p. 4.

[8]Forsyth, op. cit., p. 60.

[9]Peter Marshall, *Prayers* (U.S. Govt. Printing Office, Washington, 1949), p. 130.

[10]LeFevre, *Radical Prayer*, op. cit., p. 85.

[11]Mathew Fox, *Original Blessing* (Santa Fe, New Mexico, Bear & Co., 1989), p. 81.

[12]Michael Quoist, *Prayers* (Avon Books, The Hearst Corporation, New York, 1963), p. 19.

[13]Attributed to Nicholas Herman, *Oxford Book of Prayers* (Oxford University Press, 1985), p. 86.

[14]*Sarum Primer Prayer.* Sixteenth Century.

[15]Howard Thurman, *Meditations of the Heart* (Harper & Row, New York, 1953), p. 26.

[16]Nikos Kazantzakis, *The Savious of God, Spiritual Exercise* (Simon & Schuster, New York, 1960).

THE LORD'S PRAYER IS THE MODEL FOR ALL OUR PRAYERS   29

[1]Karl Barth, op. cit., p. 25.

[2]Perry LeFevre, *Understanding Prayer* (Westminster Press, Philadelphia, 1981), p. 83.

[3]Kierkegaard, op. cit. p. 34.

[4]Author unknown.

[5]Anonymous, *The Way of a Pilgrim,* tr. R. M. French (S. P. C. K., London, 1963), p. 1.

[6]*The Jesus Psalter.*

UNDERSTANDING DIFFERENT ASPECTS OF PRAYER   41

[1]Chester P. Michael and Marie C. Norrisey, *Prayer and Temperament* (The Open Door, Charlottesville, Virginia, 1984), p.16.

[2]Ibid., p. 25.

[3]LeFevre, *Understanding Prayer*, op. cit., p. 81.

[4]Mathew Fox, *Original Blessing*, op. cit., p. 99.

[5]Thomas Merton, *Spiritual Direction and Meditation* (Liturgical Press, Collegeville, MN. 1959), p. 6.

[6]Ibid., p. 25.

[7]Jacques Ellul, *Prayer and Modern Man*, tr. C. Edward Hopkin (Seabury Press, New York, 1970), p. 153.

[8]Forsyth, op. cit., p. 92.

[9]Saint Augustine, *Confessions* (Sheed and Ward, New York, 1942), p. 144.

[10]Benedict Groeschel, *Spiritual Passages* (Crossroads, New York, 1983), p. 152.

[11]Kenneth Leech, *True Prayer* (Harper Bros. San Francisco, 1980), p. 136.

[12]Olive Wyon, *The School of Prayer*.

[13]Saint Teresa, *The Way of Perfection*.

[14]Emily Herman, *Creative Prayer* (Harper and Row, New York, no date), p. 100.

[15]Attributed to Saint John Chrysostom.

THREE PROFOUND BENEFITS OF PRAYER   75

[1]Evelyn Underhill, *The Life of the Spirit and the Life of Today* (E. P. Dutton & Co., New York, 1922), p. 7.

[2]Ibid., p. 9.

[3]Ibid., p. 12.

[4]Heiler, Frederick, *Prayer*, tr. and ed. Samuel McComb (Oxford University Press, New York, 1958).

[5]Margaret Cooper, *Evelyn Underhill* (Harper and Row, New York, 1958), p. 90.

[6]Groeschel, op. cit., p. 148.

[7]John Baillie, *A Diary of Private Prayer* (Charles Scribner Sons, New York, 1949), p. 101.

SILENCE WILL ENHANCE OUR PRAYING   97

[1]Herman, op. cit., p. 64.

[2]Helen Waddell, *The Desert Fathers* (University of Michigan Press, Ann Arbor, 1972), p. 63. Book 11, ii.

[3]John of the Cross, *The Dark Night*, Bk. 11, chs. 14, 1; Stanzas 3, 67.

[4]Thomas Merton, *Contemplation in a World of Action* (Doubleday, Garden City, New York, 1971), p. 244.

[5]*The Cloud of Unknowing*, tr. Ira Progoff (Julian Press, New York, 1969), p. 69.

[6]Carlo Carretto, *Letters From the Desert* (Maryknoll, New York, 1972), p. 73.

[7]Ibid., p. 11.

[8]Merton, op. cit., p. 43, 44.

[9]Wyon, op. cit., p. 119.

[10]Henri J. M. Nouwen, *Cry For Mercy* (Doubleday and Company, Garden City, New York., 1981), p. 26.

PRAYER ENRICHES SEX AND SEXUALITY   111

[1]Leech, op. cit., p. 42.

[2]Johnston, op. cit., pp. 153, 154.

[3]Atrributed to Victor Frankl

[4]Davies, *Communion of Saints*, op. cit., p. 132.

POSSIBLE REASONS FOR OUR UNANSWERED PRAYERS   119

[1]*A Guide to Prayer for Ministers and other Servants*, ed. Rueben Job and Norman Shawchuk (The Upper Room, Nashville, TN. 1983), p. 240.

[2]Teresa of Avila, *Autobiography*, trans. and ed. E. Allison Peers (Doubleday, New York, 1973).

[3]*Register* (Chicago Theological Seminary, Chicago, 1990), Vol. 80. No.1, p. 46.

[4]Saint Francis of Assisi. op.cit., p. xxi.

[5]Perry LeFevre, *Radical Prayer*, op. cit., p. 92.

[6]Blase Pascal, *Penses*, tr. M. Turnell (Burns and Oates, London, 1961), p. 189.

PART TWO

WHEN WE PRAY WE ASSUME A SPIRITUAL UNIVERSE   **139**
[1]Herman, op. cit., p. 155.
[2]Ibid., p. 171.
[3]LeFevre, *Understanding Prayer*, op. cit., p. 69.
[4]Attributed to Saint Francis of Assisi, Thirteenth Century.

WHEN WE HAVE PRAYERS OF SPECIAL REQUESTS   **149**
[1]Samuel L. Clemens, *Adventures of Huckleberry Finn* (Dodd
    Mead and Company, New York, 1984), p. 12.
[2]Francois Fenelon, *On Prayer and Meditation*, tr. Milfdred W.
    Stillman (Harper & Bros., 1947, New York), p. 155.
[3]*The Communion of Saints*, ed. Harton Davies (William B.
    Erdmans Pub. Co., Grand Rapids, 1990), p. 48.

WHEN WE PRAY FOR OTHERS   **163**
[1]Anthony, S.J. deMello, *Sadhana, A Way to God* (Doubleday
    Image, New York, 1984), p. 127.
[2]LeFevre, op. cit., p. 87.
[3]Dietrich Bonhoeffer, *Life Together* (Harper & Row, New York,
    1954), p. 36.
[4]Walter Wink, *Sojourner Magazine* (Washington, Vol. 19, No. 8),
    p. 13.
[5]Ibid., p. 14.
[6]Davies, *The Communion of Saints*, op. cit., p. 129.

WHEN WE WANT, OR NEED, TO CONFESS   **175**
[1]John Baillie, *A Diary of Private Prayer* (Charles Scribner's
    Sons, New York, 1949), p. 43.
[2]Dietrich Bonhoeffer, *The Cost of Discipleship* (Macmillan Pub.
    Co., New York, 1963), p. 47.

[3]*Book of Common Prayer,* (The Church Pension Fund, New York, 1945), p. 23.

WHEN WE NEED TO FORGIVE, OR BE FORGIVEN   183
[1]Barth, *Prayer,* op. cit., p. 67.
[2]Herman, op. cit., p. 211.
[3]Wadell, op. cit., p. 96, Book IX, ix.
[4]Evelyn Underhill, *Abba* (Longmans Green and Company, New York, 1975), p. 65.
[5]*The Communion of Saints,* op. cit., p. 93.

WHEN WE ARE THANKFUL   191
[1]Walter Rauschenbusch, *Prayers of The Social Awakening* (Pilgrim Press, Boston, 1909), p. 47.
[2]James Martineau, *Home Prayers* (Longman Green, London, 1891).

WHEN WE WANT TO LOVE . . . GOD   201
[1]Forsyth, op. cit., p. 66.
[2]Galasian Sacramentary.

PART THREE

HOW PRAYER ENCOURAGES PERSONAL SALVATION   215
[1]Karl Menninger, *Whatever Became of Sin?* (Hawthorn Books, Inc., New York, 1973), p. 196.
[2]Fosdick, op. cit., p. 280.
[3]Paul Tillich, *The Eternal Now* (Scribners & Sons, New York., 1963), p. 59.
[4]Dietrich Bonhoeffer, *Life Together* (Harper and Row, New York, 1954), p. 116.
[5]Hannah Whitall Smith, *The Christian's Secret of a Happy Life* (Old Tappan, Fleming H. Revell Co., New York, 1970), p. 39.

HOW PRAYER FACILITATES SOCIAL CHANGE   227

Ellul, op. cit., p. 164.

2Soren Kierkegaard, *Purity of Heart is to Will One Thing*, trans. Douglas Steere (Harpers, Torchback Books, New York, 1956), p. 185.

3Veronica Zundel, ed., *Famous Prayers* (William R. Erdmans, Grand Rapids, 1983), p. 85.

4Ellul, op. cit., p. 94.

5Evelyn Underhill, *The Spiritual Life* (Harper Brothers, New York, 1936), p. 80.

6LeFevre, *Radical Prayer*, op. cit., p. 39.

7Thomas Katsares, *Western Mystical Tradition* (Yale University Press, New haven, 1969).

8Thomas Merton, *Contemplation in a World of Action* (Garden City, New York, Doubleday, 1971), p. 164.

9Alan Paton, *Instrument of Thy Peace* (Seabury Press, New York, 1968), p. 58.

HOW PRAYER RESISTS TEMPTATION   239

1Wadell, op. cit., p. 103.

2*Serenity Prayer*, Anonymous, but sometimes attributed to Reinhold Niebuhr.

3Dietrich Bonhoeffer, *Life Together*, trans. John Doberstein (Harper Bros. New York, 1954), p. 112.

4William Johnston, *Silent Music* (Harper and Row, New York, 1979), p. 102.

5Baron Frederich von Hugel, *The Life of Prayer* (Dent, London, 1960).

6*A Guide to Prayer for Ministers and Other Servants* (The Upper Room, Nashville, 1983), p. 283.

7Alcohol Anonymous World Service Inc., *The Twelve Steps* (John Knox Press, Louisville, Kentucky, 1976), p. 59.

8Davies, *The Communion of Saints*, op. cit., p. 17.

HOW PRAYER ENCOUNTERS SUFFERING   251

[1]Perry LeFevre, *The Prayers of Kierkegaard* (University of Chicago Press, Chicago, 1956), p. 218.

[2]Forsyth, op. cit., p. 42.

[3]Baron Von Hugel, *Letters of Baron von Hugel to His Niece*, tr. Gwendolyn Greene (Dent, Dent, London, 1950), p. xvi.

[4]Attributed to Martin Luther King, Jr.

[5]Walter Russell Bowie, *Lift Up Your Hearts* (Macmillan, New York, 1942), p. 34.

HOW PRAYER CONFRONTS EVIL   261

[1]Attributed to Bishop Muzorewa of South Africa.

[2]Saint Francis, *The Little Flowers of St Francis*, tr. Raphael Brown (Image, Doubleday, New York, 1958), p. 58.

[3]LeFevre, *Radical Prayer*, op. cit., p.

[4]Attributed to Thomas a Kempis, Fifteenth Century.

HOW PRAYER HEALS   271

[1]Kenneth Leech, *True Prayer* (Harper and Row, San Francisco, 1980), p. 64.

[2]Norman Cousins, *Head First* (E. P. Dutton, New York, 1989), p. 215.

[3]Leech, op. cit., p. 165.

[4]Ibid., p. 166.

[5]Ibid., p. 166.

[6]Kenneth Pelletier, *Mind as Slayer, Mind as Healer* (Dell Publishing Co., New York, 1977), p. 33.

[7]*New English Bible* (Oxford University Press, Oxford, England, 1977), Luke 4:15–19.